Psychology and Work:
Productivity, Change, and Employment

MASTER LECTURERS
J. Richard Hackman
Lois Wladis Hoffman
Rudolf H. Moos
Samuel H. Osipow
Louis G. Tornatzky

Edited by
Michael S. Pallak
and Robert O. Perloff

AMERICAN PSYCHOLOGICAL ASSOCIATION
WASHINGTON, D.C. 20036

Library of Congress Cataloging-in-Publication Data

Psychology and work.

    (The Master lectures; v. 5)
    Bibliography: p.
    1. Psychology, Industrial. 2. Work—Psychological
aspects. 3. Labor productivity. I. Pallak, Michael S.,
1942-   . II. Perloff, Robert O., 1921-
III. Hackman, J. Richard. IV. Series: Master lecture
series; v. 5. [DNLM: 1. Employment. 2. Psychology,
Social. 3. Work. W1 MA9309V v. 5 / BF 481 P974]
HF5548.8.P774 1986   158.7   86-7952
ISBN 0-912704-48-9 (pbk.)

Copies may be ordered from:
Order Department
P.O. Box 2710
Hyattsville, MD 20784

Published by the American Psychological Association, Inc.
1200 Seventeenth Street, N.W., Washington, D.C. 20036

Printed in the United States of America.

CONTENTS

MASTER LECTURES
Self-Study Instrument

Each year the Master Lectures are presented at the APA Convention, and attendees have an opportunity to receive credit. If you were unable to attend the Master Lectures, you may obtain Continuing Education Credit through a self-study instrument (SSI) developed to accompany each volume of this series, beginning with Volume 2. For further information about this or previous years' SSI, please write or phone:

MLS-SSI
CE Program Office
American Psychological Association
1200 Seventeenth St., N.W.
Washington, D.C. 20036
(202) 955-7719

PREFACE

Since 1974, the Master Lectures volumes have presented theory and research by leading scholars in selected areas of psychology. Presented in lecture format during the annual convention and made available in printed form to a wide readership, the Master Lectures also represent the state of the art and science of psychology presented in topic format and designed to meet several needs.

First, in light of the ongoing knowledge explosion in the field, the Master Lectures provide thoughtful perspective and substance for psychologists whose research, application, and practice may not be directly involved in the particular topic focus. In doing so, Master Lectures provide a high-quality review of current thought for everyone.

Second, and of equal importance, the annual Master Lectures volumes constitute one of several systematic efforts by which the American Psychological Association and distinguished contributors provide information and perspective to the broader public involved in the topic areas represented in the Lectures. Thus, these prestigious lectures help fulfill our responsibility to society for providing knowledge, contribution, and education regarding complex issues.

Originally initiated by the Committee on Program Innovations of the Board of Convention Affairs, the Lectures have been implemented under the aegis of the Continuing Education Committee of the Education and Training Board and staff since 1977. Previous topics were as follows:

Physiological Psychology (1974)
Developmental Psychology (1975)
Behavior Control (1976)
Brain–Behavior Relationships (1977)
Psychology of Aging (1978)
Sex and Gender in Psychology (1979)
Cognitive Psychology (1980)
Psychotherapy Research and Behavior Change (1981)
Psychology and the Law (1982)
Psychology and Health (1983)
Psychology and Learning (1984)

In 1986, the topic for the Master Lectures will be "Cataclysms, Catastrophies, and Crises: Psychological Knowledge in Action"; and in 1987, the lectures will be in the area of neuropsychology.

Psychology and Work: Productivity, Change, and Employment

The lectures in this volume are especially timely. In 1981, a (then) new federal administration stated flatly and publicly that psychology and the social sciences were not essential to economic recovery initiatives in our society. Consequently, support for the field was sharply reduced throughout the federal budget.

Ironically, 1981 also was a year in which public attention became focused on productivity and economic competition, as well as on the devastating effect of unemployment and economic displacement. It has become clear that our society has been, and continues to be, in the middle of several major social, economic, and technological transitions. Issues and problems thus have arisen that will require very different approaches and solutions to which psychology has major expertise to contribute. The economy continues to shift from hard manufacturing to a service orientation, a shift fueled in part by the rapid utilization of new technology abroad and by the rapid evolution and adoption of a new generation of information technologies in our society. A dimension that is fundamental to these issues and to the development of strategies for resolution involves questions of human behavior and functioning across a variety of settings. National discussions and policy processes that do not include psychology's systematic approach deprive our society of a critically valuable source of expertise and talent, represented by psychology's knowledge base.

These current lectures devote considerable attention to these issues and to implications for the organization of productivity and work systems. In "Work as a Human Context," Rudolf H. Moos examines the relationship between a traditional emphasis on productivity and task efficiency and a more recent emphasis on human relations that leads to concerns with organizational development and quality of life. The synthesis becomes an emphasis on the reciprocal interaction between the impact of work and employment and the impact of the social context of work as illustrated and examined throughout a series of settings.

In "Technological Change and the Structure of Work," Louis G. Tornatzky presents the implications of new computer-assisted technology and notes the resulting implied revolution for organizing systems of work and management. The process of change and integration of these new technologies has major implications for preparing the work force and for training at individual, group, and managerial levels. The issues and processes need to be viewed longitudinally with a mixture of tools including case studies, surveys, and experimentation.

Next, in "The Psychology of Self-Management in Organizations," J. Richard Hackman discusses self-management systems, a new approach that emphasizes eliciting from the work force a commitment to collective objectives. He presents key features and behaviors that distinguish self-management systems from more traditional systems that emphasize "top down" management control, and he reviews evidence about conditions that foster self-management systems and indicate the relative effectiveness of such systems.

In "Career Issues Through the Life Span," Samuel H. Osipow examines career pattern issues from a historical perspective on theory and evidence concerning a common set of assumptions that do not (or no longer) seem to obtain.

In one of the best treatments of the topic that we have seen, "Work, Family, and the Child," Lois Wladis Hoffman presents a comprehensive discussion and analysis of conditions and a structure that allows us to examine the effects of unemployment on men and of nonemployment on women. Hoffman also emphasizes the issues related to the effect of mothers' employment on husband–wife relationships, mothers' morale, and mother–child relationships. The chapter pulls together a set of vital issues related to the effect of the interaction between family dynamics and the work place.

The contributors to this volume cover core issues in psychology and work and develop a sophisticated perspective on issues that range from the individual in systems, to innovation and change, to new approaches to management and career patterns, through employment and its effect on family systems. Taken together, these lectures amply demonstrate the vitality and timeliness of psychology and its usefulness in illuminating and clarifying the trends and issues for a society that must grapple with changes already upon us.

Members of the Continuing Education Committee (Clyde Crego and Lucia Gilbert, co-chairs) are to be commended for selecting "Psychology and Work: Productivity, Change, and Employment" as a topic and these lectures in particular. The efforts and cooperation of the lectures in preparing their oral and written presentations are deeply appreciated.

Finally, special thanks go to the members of APA's Central Office staff—Barbara Hammonds and Rosemary Beierman of the Continuing Education Program Office for their efforts in preparing both the lectures and related materials and Brenda K. Bryant and Deanna Cook, members of APA's Special Publications Office, for technical assistance in preparing this volume.

Michael S. Pallak
Robert O. Perloff
Editors

RUDOLF H. MOOS

WORK AS A HUMAN CONTEXT

Rudolf H. Moos received his PhD in psychology in 1960 from the University of California at Berkeley, and then held a postdoctoral fellowship at the University of California School of Medicine in San Francisco. He then joined the Department of Psychiatry and Behavioral Sciences at Stanford University, where he currently is a professor and director of the Social Ecology Laboratory. Moos also holds an appointment as a Research Career Scientist and as Director of the Health Services Research and Development Service Field Program at the Veterans Administration Medical Center in Palo Alto.

He has published widely in several areas, including environmental and community psychology, stress and coping theory, and the impact of work settings on individuals and their families. Moos has been awarded the Hofheimer Award for Research from the American Psychiatric Association and the Distinguished Contribution Award from the Division of Community Psychology of APA.

RUDOLF H. MOOS

WORK AS A HUMAN CONTEXT

Introduction

The work force in America is composed of more than 100 million people, many of whom spend between one-third and one-half of their waking hours at work. A job can provide structure for a person's life, a sense of satisfaction and productivity that stems from completing meaningful tasks, a feeling of belonging to a valued reference group, a basis for self-esteem and personal identity, and a way to earn one's economic place in society. But many Americans are employed in bureaucratic organizations in which they pursue routine predictable tasks and feel isolated and futile. Work stress, job dissatisfaction, and a sense of pressure and frustration are common.

These contrasting experiences and effects of work are well known, but today they occur in the context of rising expectations about the quality of work life. Americans believe in the value of personal autonomy and the right to a hazard-free and reasonably satisfying work setting. Although the work force is more knowledgeable and better educated than ever before, technological developments such as

Preparation of the manuscript was supported by NIMH Grants MH16744 and MH28177, NIAAA Grants AA02863 and AA06699, and Veterans Administration Medical and Health Services Research and Development Service research funds. John Finney and Sonne Lemke made valuable comments, Ann Marten assisted in the literature review, and Adrienne Juliano competently word-processed the manuscript.

automation and robotics make it possible to simplify and routinize many jobs. Such social "progress" contributes to work stress, underutilization of individual abilities, and feelings of powerlessness and disaffection. Thus, there is a growing mismatch between the talents and aspirations of many individuals and the jobs available to them (Hackman & Oldham, 1980; Levin, 1983).

Over the past 60 years, organizational theorists have formulated several conceptual frameworks to address these issues. The one-sided emphasis on employee productivity in the 1920s led to Taylorism and the scientific school of management, which focused on specifying conditions to maximize task efficiency. The human relations approach was shaped by growing concern about employee alienation and the conviction that a narrow focus on productivity paradoxically might lead to poorer job performance. This approach emphasized the value of individual and small group relationships and spawned renewed attention to organizational development and the quality of work life. Most recently, proponents of the sociotechnical school have shown the need to consider the technological or task attributes of a job as well as the interpersonal and organizational context in which it is performed (Huse, 1980; Katz & Kahn, 1978; Staw, 1984).

These three approaches provide a gradually evolving perspective on the work environment and its connections to personal characteristics and work outcomes. Scientific management sees the environment as a set of task-relevant reinforcers that can be used to manipulate and control employee behavior; there is little regard for interpersonal issues or individual differences. The human relations school highlights the personal and social context of work but tends to neglect task attributes and, with some notable exceptions, to overlook individual differences. The sociotechnical perspective provides an inclusive conception of the organizational environment as composed of the interplay of task and social factors; however, individual differences tend to be disregarded. I build on these ideas here by offering a social-ecological perspective that considers a diversity of job-related factors, personal characteristics and person–job congruence, and the reciprocal impact of work and other social contexts on each other.

A Holistic Conceptual Framework

A social-ecological perspective can broaden theoretical approaches to contextual factors and help to address long-standing issues regarding the quality and impact of work settings. It also encompasses newer concerns about how experiences at work can affect a person's spouse and children, choice of leisure activities, and general Weltan-schauung. In brief, a social-ecological framework considers both physical and social aspects of the work place and their determinants and effects. It emphasizes how individuals select and alter work settings as well as the impact of work on the person. Moreover, it recognizes that the influence of a job carries over into other life contexts such as the family and can have consequences for family members as well as for employees. This holistic view is consistent with the idea that the meaning of work should be considered in a wider social context (Price, 1985; Wilensky, 1981).

The model shown in Figure 1 depicts the environmental system (Panel I) as being composed of organizational and work-related factors as well as of current stressors and social resources that stem from other contexts in an individual's life, such as the family and neighborhood. The personal system (Panel II) encompasses work-related factors such as the type of job (occupation) and work role, sociodemographic characteristics, and personal resources such as self-esteem, intellectual ability, general problem-solving skills, and needs and value orientations. The personal and environmental systems affect each other, as do work and non-work factors in both systems.

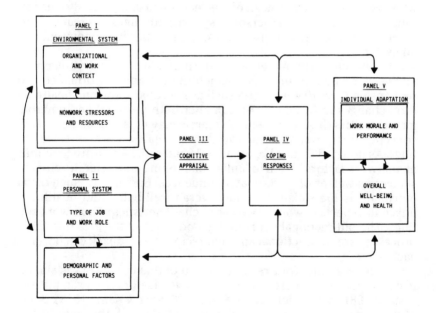

Figure 1. A model of the links between work and non-work factors and individual adaptation.

The conceptual model posits that the link between the environmental system (Panel I) and adaptation (Panel V) is affected by the personal system (Panel II), as well as by cognitive appraisal and coping responses (Panels III and IV). More specifically, cognitive appraisal (Panel III) and the environmental and personal factors (Panels I and II) that foreshadow it can shape coping responses (Panel IV) and effectiveness (Panel V). Cognitive appraisal is the outcome of an interplay between the personal and environmental systems. Consider a work group in which employees determine the allocation and sequence of specific tasks, the timing of rest breaks, and the principles underlying variations in pay. Most observers are likely to appraise such a group as high on involvement and autonomy, but an individual who is oriented toward external control (personal system) might see it as chaotic and disorganized.

The next step in the model reflects individuals' efforts to manage the environment by selecting a preferred set of coping responses. Such responses are prompted by the personal system (some people are more inclined toward active problem solving and others toward avoidance) and the environmental system (some work settings reward problem solving more than others do). An individual's use of a coping skill also may change both systems. For example, a woman who assumes an active role in office decision making may alter her attitudes (a change in the personal system) and help to create a new employee-based decision making group (a change in the environmental system).

Coping efforts ultimately affect the individual's standing on proximal work-related criteria such as job morale and performance and perhaps on more distal criteria such as life satisfaction and health. In turn, changes in these criteria can alter both personal and environmental factors (an increase in job morale may bolster a person's self-concept; more productive employees may create a more cohesive setting). As noted in Figure 1, work morale and satisfaction are functions of non-work factors linked to family functioning and other life circumstances as well as of work-related influences. Conversely, such distal outcomes as life satisfaction and overall well-being and health are linked to aspects of work as well as to characteristics of non-work settings. The bidirectional paths in the model reflect the idea that these processes are transactional and that reciprocal feedback can occur at each stage.

In general, the work-related portion of this framework is similar to conceptual models created by other investigators (for example, see Becker, 1981; Ivancevich & Matteson, 1980; Katz & Kahn, 1978). Some of these models are set in a wider context in which the cultural and economic environment is seen as affecting the organization and its structure. I recognize that macrosystem factors can alter work organizations and their employees, but an adequate treatment of these issues is beyond my scope.

Other models focus more on the organizational than the individual level of functioning. Although many work-place problems need to be considered from an organizational and societal perspective, I emphasize the individual and small-group level of analysis. This approach considers work primarily from an individual's point of view and makes it possible to integrate information in related psychological areas, such as stress and coping theory, into the literature on work stressors. Finally, research in this area abounds with methodological pitfalls that I do not discuss; there are many sources to which the interested reader can turn (e.g., Berger & Cummings, 1979; Kasl & Wells, 1985; Locke & Schweiger, 1979; Roberts & Glick, 1981). In general, the findings of controlled longitudinal studies are comparable to those obtained in cross-sectional research, as are the basic conclusions drawn from information about perceived and externally reported job characteristics. More importantly, I believe that advances in this field are most likely to stem from a renewed emphasis on conceptual issues.

The Environmental System

It is useful to consider the diversity of environmental variables in terms of four domains: physical and architectural features, organizational structure and policy, suprapersonal factors (that is, the aggregate characteristics of the individuals in a setting), and social climate. Variables in each of these domains can affect individuals directly and indirectly through the other domains. For instance, the influence of physical features on behavior and morale may be mediated by the social climate they help to create. These four domains can help to characterize work settings and explore their effects, as well as to understand other kinds of social and task-oriented contexts (Moos, 1974a, 1979; Moos & Lemke, 1984). After considering the social climate perspective, I examine the other three domains and their connections to social climate.

The Social Climate Perspective

Individuals use a process of descriptive judgment to form global ideas about an environment from perceptions of specific aspects of it. We have a tendency to ascribe human-like qualities to our environment, and social climate is the outgrowth of generalized attributions that stem from judgments of particular environmental characteristics or events (Naylor, Pritchard, & Ilgen, 1980). These perceptions are based in part on reality factors, so that a judgment of "friendliness" might stem from whether co-workers say hello in the morning, help each other with work-related tasks, take coffee and lunch breaks together, talk to each other about personal issues, and so forth. Such conditions create the social climate or atmosphere of a work setting.

As the model in Figure 1 illustrates, perceptions of social climate are the outcome of a process of concept formation that stems from the interplay between actual events and qualities of an organization (the environmental system) and an individual's values and beliefs (the personal system). From the point of view of Gestalt psychology, individuals try to create order by selecting and integrating specific perceptions into meaningful patterns. These cognitive schemas or maps are the product of a constructive process in which new information is interpreted in light of prior experience. In turn, these schemas guide subsequent information processing and shape the way in which organizational factors alter an individual's mood and behavior (Calder & Schurr, 1981; James & Sells, 1981; Salancik & Pfeffer, 1978).

From a functionalist perspective, individuals need to learn about the environment so that they can behave appropriately and attain homeostasis. Cognitive appraisal thus must be based on reasonably accurate perceptions of environmental characteristics rather than simply on idiosyncratic personal factors. But individuals are predisposed to construe reality in terms that are compatible with their current needs and beliefs. These needs may cause people to attend selectively to particular aspects of their environment. Consistent with these ideas, James, Gent, Hatter, and Coray (1979) found that employees' perceptions of their psychological influence were based both on their supervisor's actual behavior and goal-setting procedures and on personal factors.

Three Domains of Work Climate

Based on research in a variety of social environments, I have organized the underlying facets of social climate into three domains: the way in which individuals in a setting relate to each other (relationship domain), the personal growth goals toward which a setting is oriented (personal growth or goal orientation domain), and the amount of structure and openness to change that characterize it (system maintenance and change domain; Moos, 1974b, 1979, 1984). Similarly, Payne (1980) has categorized aspects of organizational contexts as supports, demands, and constraints. Supports encompass the quality of relationships with colleagues and supervisors and the adequacy of physical resources. Demands refer to aspects of an environment that command attention and stimulate employees to perform (goal orientation). The concept of constraint resembles that of system maintenance, but it is limited to conditions that confine or prevent an individual from fulfilling job demands.

The dimensions of several scales that focus on work settings can be organized using these three domains. As shown in Table 1, the six factors of Gavin and Howe's (1975) Psychological Climate Inventory reflect the three domains, as do the dimensions tapped by the Organizational Climate Index (Stern, 1970), the Psychological Climate Questionnaire (James & Sells, 1981), and the Quality of Employment Survey (Kahn, 1980). The Michigan Organizational Assessment Questionnaire (MOAQ) is a comprehensive procedure that covers employees' demographic characteristics, reactions to their jobs and organizational settings, aspects of job morale and motivation, and descriptors of the work environment (Camman, Fichman, Jenkins, & Klesh, 1983). The facets of work-group functioning, supervision, and job role characteristics tapped by the MOAQ fall into the three domains.

Some investigators have identified the goal orientation (demand, growth orientation) and system maintenance (structure, control) domains, but have tended to neglect the relationship domain. The five core job dimensions tapped by the Job Diagnostic Survey (JDS) reflect the personal growth or goal orientation area but do not explicitly consider the relationship or system maintenance and change domains (Hackman & Oldham, 1980; but see the JDS Feedback from Agents dimension, which taps a facet of the relationship domain). All three work climate domains are important, since, for example, demanding jobs may be performed effectively in contexts that are rich in social support or high on autonomy and personal control. The three sets of social climate dimensions provide a convenient framework for describing and integrating the research I cover here.

Describing and Comparing Work Climates

I have operationalized this approach by developing a Work Environment Scale (WES) to measure the three work climate domains (see Table 1). The scale is based on the idea that employees are participant observers in the work milieu and are uniquely qualified to appraise it. The WES relationship dimensions tap the extent to which employees and managers are involved with and supportive of one another. The WES personal growth or goal orientation dimensions cover the goals toward which the work setting is oriented, that is, autonomy, task orientation, and work pressure. The WES system maintenance and change dimensions deal with the amount of structure, clarity, and openness to change that characterize the work setting. These three domains of social climate factors typify different kinds of social settings (Moos, 1981; see also Moos, 1984).

Scales such as the WES can be used to depict the perceptions of individual employees and their stability over time, compare reports of

Table 1.
Dimensions of Work Climate

	Domain	
Relationship	Goal/Growth Orientation	System Maintenance and Change

Instrument: Psychological Climate Inventory (Gavin & Howe, 1975)

Esprit	Rewards	Clarity of structure
Managerial trust and consideration	Challenge and risk	Hindrance structure

Instrument: Organization Climate Index (Stern, 1970)

Closeness	Intellectual climate	Orderliness
Group life	Personal dignity	Impulse control
	Achievement standards	(constraint)

Instrument: Psychological Climate Questionnaire (James & Sells, 1981)

Work group coopera- tion and friendliness	Job challenge Job importance	Role ambiguity Role conflict
Leadership facilitation and support	Job variety	
Organizational concern and identification		

Instrument: Quality of Employment Survey (Kahn, 1980)

Relationships with co-workers	Task content (challenge)	Resource adequacy Wages
Supervision	Autonomy and control	
	Working conditions (demand)	
	Promotions	

Instrument: Michigan Organizational Assessment Questionnaire—
Modules 3, 4, & 5 (Camman et al., 1983)

Work group cohesion	Participation in decision making	Role conflict
Openness of communication	Production orientation	Role clarity Work group clarity
Internal fragmentation	Role overload	Supervisor control
Supervisor-subordinate communication and consideration		Supervisor goal setting and problem solving Decision centralizations

Instrument: Work Environment Scale (Moos, 1981)

Involvement	Autonomy	Clarity
Peer cohesion	Task orientation	Control
Supervisor support	Work pressure	Innovation
		Physical comfort

employees and managers, and describe and contrast different work settings. Figure 2 shows the WES profiles for 36 high-technology production workers and 30 fire fighters from a county department. The production workers saw a supportive, task-oriented, and physically comfortable work milieu that was characterized by clear expectations and an emphasis on innovation. Employees reported little work pressure or time urgency. These findings were consistent with the employees' jobs, which were individually paced and highly independent. The plant was well known for its congenial work environment and low employee turnover.

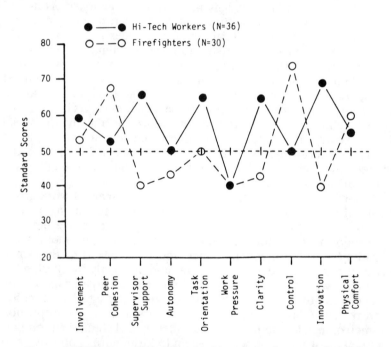

Figure 2. WES Form R Profiles for hi-tech workers and fire fighters.

The fire fighters viewed their job setting as cohesive but rigidly controlled and lacking in clarity and innovation. They mistrusted their supervisors, whom they saw as being autocratic and arbitrary. In fact, the supervisors had instituted a strict timekeeping system and rigid job requirements. The unusually high level of supervisor control may have heightened the cohesiveness of co-workers by inducing the employees to stand up for each other. This type of information can be used to track changes in a work group, to compare employees' actual and preferred job climates, and to provide feedback to work groups and help to improve them (Moos, 1981).

The Determinants of Work Climate

Work groups vary widely in the quality of interpersonal relationships, the emphasis on task orientation and work pressure, and the level of clarity and organization. This finding raises an intriguing question. Why do social climates develop in such disparate ways, that is, what leads to an emphasis on supervisor support, or task orientation, or work pressure? How is social climate influenced by other domains of the environmental system and how does it mediate their impact?

To address this question, my colleagues and I have conceptualized the work environment as a dynamic system composed of four domains: physical and architectural features, organizational structure and policies, suprapersonal factors (employees' aggregate background and personal characteristics), and social climate. We have formulated a model of the relationships among the four sets of environmental domains and their connections to the organizational context (see Figure 3). In essence, the model posits that the impact of architectural, organizational, and suprapersonal factors stems in part from the social climate they help to promote. More specifically, the social climate can alter the impact of the other three domains on employee morale and performance. This perspective is consistent with the sociotechnical school, which accents the interplay between physical (technical) and organizational factors.

According to the model, physical features can affect work-group climate directly (open-plan offices may facilitate cohesion) or indirectly by altering organizational factors (greater distance between work groups may promote more flexible policies and autonomy). Organizational structure can influence social climate directly (small work groups tend to be more cohesive) and indirectly by altering the individuals who select a work group (hierarchical organizations may attract competitive persons who tend to create more task orientation and work demands). Human aggregate factors, such as the proportion of women or men in a setting, also can affect social climate. In comparison to men, for instance, women seem to form more supportive and less structured social groups (Moos, 1979).

As I noted earlier, each of these processes is reciprocal. The social climate of a work group can influence the type of people who select it (achievement-oriented individuals may favor task-oriented work settings), organizational policies (employee autonomy can promote formal channels for grievances), and physical parameters. Employees in a cohesive work group may elect to partition an open-plan office to control noise and create privacy. Finally, aspects of the company or facility in which a work group is located (that is, the organizational context) can affect each of the four sets of environmental descriptors.

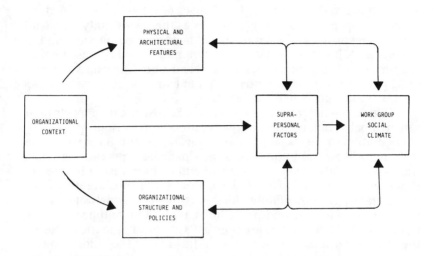

Figure 3. A model of the interconnections among domains of work context factors.

Physical and architectural features. Studies of open-plan offices illustrate some of the effects of physical features on social climate. Proponents of the human relations approach posit that the absence of interior walls and barriers in open-plan offices will facilitate social relationships and promote job satisfaction and performance. The increased communication in open-plan offices is thought to enhance feedback by enabling employees and supervisors to share work-related and personal information. In contrast, the sociotechnical approach emphasizes the value of physical boundaries in constructing private, defensible space. Boundaries can clarify the nature of the work process, increase task identity and friendship formation, and create autonomy by making it less likely that co-workers and supervisors will constrict an employee's discretion.

Employees who move from conventional to open-plan offices describe an increase in non-work-related conversations while the amount of work-related conversation remains stable. But such offices may not provide enough privacy to support the formation of close friendships or to permit supervisors to offer candid evaluations to subordinates. Employees in open-plan offices report less job autonomy and task identity, fewer leadership opportunities, and a reduction in co-worker and supervisor feedback. Thus, a change in physical features can alter the work climate and employee motivation and morale (Oldham & Brass, 1979). The impact of office physical features seems to depend on such social factors as the opportunity for friendship and feedback and such technical factors as autonomy and task identity and significance (Oldham & Rotchford, 1983). These findings support the sociotechnical perspective and affirm the value of considering physical and social factors together (for a general overview, see Becker, 1981, and Wineman, 1982).

Organizational structure and policies. Some primary aspects of organizational structure are (1) organizational and work-group size, (2) configuration or the "shape" of an organization and the span of control (that is, how many employees each manager supervises), (3) centralization or how much the locus of authority is vested in one or a small group of individuals, (4) specialization or the extent to which each person performs different functions, and (5) formalization or the degree to which rules and procedures are written and precisely defined. The first two aspects are seen as "structural" qualities, whereas the other three are "structuring" qualities in that they index policies that shape or constrain behavior. A vast amount of research has generated only a few dependable findings linking these factors to work-group climate or performance (see Berger & Cummings, 1979; Dalton, Todor, Spendolini, Fielding & Porter, 1980).

The most robust findings involve size and centralization. Large organizations typically are highly formalized and bureaucratic and composed of work groups that are oriented toward rules, conventionality, and supervisor control. Employees in larger work groups tend to perform more specialized tasks and to report less group cohesiveness. Centralized organizations also are more formalized and accent task orientation and manager control more than autonomy or innovation. In general, the connection between a structural variable (such as size) and an outcome criterion (such as job involvement or motivation) is mediated by processes linked to size (formalization, centralization) and the social climate they create, as well as by personal characteristics of employees.

Suprapersonal factors. When individuals come together in a social group, be it a work group, a college dormitory, or a congregate living unit for older people, they bring with them values, norms, and abilities. Because of selective mechanisms, groups draw their members in a nonrandom manner from the general population and produce distinctive blends of individual characteristics. The aggregate of the members' attributes (the suprapersonal environment) in part defines the subculture that forms in a group, and, in turn, the morale and behavior of its members. Thus, the type of work force attracted and retained by an organization can shape its culture and viability.

Holland's (1985) theory has spawned an extensive body of research on aggregate personal characteristics. Holland proposes that people's vocational choices are expressions of their personalities and that occupations can be categorized into six groups, with each group representing a distinct personality type. Since people in an occupational group have similar personalities, they should respond to situations in similar ways and create characteristic work climates. Thus, Holland has described six types of work settings linked to the six personality types: realistic, investigative, artistic, social, enterprising, and conventional. The type of environment is influenced by the modal personality of group members. In this way, an average background characteristic of a group (that is, the dominant vocational preference) creates a particular milieu with unique demands, rewards, and opportunities.

In a test of Holland's theory, my colleagues and I found that employees in realistic occupations (such as engineers and air traffic controllers) tend to see their work groups as having a high level of control and as lacking in autonomy and innovation. These groups also showed low levels of involvement, cohesiveness, and supervisor support. In contrast, employees in social-type work settings (such as social workers and bartenders) reported relatively high emphasis on the relationship areas and on clarity and innovation. As expected, investigative work settings (such as those populated by physicists and computer operators) strongly accentuated autonomy and innovation and showed especially low levels of control. These findings support Holland's ideas and indicate that modal personal characteristics can influence work group climate (Moos, 1981).

Examining the overall model. Few, if any, studies have looked at all of the environmental domains and connected them with each other and with work group performance. Parasuraman and Alutto (1981) linked organizational factors to perceived work stressors among employees in a food processing firm. Compared to administrative employees, those who were engaged in food production reported more technical problems and greater work demands and role frustration. This was thought to stem from their reliance on complex machinery and the presence of explicit performance criteria. Supervisors experienced more stressors indicative of qualitative overload and time constraints, whereas role frustration was more prevalent among employees in lower-level positions. Task complexity and close supervision contributed to interunit conflict, role frustration, and efficiency problems, even after contextual and job-level factors were considered. Thus, technical and social factors combine to produce work stressors (for ideas on the antecedents of work support, see House, 1983).

Jones and James (1979) found that organizational structure and suprapersonal factors were predictably linked to the work climate in 160 Navy ship divisions. The types of work climates identified varied from cooperative and friendly, to enriched and warm but uninvolved, constricted and alienating, and ambiguous and conflicted. These climates seemed to reflect basic variations in group functions and in their technology and resources, structural factors, and personnel composition, and these factors were linked to their performance. Divisions with cooperative and friendly work climates performed most effectively, whereas those with cold and unsupportive climates functioned least well. The warm and friendly climates were associated with complex technology, little task specialization, flat configurations, small size, and work-group members of high-average intelligence and education. In contrast, the cold and unsupportive climates were associated with routine technology, a broad span of control and large size, less interdependence with other work groups, and personnel with low-average intelligence and education. Consistent with the model presented earlier, such findings imply that contextual, policy, and suprapersonal factors help to create certain psychological climates, which combine with them to influence work-group effectiveness.

The Impact of Work Milieus

A considerable body of research has examined the connections between specific facets of work settings and employee satisfaction, performance, and well-being. Most of the studies have tried to link work-related aspects of the environmental system (Panel I in the model) directly to adaptation (Panel V), though some have considered the role of personal factors (Panel II) and cognitive appraisal (Panel III). Because work-group climate can shape the influence of other environmental factors, I emphasize studies that have considered it.

Job Morale and Performance

Not surprisingly, work climates that are cohesive and accepting, are oriented toward independence and autonomy, and provide meaningful and challenging tasks tend to produce good employee morale and to reduce turnover intentions. Considerate supervisors who specify clear goals and encourage participation in decision making also promote these outcomes, as well as employees' experiences of being challenged and pleased with intrinsic and extrinsic job rewards. Well-organized work settings in which individuals do not feel hindered by bureaucratic policies also tend to create better morale. Role ambiguity and overload and group conflict have the converse effect, as do situational constraints and highly structured tasks and leaders (Fisher & Gitelson, 1983; Hendrix, Ovalle, & Troxler, 1985; O'Connor-Pooyan, Weekley, Peters, Frank, & Erenkrantz, 1984; Pierce, Dunham, & Cummings, 1984).

Indices of Strain: Substance Use and Abuse

The work-related economic and social costs of substance abuse may be much greater than is commonly suspected. The detrimental effect of problem drinking on the individual is well known, but the impact on co-workers and supervisors has been overlooked. Alcohol consumption and adverse consequences of drinking have been associated with lack of challenge, role conflict and ambiguity, and high work demands. Employees who report more work-related problems tend to cite a wider variety of reasons to justify drinking (such as to relax and cope with job pressure). Thus, work problems may increase alcohol consumption by making an individual more likely to justify drinking as a response to job stressors (Fennell, Rodin, & Cantor, 1981).

Daily self-reported cigarette, coffee, and alcohol consumption were measured in a longitudinal field study of Navy petty officers who were performing a job with known systematic variation in stress (Conway, Vickers, Ward, & Rahe, 1981). Cigarette smoking and coffee drinking were positively associated with perceived stress, but alcohol consumption tended to lessen under stress. This decline was attributed to ecological constraints, in that officers often remained on the base during peak demand periods. The lack of easy access to alcohol was thought to explain the reduced consumption during these times. There also were wide individual differences in the tendency to increase or decrease habitual substance use in response to varying levels of stress. Such findings point to the need to consider the social context and individual variations in research on the impact of work (see also Westman, Eden, & Shirom, 1985).

Indices of Strain: Mental and Physical Symptoms and Medical Conditions

A substantial number of researchers have examined the links between work settings and health-related criteria. Four main facets of work-group climate have been associated with employee strain and lack of mental and physical well-being: high job demands as indexed by heavy work load and time pressure, insufficient opportunity to participate in decision making and to organize and pace the work, high level of supervisor control, and role ambiguity or lack of clarity about the job and criteria for adequate performance (Billings & Moos, 1982b).

Karasek (1979) has posited that strain is most likely to occur when job demands (task orientation and work pressure) are high and the individual has little discretion in deciding how to meet them (low autonomy , high control). When employees are allowed to make decisions about their work, high job demands can be stimulating and can promote active problem solving and innovation. These ideas were tested among representative groups of working men in the United States and Sweden. Men who held jobs that were demanding and lacking in autonomy were more likely to report mental exhaustion, depression, and insomnia; to consume more sleeping pills and tranquilizers; and to take more sick leave. These problems declined among men who shifted to less stressful jobs. At every level of job demand, men who were able to use their skills to make decisions experienced less strain. These findings held when job characteristics were rated by experts as well as by the men themselves; therefore, they are not influenced by potential artifacts of self-report.

The Position Analysis Questionnaire (PAQ) provides a composite picture of job characteristics obtained from ratings conducted by personnel specialists, supervisors, or job incumbents. Shaw and Riskind (1983) found some predictable associations between the independently derived PAQ dimensions and work strains reported by individuals in varied blue-collar, clerical, and professional occupations. Employees in jobs rated as encompassing controlled manual activities experienced more anxiety and depression, job dissatisfaction, and physical symptoms. Conversely, individuals located in responsible, challenging jobs with some decision-making latitude tended to report less negative affect and fewer symptoms and illnesses.

Mass psychogenic illness. Other researchers have considered episodes of "mass psychogenic illness" in work settings (e.g., Schmitt & Fitzgerald, 1982). These occur when employees experience symptoms such as headache, dizziness, and fatigue that cannot be traced to exposure to chemicals or other physical factors in the work place. Employees who report high work pressure, lack of autonomy and clarity, and poor relationships with their peers and supervisors tend to complain of more symptoms during such episodes. Similarly, the average number of symptoms reported by employees is higher in work groups characterized by these social climate factors. Thus, a lack of coworker and supervisor support may intensify the effects of high work demands and low autonomy on the prevalence of physical and mental symptoms.

Coronary heart disease and other medical conditions. Indices of job pressure or stress (such as work overload and role conflict) have been implicated in the development of varied medical conditions. After considering potential confounding factors (such as age, education, amount of cigarette smoking), House and his co-workers (House, McMichael, Wells, Kaplan, & Landerman, 1979) found that job stressors were related to self-reported angina, ulcers, and neurotic symptoms and to medical evidence of hypertension and other heart disease risk factors. Job stressors also were associated with respiratory and dermatological symptoms, but only among workers who were exposed to potentially noxious physical or chemical agents. There were some logically consistent connections between specific stressors and symptoms. For instance, angina was linked to stressors involving performance and achievement, whereas ulcer symptoms were related primarily to interpersonal tension and lack of self-esteem.

In an extension of his earlier work, Karasek and his colleagues (Karasek, Baker, Marxer, Ahlbom, & Theorell, 1981) obtained six-year follow-up data on their sample of employed Swedish men. Initially asymptomatic persons who developed a myocardial infarction or other signs of coronary heart disease (CHD) over the six years were matched with their asymptomatic peers who did not. The psychosocial characteristics of the work situation were indexed by the perceptions of working men from the nationwide interview survey rather than by the reports of the individuals who had CHD. High work demands in conjunction with low autonomy were predictive of new cases of CHD, even after considering risk factors such as age, obesity, and smoking. These associations were stronger among individuals whose work climate remained stable. Alfredsson, Karasek, and Theorell (1982) concluded that work demands are especially harmful when environmental constraints prevent optimal coping with them (low control) or when coping does not increase the chance for personal growth.

The Interplay of Work Climate Factors

Job characteristics and their social context. Hackman and Oldham (1980) posit that the motivating potential of a job increases with the identity and significance of the task, the variety of skills needed to perform it, and the level of autonomy and feedback. In fact, such job dimensions are linked to internal motivation as well as to higher work satisfaction and performance and less absenteeism. As I noted earlier, these five job conditions tap primarily the personal growth domain of work climate. Their impact should be moderated by contextual and social factors, such as the quality of relationships among employees and supervisors, as well as by individual growth needs. In a well-controlled experimental test of these ideas, Orpen (1979) found that job enrichment had a stronger and more favorable impact on attitudes among clerical employees with high growth needs and among those who were satisfied with contextual and social job factors. Moreover, some of the effects of job enrichment were thought to be due to interpersonal factors in that members of enriched groups worked together as a team more often than did their counterparts in unenriched jobs.

The social context may be more important than objective job conditions in determining perceptions of core task attributes and affective reactions to them. Griffin (1983) conducted a field experiment in which jobs were enriched for one group of employees, and supervisors of another group were trained to provide positive feedback. A third group of employees received both enriched tasks and positive feedback. Such feedback affected employees' views of their job-related tasks and their satisfaction with them as strongly as did job enrichment. More generally, socially provided information (such as job descriptions, role models, and verbal cues from peers and supervisors) can influence task perception and job motivation as much as do presumably more concrete aspects of a job.

Work stressors and work support. Job strains and health outcomes that are caused by psychosocial stressors should be affected by social support. According to Payne (1980), work groups can offer access to information about company ideologies and norms, supply guidance and feedback, stimulate cognitive reappraisal, and provide practical help in problem solving. Employees who enjoy cohesive relationships with their co-workers and supervisors do seem to experience fewer work stressors and to react less negatively to them (House, 1983). LaRocco, House, and French (1980) examined these ideas among a diverse group of more than 600 men in 23 occupations. Job-related support (as indexed by perceived help from supervisors and co-workers) had a beneficial impact on job-related strain (dissatisfaction and boredom) and health (depression and somatic symptoms), irrespective of the magnitude of work stressors. These sources of support also mitigated the impact of job stressors and strains on the health indices.

Social support can help individuals to manage stressors as well as to moderate their effects. The typical buffering hypothesis predicts an association between stressors and strain among employees who lack work support, but no (or a reduced) link among those with high support. If the main function of support is to help individuals cope with stressors, however, then support should reduce strain among highly stressed individuals. No relation would be expected between support and strain among individuals not under stress. When Seers and his colleagues (Seers, McGee, Serey, & Graen, 1983) examined these ideas in nine branches of a federal agency, their findings were more consistent with the coping than with the buffering perspective. For instance, social support from peers and the branch manager was associated with greater satisfaction with the immediate supervisor under conditions of high but not of low role conflict. In general, work-related support was more beneficial in coping with role conflict than with role ambiguity.

Relationship, goal, and system maintenance domains. In conjunction with a considerable body of other research, the studies just reviewed affirm the value of examining the interplay of relationship, goal orientation, and system maintenance factors in searching out the consequences of varying work climates. Work groups characterized by strong goal orientation and the opportunity for independent action tend to promote performance and to reduce absenteeism. Conversely, the combination of high job demands and lack of freedom seems to have an especially detrimental impact on health and satisfaction.

There is growing recognition of the importance of interpersonal relationships in moderating these associations. Co-workers and supervisor support improve job attitudes and morale as well as employees' motivation and commitment. But support in the absence of goal direction diminishes satisfaction and productivity, whereas the combination of consideration and structure promotes them (Tjosvold, 1984). Cohesive relationships amplify the influence of autonomy and task orientation and moderate the problematic consequences of highly demanding and constrained work settings.

Aside from their role in regulating and structuring a work setting, the system maintenance factors also can promote goal orientation and personal growth. Clear expectations about job tasks and policies, adequate performance feedback, and moderate organization and structure all contribute to satisfaction and effectiveness. In the relative absence of these system maintenance factors (that is, when job roles are ambiguous, feedback is sparse, and organizational policies are lax), there is a prevalence of health and behavioral problems. But an overemphasis on these factors (especially in the relative absence of autonomy) restricts employees' opportunities for personal development and may create tension and rigidity. Thus, all three sets of climate factors need to be considered in examining the impact of work settings (Moos, 1981, 1984).

Personal Characteristics as Moderating Factors

The discussion thus far implies that certain kinds of work climates typically have beneficial (or harmful) consequences. According to my model, however, such effects can be altered by personal factors. As I noted earlier, job challenge and enrichment seem to benefit most employees, but those who have high personal growth needs react more positively to it (Hackman & Oldham, 1980; Kemp & Cook, 1983; Orpen, 1979). Role clarity improves performance for competent employees more than it does for their less competent counterparts (McEnrue, 1984). Conversely, work structure may be more important for individuals whose growth needs are not as great. Such findings imply that an optimal match between person and environment can contribute to morale and reduce the dysfunctional consequences of some work settings.

Type A and Type B managers. Type A managers presumably have a competitive, hard-driving style and enjoy exercising control over their environment; therefore, a rigid, bureaucratic work setting should present a special threat or challenge to such managers. To test this idea, Chesney and Rosenman (1980) identified three groups of managers: a group in an internally controlled environment, a middle group, and a group in an externally controlled setting. As predicted, Type A managers in the externally controlled milieu reported more anxiety than did those in the freer one. Type B managers in the externally controlled setting reported less anxiety than did their Type B counterparts in more autonomous work situations. Type A employees who saw their work as encouraging autonomy and cohesiveness tended to have lower blood pressure than those who did not, whereas the reverse was true of Type Bs (Chesney et al., 1981). An extroverted, assertive Type A person may feel congruent in a cohesive, independent setting. More introverted Type Bs seem to be more comfortable in a structured setting that does not highlight autonomy or peer interaction.

Person–environment fit theory. French and his colleagues (French, Caplan, & Van Harrison, 1982) have formulated and tested a person–environment (P–E) congruence framework. Objective characteristics of the environment and the person index "objective" P–E fit. Similarly, indices of the perceived environment and of self-assessed personal characteristics can form a measure of subjective P–E fit. Objective and subjective measures of P–E congruence are only moderately related, and, in comparison to objective incongruence, perceived incongruence is more closely linked to employee morale and health.

The studies conducted by these investigators point to a U-shaped relationship between some aspects of P–E fit and indices of morale and strain. For instance, depression tends to be lowest for employees with good fit on job complexity and increases with both too little and too much complexity, either of which can prevent an individual from gaining a sense of self-esteem. Both too much and too little responsibility are associated with work-load dissatisfaction as well as anxiety and anger. In general, measures of P–E fit account for as much or more of the variance in work strain as do the additive effects of the component person and environment indices. These studies need to be broadened to include independently observed aspects of work settings and to distinguish between two aspects of congruence (a person's abilities in relation to job demands and the correspondence of a person's needs with environmental opportunities) (Caplan, 1983; French et al., 1982; Kahn, 1980).

Holland's congruence model. As noted earlier, Holland (1985) has proposed that people's personalities and occupations can be categorized into six types, each of which is associated with a distinctive work climate. Individuals who are congruent with their occupational environment (that is, who share the dominant interests and values of their work group) should be more satisfied and healthier than those who are not. Thus, realistic people should feel better in realistic environments, investigative people in investigative environments, and so on. Conversely, an investigative person who is relatively analytic and asocial may not fit well into a conventional environment that stresses conformity and control.

In general, processes of self-selection, job attrition, and gradual personality change seem to produce reasonably high P–E congruence. Individuals who are incongruent with their work settings tend to be less satisfied and productive in them. For instance, Furnham and Schaeffer (1984) found that employees with a poor P–E fit reported less job satisfaction and higher levels of mental distress. Investigators need to learn more about how people cope with incongruent work settings and about the factors that impel them to leave their jobs, try to modify them, or adapt to the situation and change their needs accordingly. Studies of "off quadrant" cases (that is, people who are satisfied even though their needs are not met by the work situation, and vice versa) can help to identify some of the salient issues, such as how individuals view their overall career progression (Scarpello & Campbell, 1983).

Job longevity. Another approach to P–E congruence is to examine the influence of a person's longevity on the job. In a perceptive analysis, Katz (1980) has formulated a three-stage framework of job longevity: a socialization stage, a period of innovation, and an adaptation phase. He posits that employees in the socialization phase try to establish personal acceptance and are reactive to supervisor and peer feedback, but they are not concerned about job properties such as task autonomy or variety. Newcomers may profit more from directive than participative goal setting, because knowing the supervisor's expectations helps to reduce uncertainty. In the innovation phase, employees are more responsive to the richness and challenge of their work and may react positively to job redesign. As employees move to the adaptation stage, even challenging jobs become routine, and the importance of contextual factors such as good relationships and working conditions increases. Thus, sources of job satisfaction and performance may change systematically with the length of time a person is in a given job.

The Work Climate of Health Care Settings

There is considerable interest now in identifying the special stressors involved in "people-processing" jobs such as teaching, law enforcement, and health care. For example, many health care workers assume responsibility for acutely ill people, function in situations that demand quick decisive action, and fill difficult and contradictory "boundary roles" by balancing the interests of patients with those of their families and the community. More than five million people are employed in the health care sector. Many of these health professionals have physical and mental health problems that can compromise the quality of patient care. Although research in this area has proceeded independently of the main body of studies on work settings, most of the issues are similar and the framework set forth earlier can help investigators to examine them.

Special problems seem to exist in health care work settings. The Work Environment Scale (WES) described earlier has been given to more than 1,600 employees in a variety of health care facilities. In comparison to a sample of more than 1,400 employees in business and industrial work settings, health care employees report less job involvement and less cohesiveness among co-workers and less support from supervisors. Moreover, health care settings are seen as lacking in autonomy and clarity, as less physically comfortable, and as placing more emphasis on work demands and supervisor control (see Figure 4). From the sociotechnical perspective, these differences probably reflect both the stressful and emotionally difficult nature of health care tasks and the problem of working in large, underbounded, but highly structured organizations (for examples of WES profiles for specific health care settings, see Moos, 1981).

The Impact of Health Care Work Climates

Morale and performance. Several aspects of health care work climates have been linked to employee morale and performance. For instance, Brady, Kinnaird, & Friedrich (1980) found that mental health center staff who see their work settings as having high levels of cohesiveness and supervisor support, as well as autonomy and innovation, report higher job satisfaction. Social workers who view their work as being well-defined and challenging, and view the work place as being supportive and physically comfortable, tend to be more satisfied with their jobs and to report less depression and somatic symptoms (Jayaratne & Chess, 1983, 1984). Nurses who report role ambiguity, little influence in decision making, and lack of feedback about the quality of their work also are more likely to experience emotional exhaustion and alienation (Maslach & Jackson, 1982). In general, human services workers tend to do better in a human relations rather than a rationalistic administrative context.

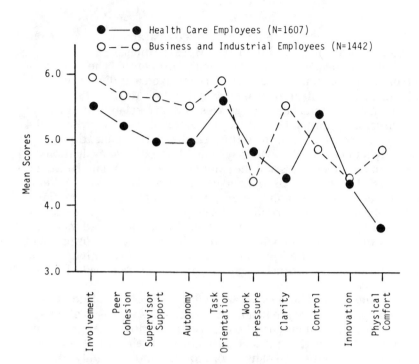

Figure 4. WES Form R profiles for health care and business/industrial work settings.

The findings just described are subject to the limitations of cross-sectional self-report methods. But a recent experimental study sustains the idea that variations in work climate are causally implicated in health care employees' satisfaction and performance (Parkes, 1982). Student nurses were assigned successively to four combinations of ward types, such that two factors—type of nursing (medical/surgical) and sex of patients (male/female)—were varied systematically. Each student nurse experienced both medical and surgical nursing and worked with both men and women patients.

Work support and job discretion were related to changes in student nurses' morale and physical symptoms. Specifically, when nurses were moved to a ward that they saw more favorably, affective symptoms decreased and work satisfaction increased. Moreover, an increase in perceived work support was associated with improved performance, whereas a decrease in support foreshadowed poorer performance. In comparison to wards for women, the student nurses saw wards for men more favorably and were more satisfied with them. Task discretion and work support reduced the differences between these two types of units by increasing nurses' morale and diminishing their negative affect. These findings are comparable to those we encountered in business and industrial work settings.

Organizational communication and performance. The quality of personal relationships in the work place is linked to indices of individual satisfaction and performance. Snyder and Morris (1984) have shown that communication processes also are related to objective measures of performance at the organizational level. They tapped 4 aspects of communication within 12 district organizations of a federally funded social services system. More positive evaluations of the quality of supervisors and the extent to which job-related information was shared were associated with lower work loads (clients served per employee) and higher organizational efficiency (relative and total costs of the operation). The employees of these 12 organizations were primarily women. Snyder and Morris speculated that communication processes may be less strongly related to performance in organizations populated primarily by men, where sensitivity to the social network and informal communication skills may be less developed.

The interplay of work climate domains. Work climate factors need to be considered jointly in health care settings as well as in other settings. Thus, hospital nurses who experience positive peer group and supervisory interaction manage to maintain their morale and performance even in the face of high role conflict and ambiguity. Organizational efforts to expedite the flow of work can buffer the impact of conflicting role demands and improve performance (Bedeian, Mossholder, & Armenakis, 1983). There also is evidence that challenging work can compensate for an unfavorable organizational climate. Ferris and Gilmore (1984) found that job complexity was a good predictor of satisfaction among nurses who were critical of the work climate of a skilled nursing facility, whereas it explained little of the variance in satisfaction when the climate was seen as being positive.

It may be important to distinguish between job stressors and job enrichers in human service work, as well as between client-related and nonclient job characteristics. Eisenstat and Felner (1984) found that job enrichers such as task significance and identity, autonomy, and positive feedback from staff were related to job satisfaction and feelings of personal accomplishment, but they did not seem to diminish the level of emotional exhaustion. Conversely, job stressors such as role conflict, ambiguity, and work pressure were associated with emotional exhaustion, but they did not diminish feelings of personal accomplishment. Positive feedback from clients helped to promote employees' feelings of personal accomplishment and commitment to clients, whereas positive feedback from staff was related to job involvement and morale. Positive feedback from patients and co-workers may be more important than supervisor feedback in facilitating hospital staff nurses' performance.

The role of personal factors. Studies in this area are beginning to examine personal characteristics as moderators of the links between job stressors and performance. Jamal (1984) noted that role conflict and overload were linked to poorer motivation and performance, less interest in patient care, and higher absenteeism and tardiness among hospital nurses. But nurses who had high organizational and professional commitment continued to work effectively in the face of these work stressors. Correspondence between occupational needs and rewards has been linked to job satisfaction among nurses and social workers. In a methodologically sophisticated study, Tziner (1983) asked one group of social workers to rate occupational rewards. Congruence between these rewards and the occupational needs of a second group of social workers was associated with their job satisfaction. This unique procedure effectively overcomes the potential method bias of having the same individuals judge job congruence and satisfaction.

The Determinants of Health Care Work Climates

The prevalence of staff demoralization and dysfunction varies widely among health care settings and is linked to their work climate. In turn, the work climate is a function of the organizational context (such as profit versus nonprofit ownership) and the three domains of the environmental system mentioned earlier (see Figure 3). Specifically, physical features, policy, and both staff and patient characteristics affect the work stressors faced by staff, as well as the resources available to cope with them.

Physical and organizational factors. Some investigators have linked the physical and organizational features of health care settings to aspects of their social environment and staff morale. Not surprisingly, staff working in newer, more pleasant physical facilities report higher satisfaction. Moreover, when staff in residential care settings have more adequate physical facilities, they tend to establish clearer policies and to provide residents with more choice in their everyday activities and more control over facility policies (Moos & Lemke, 1980).

Two organizational factors, job formalization and centralized decision making, have been linked to lack of support and less emphasis on autonomy and clarity. There also is more employee tension and dissatisfaction in programs that are not well-staffed and in those in which staff members have more extensive contact with patients. For instance, in comparison to state psychiatric hospital personnel in reasonably well-staffed admission units, personnel working in a poorly staffed admission area saw their work climate as being more demanding and as lower on autonomy, clarity, and the quality of co-worker and supervisor relationships (Drude & Lourie, 1984).

The structure and distribution of the work week is another important organizational factor. Eaton and Gottselig (1980) examined the effects on intensive care unit nurses of moving from 8-hour to 12-hour shifts. The modification heightened the emphasis on job autonomy and innovation and reduced supervisor control. These changes were linked to expectations that nurses exercise more initiative and freedom in fulfilling their responsibilities. There also was a decrease in work clarity, which may have occurred because of the need to share leadership roles during the night shift.

Task and suprapersonal factors. The primary task performed by health care personnel can influence the work climate. For example, health care work is thought to be more difficult for staff involved in patient care than for administrative and maintenance staff. Consistent with this idea, I found that patient care staff saw their work climate somewhat more negatively than personnel not involved in patient care. Specifically, they experienced their work as being more demanding and reported a lack of autonomy and job clarity and less support from co-workers and supervisors (Moos, 1981). Other studies have shown that staff who spend more time in direct patient care experience more emotional exhaustion (Maslach & Jackson, 1982).

Mohl and his colleagues (Mohl, Denny, Mote, & Coldwater, 1982) reasoned that both the type of patient care task and social systems factors (such as authority patterns and the division of labor) affect nurses' attitudes and stress levels. They looked at the work climate of two general medical (GMUs) and two intensive care units (ICUs). The ICU staff saw their work milieu as being more absorbing and cohesive as well as providing more autonomy, task orientation, clarity, and innovation, and as being less pressured. Thus, the ICU's primary task creates a particular work climate. However, social systems factors also were important in that one ICU was higher than the other on supervisor support and lower on staff distress. These findings are consistent with the sociotechnical perspective in highlighting the salience of both task and social characteristics.

Work settings, treatment milieus, and patient outcomes. Some studies have explored the relations among human service work environments, employees' job attitudes, and employees' attitudes and behavior toward clients. For instance, Johnson (1981) noted that cohesiveness among staff in group residential facilities was associated with a more supportive treatment environment that highlighted client autonomy and self-understanding. Holland and his colleagues (Holland, Konick, Buffum, Smith, & Petchers, 1981) posited that highly centralized, hierarchical organizational structures are associated with routinized, impersonal patterns of care. In turn, these custodial practices tend to make patients more passive. Decentralized or participative organizational structures in which decisions are made by staff in close contact with patients typically promote more individualized patterns of care.

When the researchers tested these ideas, they found that programs that admitted residents who were functioning better at intake (suprapersonal factor) were able to be less centralized (organizational factor). These two factors promoted staff and resident participation in treatment decisions, which, in turn, fostered individualized resident management practices and better resident outcomes. Residents' behavior showed more improvement in programs in which staff were more satisfied with their jobs. Thus, staff work attitudes are enhanced by better patient functioning, because it promotes the involvement of staff and patients in treatment decisions. These attitudes then have positive consequences for staff in terms of job satisfaction and for residents in terms of improvement in functioning and behavior.

Cherniss and Krantz (1983) believe that low morale stems primarily from loss of commitment and moral purpose in work rather than from the presumed stressors of long hours and arduous caretaking tasks. They have pointed out that a formal belief system can reduce the ambiguity and conflict of human service work, provide moral support and a rationale for difficult decisions, develop commitment by highlighting intrinsic rewards and valuing routine or aversive tasks, and contribute to self-selection and a better person–environment match. These factors have a positive impact on work climate by promoting job involvement and cohesiveness, trust and rapport among staff and supervisors, and greater choice and autonomy in everyday work activities. Cherniss and Krantz surmised that an ideology based only on "empirical support" or vague humanism cannot sustain human service workers. Such reasoning highlights the salience of the social and value context in which a job is performed.

Improving Health Care Work Settings

Individual and group coping strategies. Shinn and Morch (1983) have proposed a tripartite model of coping with work stressors. There are coping strategies used by individuals (setting limits on one's activities, focusing on the positive aspects of work), strategies undertaken by groups of individuals to aid one another (mutual support groups), and strategies initiated by agencies themselves (changing job designs, developing training programs, providing recreational facilities). Group and agency strategies were associated with greater job satisfaction and less alienation among child care workers, but individual coping responses did not seem to reduce the strain produced by work stressors. However, there was some evidence that problem-focused strategies (such as building job competence and changing one's approach to the job) were associated with less strain, whereas emotion-focused strategies (concentrating on non-job concerns and taking breaks) were linked to more strain. Shinn and Morch concluded that instrumental coping may have some positive effects but that individuals by themselves can make only limited changes in work conditions (see also Shinn, Rosario, Morch, & Chestnut, 1984).

Survey feedback and process consultation. One type of group approach is to provide supervisors and staff with information about the work climate and use it to increase communication among them. Such information may help to modify a work setting by identifying potential areas for change and monitoring the results of change efforts. Indices of employee expectations of the changeability of selected facets of work climate can aid in the process of organizational diagnosis and program modification (Pond, Armenakis, & Green, 1984).

In an example of a feedback and consultation project, my colleagues and I used the WES to help identify and reduce work stressors among staff in an intensive care unit (Koran, Moos, Moos, & Zasslow, 1983). Ward staff were quite dissatisfied and were showing dysfunctional reactions (such as mild depression and withdrawal from patients) that seemed to be due to high work demands, role ambiguity, and lack of autonomy and supervisor support. The feedback process was used to identify target areas for change and a number of innovations were instituted: Group discussions clarified areas of responsibilities for technicians and nurses, work shifts were increased from 8 to 10 hours, and regular times were established for meetings between nurses and physicians. Staff felt that the work climate improved, as was shown by increases in job involvement and cohesiveness, more staff autonomy and clarity, and less work pressure. Survey feedback and process consultation can help make health care work environments more satisfactory for their employees.

Monitoring the impact of change. Information about work climate also can be used to monitor and track the process of independently initiated changes. For example, Wilderman and Mezzelo (1984) examined the effects on work climate of implementing a direct service model in a community mental health center. Greater regularity and structure in the setting were accompanied by increases in clarity and supervisor control. Consistent with the fact that staff spent more time with clients and less with their colleagues, however, there was a decline in cohesiveness among the counselors themselves.

Quality assurance (QA) programs are being instituted in many health care settings, but little is known about their effects on staff morale. To address this issue, Sinclair and Frankel (1982) compared two outpatient treatment programs. One unit of each program was selected randomly to participate in QA activities; the other unit was designated as a control. Contrary to the concern that QA activities might result in a decline in morale, there were no significant negative changes in staff perceptions of the work environment. In fact, clinicians in the experimental group reported an increase in supervisor support and a decrease in control. Moreover, clinicians who provided higher quality services saw the work climate as being more cohesive and independent and less pressured. A well-managed QA program may have positive effects on health care work environments.

Considerable emphasis has been placed on increased participation in decision making as a way to counter role conflict and ambiguity and promote job satisfaction and well-being. Jackson (1983) tested these ideas in a hospital outpatient facility among nursing and clerical employees, who were assigned randomly to an increased participation or a control condition. Participation had a positive impact on perceived influence and job satisfaction and helped to reduce role conflict and ambiguity as well as emotional strain and absenteeism. Overall, involvement in decision making may lessen role strains and enhance valued individual and organizational outcomes.

Work in an Ecological Perspective

To fully understand the determinants and impacts of work settings, one needs to consider their links to other aspects of an individual's life context. Bronfenbrenner (1979) has defined the mesosystem as the interrelation between two or more microsystems, such as work and family or school and family. The exosystem is composed of settings that can affect a person even though the person does not take an active part in them (such as the influence of a person's work setting on his or her spouse). Recent research on the influence of work is beginning to examine mesosystem and exosystem relationships.

Links Between Work and Family

Investigators have noted both positive and negative connections between experiences at work and in the family (Greenhaus & Beutell, 1985). Piotrkowski (1979) identified three patterns of work–family interface. One is a pattern of positive carryover when personal gratification and information from work enrich the family. A more common pattern is one of negative carryover in which work overload and job-role conflict cause strain that creates tension in the family. The third pattern occurs when individuals try to conserve their energy and privacy and become less available to family members.

According to Piotrkowski (1979), work and family settings compete for scarce personal resources. As work stressors increase, families often have fewer interpersonal resources available to buffer them. Similarly, role theory implies that a person who fulfills both work and family roles may experience interrole conflict and work overload. From the social support perspective, however, location in a family may reduce the impact of work stressors on strain. In general, employment, marriage, and parenthood are associated with good physical health among both women and men. Verbrugge (1983) found that employed married parents tend to be the most healthy, whereas persons with none of these roles tend to have the poorest health. Notwithstanding these findings, combined work and family responsibilities can have detrimental consequences.

As noted earlier, human service work can be especially demanding. Jackson and Maslach (1982) examined the impact of the problematic aspects of police work (long irregular hours, concern about personal safety, adverse public opinion) on male officers and their wives. In general, officers who reported more work-related exhaustion and alienation were more likely to be described by their wives as coming home angry or upset, being physically exhausted, complaining about work problems, and having difficulty sleeping. These women felt isolated socially, noted that their husbands withdrew from family activities, and were dissatisfied with the quality of their family life. Thus, job tensions endemic to police work can disrupt the family and produce negative attitudes among wives toward their husbands' careers.

When Cooke and Rousseau (1984) examined similar ideas in a representative group of public school teachers, they found that high job-role expectations were linked to interrole conflict and overload, which were associated with more physical symptoms and lack of job and life satisfaction. Family roles also contributed to interrole conflict, which led to more physical strain, The association between job-role expectations (taking on extra duties, finishing job tasks by staying overtime) and perceived overload was progressively stronger among single teachers, those who were married, and those who had children. Finally, once interrole conflict was considered, family roles helped to buffer physical strain. Thus, family role expectations can promote strain among workers due to interrole conflict, but they also can provide the support to reduce it.

Most of the research on the impact of work has been conducted on men. However, the recent influx of women into the work force is beginning to spawn studies that consider women's multiple work and family roles. Warr and Parry (1982) posit that the link between a woman's employment status and her well-being is mediated by the quality of her family and social environment as well as by her occupational involvement and work relationships. They believe that a job can provide respite from domestic stress and fulfill unmet needs, such as for economic resources, adult company and support, or temporal routine and structure. Paid employment does seem to be most beneficial for women when occupational involvement is high, the job is attractive, and the nonoccupational milieu is adverse. There is a closer association between employment status and psychological well-being among working-class women than among their middle-class counterparts.

Results from the Framingham study (Haynes & Feinleib, 1980) tend to support the view that interrole conflict can have adverse consequences. The findings showed no increased risk of coronary heart disease (CHD) among working women as compared to housewives. But there was greater risk among women clerical workers with significant family responsibilities. Specifically, working women who had three or more children were more likely to develop CHD than were working women without children (11% versus 6.5%) or housewives with the same number of children (4.4%). Women clerical workers who were married to blue-collar men and had children were more than three times as likely to develop CHD as were nonclerical working mothers (21.3% versus 6%). There was no excess risk among women clerical workers married to men with white-collar jobs. Overall, women's involvement in multiple roles does not detract from their mental or physical health unless they lack support from significant others and evaluate their role performance negatively (Haw, 1982).

Work involvement may diminish an individual's available time and energy for the family and thereby contribute to family members' psychological distress. Kessler and McRae (1982) found that paid employment was associated with improved mental health among married women. This seemed to be due to objective changes in women's life situations coincident with their move out of the home and into the labor force. But their husbands reported increased housework or child care responsibilities (see also Jackson & Maslach, 1982).

Studies by my colleagues and me support these ideas. We found that salient features of work and family settings influenced each other. High stress in a married woman's job setting was associated with her husband's reports of less positive family relationships and more physical symptoms. Moreover, work pressure encountered by the spouses of married alcoholics was related to more conflict and less cohesiveness among their families. In turn, these family factors were linked to poorer treatment outcome for the alcoholic patient. By reducing the adaptive energy available to manage conflicts and maintain a cohesive family unit, stress in the work place can adversely affect the functioning of spouses and families (Billings & Moos, 1982a,b; Moos & Moos, 1984).

Work and Leisure Patterns

As noted earlier, some researchers have speculated about the connections between work and leisure activities. Kabanoff (1980) reviewed three perspectives on this issue. The compensation hypothesis suggests that individuals will "let off steam" in efforts to make up for deprivations experienced at work. The generalization theory argues for a direct carryover from work to leisure, that is, alienation from work is associated with alienation from leisure pursuits. The idea is that routine work is linked to narrow and restricted activities that promote passivity and impede personal growth. The segmentalist position argues that social experience is compartmentalized and the worlds of work and leisure thus are basically independent of each other.

Kabanoff and O'Brien (1980) have argued for the holistic assumption that there are connections between work and leisure activities. They asked respondents to describe their jobs on five task attributes covering autonomy, variety, skill utilization, work pressure, and social interaction. Respondents' leisure activities were rated by independent judges on the same five attributes. There was some support for the generalization hypothesis, in that people whose jobs were more varied and skilled engaged in leisure activities that also were characterized by these attributes. There also was evidence for a compensation effect in which work that is incongruent with a person's dominant orientation may be counterbalanced by leisure activities that are congruent with it. Persons who had high internal control and undemanding jobs with little autonomy tended to be involved in more demanding leisure pursuits. Conversely, externally oriented persons in pressured jobs that entailed independent decision making chose less demanding leisure.

More generally, patterns of work satisfaction may spill over to influence fulfillment and satisfaction in non-work areas (Staines, 1980). Such findings are consistent with Wilensky's (1981) views on the centrality of work and imply that the detrimental impact of work stressors on family life may outstrip the power of the family to buffer them. Rice (1984) has integrated these perspectives by emphasizing the salience of work in determining the perceived quality of life. Changes in the work place affect quality of life directly as well as indirectly through their influence on non-work domains, such as health, housing, leisure, and the family. For instance, the quality of leisure and family life may depend on work schedules and the level of health and energy that results in part from working conditions.

Work Factors, Personal Orientations, and Social Participation

Some researchers have linked specific aspects of work to an individual's values and patterns of interaction in family and leisure settings (mesosystem relationships). Kohn and Schooler (1983) identified a connection between job conditions that promote self-direction and flexibility (substantive complexity of work, relative freedom from routine, and lack of close supervision) and better intellectual functioning, a more positive self-concept, and greater interest in social issues. These findings were similar for employed women and men.

Kohn and Schooler believe that structural job conditions alter a person's way of dealing with the larger world. A job influences people's values and cognitive processes by confronting them with demands that must be met. Employees whose jobs require intellectual flexibility learn to exercise their cognitive ability in leisure time activities as well as on the job. Conversely, the long-term consequence of ideational flexibility is an increased likelihood of attaining a self-directed job. Comparable findings have been obtained among employees in Japan and Poland (Naoi & Schooler, 1984; Slomczynski, Miller, & Kohn, 1981). They support the idea that the conditions of work affect an individual's perspective toward the world in Asian and European countries and in socialist as well as capitalist societies.

Brousseau (1978) conducted a longitudinal study that supports these ideas. He assessed personal characteristics among new employees and measured aspects of their jobs by use of the Job Diagnostic Survey (JDS). Task identity and significance were associated with increases in employees' orientation toward activity and freedom from depression over a six-year follow-up. These relationships were stronger as job tenure increased. Moreover, they held both for self-reported job conditions and for average job characteristic scores based on all persons in a job category. Brousseau concluded that more complex jobs promote cognitive differentiation and the capacity for abstract thought, which contribute to an individual's active orientation, self-confidence, and well-being.

Schneewind, Beckmann, and Engfer (1983) have carried this perspective one step further in their studies of West German men and their families. They have shown that a man's ecological context (amount of living space, economic status) and job experiences (such as stimulation and autonomy) can influence the quality of his family environment. More specifically, an impoverished social context and a monotonous and constraining job are linked to a controlling and nonstimulating family climate. These conditions contribute to the father's and his son's authoritarianism and external control orientation. Conversely, an emotionally stimulating and well-organized family milieu is related to children's orientations toward internal control. Thus, characteristics of parents' work settings can change their orientation to the world and affect the outlook of their children (see also Moos & Fuhr, 1982).

Future Prospects

The growth of psychological research and a focus on the role of the individual in the work place is a welcome trend that can complement the more established sociological focus on organizational processes. This person-oriented perspective will be especially valuable in addressing emerging issues in the work setting. Important foci for future research include office automation and computer technology, the formation of work-site intervention and prevention programs, consideration of the active ways in which individuals shape and manage work, and the emergence of a holistic framework that encompasses the links between work and other life contexts.

Office Automation and Computer Technology

Computer-assisted technology and robotics will grow rapidly in the next decade and beyond. Work-place automation can alter individuals' control over their jobs and affect the work climate and its links to performance and health. Alcalay and Pasick (1983) have reasoned that technological innovations increase control for management and other professional workers but decrease it for clerical and blue-collar employees. Computer-based systems tend to increase job challenge and productivity and to heighten performance standards, but they also make the work environment more tense and demanding (Gutek, Bikson, & Mankin, 1984). Moreover, automation can lessen perceived control over work procedures and diminish the opportunity to interact with co-workers. Technology also may have an adverse impact on job complexity and lead to a routinization of work and eventually to intellectual rigidity and diminished self-efficacy.

An underlying question is how much technology inevitably shapes or determines the structure of work and employees' activities. Investigators need to examine the ways in which complex technology alters job strain and individuals' control over their jobs and inhibits the formation of social bonds at work. Future research can examine whether blue-collar or lower status employees are more likely to experience such consequences. Preventive strategies can be identified, such as providing job variation, designing technical operations so that people can work in pairs or groups, establishing communication channels to provide feedback, and allowing employees to participate in the selection of equipment and work space design when possible.

Work-Site Intervention and Prevention Programs

Poor job design and harsh work climates may create multiple problems, but job redesign and intervention programs can help to alleviate them. The organizational development (OD) and quality of working life (QWL) approaches provide two major perspectives on how to improve work settings. The OD perspective stems from Lewin's concepts of ecological psychology and his recognition of the open-system nature of persons and groups. The methods used to change organizations focus primarily on interpersonal and intragroup phenomena. In contrast, QWL programs tend to consider the entire work setting in a systems framework and to follow a sociotechnical approach (Huse, 1980).

Such intervention programs typically increase morale and job satisfaction and lead to a reduction in absenteeism. Employees report that they have more responsible and complex work roles, are more involved in decision making, and enjoy more latitude and freedom in their work. Moreover, performance and productivity either remain stable or show moderate improvement (Faucheux, Amado, & Laurent, 1982; see also Cummings, 1982; Huse, 1980). About 70 percent of OD interventions show positive effects, especially when they entail job redesign and are enhanced by system-wide commitment (Schneider, 1985). But enriched jobs may not have beneficial effects on employees in highly bureaucratic organizations. Moreover, short-term changes often fade out quickly over time. Attention to the interdependent role of contextual and personal factors should help to formulate more powerful intervention programs and maximize their effectiveness.

From the perspective of prevention, the work place is the most organized and structured aspect of many people's lives. It thus provides an attractive focus for physical fitness, stress management, and other health promotion programs (House, 1983; Murphy, 1984; Pate & Blair, 1983). In comparison to the usual community-based treatment, for example, work-site weight loss and hypertension control programs may be especially helpful and cost-effective. More basic changes in the conditions of work, such as adapting shift rotations to natural circadian rhythms, can improve employees' subjective well-being and reduce health risk factors (Orth-Gomer, 1983). Work settings provide ready-made channels of communication and efficient ways of developing and maintaining prevention programs.

Investigators need to learn more about the characteristics of effective intervention and prevention programs. Future studies can focus on the role of cohesiveness and support in the outcome of work-site health promotion programs, the identification of potentially successful participants, the way in which benefits can be maintained over time, and the issue of cost–benefit ratios (Murphy, 1984). Some programs teach employees more efficient coping strategies but do not eliminate sources of work stress. Rather than just helping individuals to adapt to poorly designed and potentially noxious job settings, however, we should pursue approaches that seek fundamental improvements in the conditions of work. Stress management and health promotion programs need to be planned in conjunction with OD and QWL approaches.

Individual and Group Coping Processes

Although there are some notable exceptions (e.g., Shinn & Morch, 1983), the essential thrust of research on work emphasizes the impact of organizational conditions on employees. Studies of the active ways in which individuals select and shape work milieus should prove fruitful. For example, there is a large body of research on the effects of performance feedback on employee behavior. As noted by Ashford and Cummings (1983), however, seeking information and feedback also is a coping style that individuals employ to reduce uncertainty, find out how they are perceived and evaluated, understand the expected outcome of their behavior, or learn how to achieve their goals. As the model in Figure 1 indicates, both personal and contextual factors are determinants of such coping processes and their outcomes. One area in which these issues should be considered concerns how newcomers experience and learn about unfamiliar organizational settings (Feldman & Brett, 1983; Louis, 1980).

New studies in this area should consider stress and coping theory and information about how individuals manage a diversity of life transitions and crises (Lazarus & Folkman, 1984; Moos, 1985). In one example, Menaghen and Mervis (1984) considered the effectiveness of individual coping efforts on job distress and occupational problems. None of the coping strategies helped to reduce occupational problems. However, a propensity to use optimistic comparisons and to refrain from restricting one's expectations were associated with less concurrent occupational distress and reductions in distress over time. These two coping skills also help to lessen emotional distress in the areas of marriage and parenting, implying that they may be generally efficacious. Longitudinal research on these issues should be anchored in a conceptual framework that encompasses work and other life contexts (for examples, see Bhagat, McQuaid, Lindholm, & Segovis, 1985; Parasuraman & Alutto, 1984).

Toward a Holistic Approach to Work

Because of the centrality of work in modern life, it may influence family and leisure patterns and partners and children, as well as a person's health, self-concept, and personal orientation. As new work patterns are developed, it is important to recognize that the style of organizational control may alter the way in which family and work settings affect each other. Type A organizations are exemplified by specialized career paths, short-term employment, formalized performance evaluation systems, and strict contractual relationships between management and employees. In contrast, Type Z organizations rely on a process of employee socialization that includes long-term employment contracts, nonspecialized career paths, and informal performance appraisal systems (Ouchi, 1981). Bhagat (1983) has posited that there should be less adverse impact of life strain on job involvement and performance in Type Z than in Type A settings. Type Z companies emphasize long-term effectiveness and thus are more tolerant of fluctuations in work productivity.

One neglected issue involves further specifying the salient aspects of participation in decision making in the work place. In general, a participative job setting benefits employees and their families. More research is needed to identify the precise sources of these benefits, such as the complexity of the work itself, the degree of autonomy and power of the individual or the work group, the amount of joint problem solving and decision making, and the social context in which the work is conducted. A related point to consider is the precise ways in which work experiences generalize to other contexts. For instance, individuals may develop new ideas and employ them in other settings, such as when participation in team meetings at work promotes joint decision making in the family.

Researchers also need to examine "negative spillover," such as when participative work creates new work stressors (unexpected overtime, tension that stems from feeling responsible for production deadlines, work that is too demanding) that interfere with family or leisure pursuits, elicits frustration that spawns authoritarian and short-tempered behavior with children, or promotes personal growth that is threatening to a person's spouse (Crouter, 1984). In addition, work groups can become too powerful and autocratic, set arbitrary limits on individual productivity, scapegoat and isolate nonconformists, and restrict personal initiative or foment resentment among those whose ideas are rejected (Locke & Schweiger, 1979). Evaluations of the impact of work need to include formative procedures and process approaches to identify the precise aspects of work conditions linked to different outcomes and to encompass costs as well as benefits to individuals in their life outside of work.

Karasek (1981) has speculated that the pervasive job constraints experienced in advanced industrial societies may lead to passive leisure activities and a gradual withdrawal from meaningful social participation. He proposed that work settings should become an integral part of the educational system of a modern society. They can help to promote cognitive development and personal maturity, serve to foster social competence and self-esteem, and influence the academic and social orientation of the next generation. Such considerations provide a compelling rationale for redesigning our current system of work.

References

Alcalay, R., & Pasick, R. (1983). Psychosocial factors and the technologies of work. *Social Science and Medicine, 17,* 1075–1084.

Alfredsson, L., Karasek, R., & Theorell, T. (1982). Myocardial infarction risk and psychosocial work environment: An analysis of the male Swedish working force. *Social Science and Medicine, 16,* 463–467.

Ashford, S., & Cummings, L. L. (1983). Feedback as an individual resource: Personal strategies of creating information. *Organizational Behavior and Human Performance, 32,* 370–398.

Becker, F. D. (1981). *Workspace: Creating environments in organizations.* New York: Praeger.

Bedeian, A., Mossholder, K., & Armenakis, A. (1983). Role perception-outcome relationships: Moderating effects of situational variables. *Human Relations, 36,* 167–184.

Berger, C., & Cummings, L. (1979). Organizational structure, attitudes and behaviors. In B. M. Staw (Ed.), *Research in organizational behavior* (Vol. 1, pp. 169–208). Greenwich, CT: JAI Press.

Bhagat, R. (1983). Effects of stressful life events on individual performance effectiveness and work adjustment processes within organizational settings: A research model. *Academy of Management Review, 8,* 660–671.

Bhagat, R., McQuaid, S., Lindholm, H., & Segovis, J. (1985). Total life stress: A multimethod validation of the construct and its effects on organizationally valued outcomes and withdrawal behaviors. *Journal of Applied Psychology, 70,* 202–214.

Billings, A., & Moos, R. (1982a). Social support and functioning among community and clinical groups: A panel model. *Journal of Behavioral Medicine, 5,* 295–311.

Billings, A., & Moos, R. (1982b). Work stress and the stress-buffering roles of work and family resources. *Journal of Occupational Behaviour, 3,* 215–232.

Brady, C., Kinnaird, K., & Friedrich, W. (1980). Job satisfaction and perception of social climate in a mental health facility. *Perceptual and Motor Skills, 51,* 559–564.

Bronfenbrenner, U. (1979). *The ecology of human development.* Cambridge, MA: Harvard University Press.

Brousseau, K. (1978). Personality and job experience. *Organizational Behavior and Human Performance, 22,* 235–252.

Calder, B., & Schurr, P. (1981). Attitudinal processes in organizations. In L. Cummings & B. Staw (Eds.), *Research in organizational behavior* (Vol. 3, pp. 282–302). Greenwich, CT: JAI Press.

Cammann, C., Fichman, M., Jenkins, G. D., & Klesh, J. (1983). Assessing the attitudes and perceptions of organizational members. In S. Seashore, E. Lawler, P. Mirvis, & C. Cammann (Eds.), *Assessing organizational change: A guide to methods, measures and practices* (pp. 72–138). New York: Wiley.

Caplan, R. (1983). Person–environment fit: Past, present, and future. In C. Cooper (Ed.), *Stress research: Issues for the 80's* (pp. 35–78). New York: Wiley.

Cherniss, C., & Krantz, D. (1983). The ideological community as an antidote to burnout in the human services. In B. A. Farber (Ed.), *Stress and burnout in the human service professions* (pp. 198–212). New York: Pergamon Press.

Chesney, M., & Rosenman, R. (1980). Type A behavior in the work-setting. In C. L. Cooper & R. Payne (Eds.), *Current concerns in occupational stress* (pp. 186–212). New York: Wiley.

Chesney, M., Sevelius, G., Black, G., Ward, M., Swan, G., & Rosenman, R. (1981). Work environment, Type A behavior and coronary heart disease risk factors. *Journal of Occupational Medicine, 23,* 551–555.

Conway, T., Vickers, R., Ward, H., & Rahe, R. (1981). Occupational stress and variation in cigarette, coffee and alcohol consumption. *Journal of Health and Social Behavior, 22,* 155–165.

Cooke, R., & Rousseau, D. (1984). Stress and strain from family roles and work role expectations. *Journal of Applied Psychology, 69,* 252–260.

Crouter, A. (1984). Participative work as an influence on human development. *Journal of Applied Developmental Psychology, 5,* 71–90.

Cummings, L. (1982). Organizational behavior. *Annual Review of Psychology, 33,* 541–579.

Dalton, D., Todor, W., Spendolini, M., Fielding, G., & Porter, L. (1980). Organization, structure and performance: A critical review. *Academy of Management Review, 5,* 49–64.

Drude, K., & Lourie, I. (1984). Staff perceptions of work environment in a state psychiatric hospital. *Psychological Reports, 54,* 263–268.

Eaton, P., & Gottselig, S. (1980). Effects of longer hours, shorter week on intensive care nurses. *Dimensions in Health Service, 57,* 25–27.

Eisenstat, R., & Felner, R. (1984). Toward a differentiated view of burnout: Personal and organizational mediators of job satisfaction and stress. *American Journal of Community Psychology, 12,* 411–430.

Faucheux, C., Amado, G., & Laurent, A. (1982). Organizational development and change. *Annual Review of Psychology, 33,* 343–370.

Feldman, D., & Brett, J. (1983). Coping with new jobs: A comparative study of new hires and job changers. *Academy of Management Journal, 26,* 258–272.

Fennell, M., Rodin, M., & Cantor, G. (1981). Problems in the work-setting, drinking and reasons for drinking. *Social Forces, 60,* 114–132.

Ferris, G., & Gilmore, D. (1984). The moderating role of work context in job design research: A test of competing models. *Academy of Management Journal, 27,* 885–892.

Fisher, C., & Gitelson, R. (1983). A meta-analysis of the correlates of role conflict and ambiguity. *Journal of Applied Psychology, 68,* 320–333.

French, J. R. P., Caplan, R., & Van Harrison, R. (Eds.). (1982). *The mechanisms of job stress and strain.* New York: Wiley.

Furnham, A., & Schaeffer, R. (1984). Person-environment fit, job satisfaction and mental health. *Journal of Occupational Psychology, 57,* 295–307.

Gavin, J., & Howe, J. (1975). Psychological climate: Some theoretical and empirical considerations. *Behavioral Science, 20,* 228–240.

Greenhaus, J., & Beutell, N. (1985). Sources of conflict between work and family roles. *Academy of Management Review, 10,* 76–88.

Griffin, R. (1983). Objective and social sources of information in task redesign: A field experiment. *Administrative Science Quarterly, 28,* 184–200.

Gutek, B., Bikson, T., & Mankin, D. (1984). Individual and organizational consequences of computer-based office information technology. In S. Oskamp (Ed.), *Applied social psychology annual: Applications in organizational settings* (Vol. 5, pp. 231–254). Beverly Hills, CA: Sage.

Hackman, J. R., & Oldham, G. (1980). *Work redesign*. Reading, MA: Addison Wesley.

Haw, M. A. (1982). Women, work, and stress: A review and agenda for the future. *Journal of Health and Social Behavior, 23,* 132–144.

Haynes, S., & Feinleib, M. (1980). Women, work, and coronary heart disease: Prospective findings from the Framingham Heart Study. *American Journal of Public Health, 70,* 133–141.

Hendrix, W., Ovalle, N., & Troxler, R. G. (1985). Behavioral and physiological consequences of stress and its antecedent factors. *Journal of Applied Psychology, 70,* 188–201.

Holland, J. (1985). *Making vocational choices: A theory of careers.* Englewood Cliffs, NJ: Prentice-Hall.

Holland, T., Konick, A., Buffum, W., Smith, M. K., & Petchers, M. (1981). Institutional structure and resident outcomes. *Journal of Health and Social Behavior, 22,* 433–444.

House, J. (1983). *Work stress and social support.* Reading, MA: Addison Wesley.

House, J., McMichael, A., Wells, J., Kaplan, B., & Landerman, L. (1979). Occupational stress and health among factory workers. *Journal of Health and Social Behavior, 20,* 139–160.

Huse, E. (1980). *Organization development and change.* St. Paul, MN: West.

Ivancevich, J., & Matteson, M. (1980). *Stress and work: A managerial perspective.* Glenview, IL: Scott Foresman.

Jackson, S. (1983). Participation in decision-making as a strategy for reducing job-related strain. *Journal of Applied Psychology, 68,* 3–19.

Jackson, S., & Maslach, C. (1982). After-effects of job-related stress: Families as victims. *Journal of Occupational Behavior, 3,* 63–77.

Jamal, M. (1984). Job stress and job performance controversy: An empirical assessment. *Organizational Behavior and Human Performance, 33,* 1–21.

James, L., Gent, M., Hatter, J., & Coray, K. (1979). Correlates of psychological influence: An illustration of the psychological climate approach to work environment perceptions. *Personnel Psychology, 32,* 563–588.

James, L., & Sells, S. (1981). Psychological climate: Theoretical perspectives and empirical research. In D. Magnusson (Ed.), *Toward a psychology of situations: An interactional perspective* (pp. 275–295). Hillsdale, NJ: Erlbaum.

Jayaratne, S., & Chess, W. (1983). Job satisfaction and burnout in social work. In B. A. Farber (Ed.), *Stress and burnout in the human service professions* (pp. 129–141). New York: Pergamon Press.

Jayaratne, S., & Chess, W. (1984). The effects of emotional support on perceived job stress and strain. *Journal of Applied Behavioral Science, 20,* 141–153.

Johnson, S. (1981). Staff cohesion in residential treatment. *Journal of Youth and Adolescence, 10,* 221–232.

Jones, A., & James, L. (1979). Psychological climate: Dimensions and relationships of individual and aggregated work environment perceptions. *Organizational Behavior and Human Performance, 23,* 201–250.

Kabanoff, B. (1980). Work and nonwork: A review of models, methods, and findings. *Psychological Bulletin, 88,* 60–77.

Kabanoff, B., & O'Brien, G. (1980). Work and leisure: A task attributes analysis. *Journal of Applied Psychology, 65,* 596–609.

Kahn, R. (1980). *Work and health.* New York: Wiley.

Karasek, R. (1979). Job demands, job decision latitude, and mental strain: Implications for job redesign. *Administrative Science Quarterly, 24,* 285–307.

Karasek, R. (1981). Job socialization and job strain: The implication of two related psychosocial mechanisms for job design. In B. Gardell & G. Johansson (Eds.), *Working life* (pp. 75–94). New York: Wiley.

Karasek, R., Baker, D., Marxer, F., Ahlbom, A., & Theorell, T. (1981). Job decision latitude, job demands, and cardiovascular disease: A prospective study of Swedish men. *American Journal of Public Health, 71,* 694–705.

Kasl, S. & Wells, J. (1985). Social support in the middle years: Work and the family. In S. Cohen & S. L. Syme (Eds.), *Social support and health* (pp. 175–198). New York: Academic Press.

Katz, R. (1980). Time and work: Toward an integrative perspective. In B. Staw & L. Cummings (Eds.), *Research in organizational behavior* (Vol. 2, pp. 81–127). Greenwich, CT: JAI Press.

Katz, D., & Kahn, R. (1978). *The social psychology of organizations.* New York: Wiley.

Kemp, N., & Cook, J. (1983). Job longevity and growth needs strength as joint moderators of the task design-job satisfaction relationship. *Human Relations, 36,* 883–898.

Kessler, R., & McRae, J. (1982). The effect of wives' employment on the mental health of married men and women. *American Sociological Review, 47,* 216–227.

Kohn, M., & Schooler, C. (1983). *Work and personality: An inquiry into the impact of social stratification.* Norwood, NJ: Ablex.

Koran, L., Moos, R., Moos, B., & Zasslow, M. (1983). Changing hospital work environments: An example of a burn unit. *General Hospital Psychiatry, 5,* 7–13.

LaRocco, J., House, J., & French, J. (1980). Social support, occupational stress, and health. *Journal of Health and Social Behavior, 21,* 202–218.

Lazarus, R., & Folkman, S. (1984). *Stress, appraisal, and coping.* New York: Springer.

Levin, H. (1983). The workplace: Employment and business interventions. In E. Seidman (Ed.), *Handbook of social intervention* (pp. 499–521). Beverly Hills, CA: Sage.

Locke, E., & Schweiger, D. (1979). Participation in decision making: One more look. In B. M. Staw (Ed.), *Research in organizational behavior* (Vol. 1, pp. 265–339). Greenwich, CT: JAI Press.

Louis, M. R. (1980). Surprise and sense-making: What newcomers experience in entering unfamiliar organizational settings. *Administrative Science Quarterly, 25,* 226–251.

Maslach, C., & Jackson, S. (1982). Burnout in health professions: A social psychological analysis. In G. Sanders & J. Suls (Eds.), *Social psychology of health and illness* (pp. 227–251). Hillsdale, NJ: Erlbaum.

McEnrue, M. (1984). Perceived competence as a moderator of the relationship between role clarity and job performance: A test of two hypotheses. *Organizational Behavior and Human Performance, 34,* 379–386.

Menaghan, E., & Mervis, E. (1984). Coping with occupational problems: The limits of individual efforts. *Journal of Health and Social Behavior, 25,* 406–423.

Mohl, P., Denny, N., Mote, T., & Coldwater, C. (1982). Hospital unit stressors that affect nurses: Primary task versus social factors. *Psychosomatics, 23,* 366–374.

Moos, R. (1974a). *Evaluating treatment environments: A social ecological approach.* New York: Wiley.

Moos, R. (1974b). *The Social Climate Scales: An overview.* Palo Alto, CA: Consulting Psychologists Press.

Moos, R. (1979). *Evaluating educational environments: Procedures, methods, findings and policy implications.* San Francisco, CA: Jossey-Bass.

Moos, R. (1981). *Work Environment Scale manual.* Palo Alto, CA: Consulting Psychologists Press.

Moos, R. (1984). Context and coping: Toward a unifying conceptual framework. *American Journal of Community Psychology, 12,* 5–25.

Moos, R. (1985). Evaluating social resources in community and health care contexts. In P. Karoly (Ed.), *Measurement strategies in health psychology* (pp. 433–459). New York: Wiley.

Moos, R., & Fuhr, R. (1982). The clinical use of social-ecological concepts: The case of an adolescent girl. *American Journal of Orthopsychiatry, 52,* 111–122.

Moos, R., & Lemke, S. (1980) Assessing the physical and architectural features of sheltered care settings. *Journal of Gerontology, 35,* 571–583.

Moos, R., & Lemke, S. (1984). Supportive residential settings for older people. In I. Altman, M. P. Lawton, & J. Wohlwill (Eds.), *Elderly people and the environment* (pp. 159–190). New York: Plenum.

Moos, R., & Moos, B. (1984). The process of recovery from alcoholism: III. Comparing functioning in families of alcoholics and matched control families. *Journal of Studies on Alcohol, 45,* 111–118.

Murphy, L. (1984). Occupational stress management: A review and appraisal. *Journal of Occupational Psychology, 57,* 1–15.

Naoi, A., & Schooler, C. (1984). Occupational conditions and psychological functioning in Japan. *American Journal of Sociology, 90,* 729–752.

Naylor, J., Pritchard, R., & Ilgen, D. (1980). *A theory of behavior in organizations.* New York: Academic Press.

O'Connor-Pooyan, A., Weekly, J., Peters, L., Frank, B., & Erenkrantz, B. (1984). Situational constraint effects on performance, affective reactions and turnover: A field replication and extension. *Journal of Applied Psychology, 69,* 663–672.

Oldham, G., & Brass, D. (1979). Employee reactions to an open-plan office: A naturally occurring quasi-experiment. *Administrative Science Quarterly, 24,* 267–284.

Oldham, G., & Rotchford, N. (1983). Relationships between office characteristics and employee reactions: A study of the physical environment. *Administrative Science Quarterly, 28,* 542–556.

Orpen, C. (1979). The effects of job enrichment on employee satisfaction, motivation, involvement, and performance: A field experiment. *Human Relations, 32,* 189–217.

Orth-Gomer, K. (1983). Intervention on coronary risk factors by adapting a shift work schedule to biologic rhythmicity. *Psychosomatic Medicine, 45,* 407–415.

Ouchi, W. G. (1981). *Theory Z.* Reading, MA: Addison-Wesley.

Parasuraman, S., & Alutto, J. (1981). An examination of the organizational antecedents of stressors at work. *Academy of Management Journal, 24,* 48–67.

Parasuraman, S., & Alutto, J. (1984). Sources and outcomes of stress in organizational settings: Toward the development of a structural model. *Academy of Management Journal, 27,* 330–350.

Parkes, K. (1982). Occupational stress among student nurses: A natural experiment. *Journal of Applied Psychology, 67,* 784–796.

Pate, R. R., & Blair, S. N. (1983). Physical fitness programming for health promotion at the worksite. *Preventive Medicine, 12,* 632–643.

Payne, R. (1980). Organizational stress and social support. In C. L. Cooper & R. Payne (Eds.), *Current concerns in occupational stress* (pp. 269–298). New York: Wiley.

Pierce, J., Dunham, R., & Cummings, L. L. (1984). Sources of environmental structuring and participant responses. *Organizational Behavior and Human Performance, 33,* 214–242.

Piotrkowski, C. (1979). *Work and the family system: A naturalistic study of working class and lower middle class families.* New York: Free Press.

Pond, S., Armenakis, A., & Green, S. (1984). The importance of employee expectations in organizational diagnosis. *Journal of Applied Behavioral Science, 20,* 167–180.

Price, R. (1985). Work and community. *American Journal of Community Psychology, 13,* 1–12.

Rice, R. (1984). Organizational work and the overall quality of life. In S. Oskamp (Ed.), *Applied social psychology annual: Vol. 5. Applications in organizational settings* (pp. 155–178). Beverly Hills, CA: Sage.

Roberts, K., & Glick, W. (1981). The job characteristics approach to task design: A critical review. *Journal of Applied Psychology, 66,* 193–217.

Salancik, G., & Pfeffer, J. (1978). A social information processing approach to job attitudes and task design. *Administrative Science Quarterly, 23,* 224–253.

Scarpello, V., & Campbell, J. (1983). Job satisfaction and the fit between individual needs and organizational rewards. *Journal of Occupational Psychology, 56,* 315–328.

Schmitt, N., & Fitzgerald, M. (1982). Mass psychogenic illness: Individual and aggregate data. In M. Colligan, J. Pennebaker, & L. Murphy (Eds.), *Mass psychogenic illness: A social psychological analysis* (pp. 87–100). Hillsdale, NJ: Erlbaum.

Schneewind, K., Beckmann, M., & Engfer, A. (1983). *Eltern und kinder: Umwelteinflusse auf das familiare verhalten.* Stuttgart, West Germany: Kollhammer.

Schneider, B. (1985). Organizational behavior. *Annual Review of Psychology, 36,* 573–611.

Seers, A., McGee, G., Serey, T., & Graen, G. (1983). The interaction of job stress and social support: A strong inference investigation. *Academy of Management Journal, 26*, 273–284.

Shaw, J., & Riskind, J. (1983). Predicting job stress using data from the position analysis questionnaire. *Journal of Applied Psychology, 68*, 253–261.

Shinn, M., & Morch, H. (1983). A tripartite model of coping with burnout. In B. A. Farber (Ed.), *Stress and burnout in the human service professions* (pp. 227–240). New York: Pergamon Press.

Shinn, M., Rosario, M., Morch, H., & Chestnut, D. (1984). Coping with job stress and burnout in the human services. *Journal of Personality and Social Psychology, 46*, 864–876.

Sinclair, C., & Frankel, M. (1982). The effect of quality assurance activities on the quality of mental health services. *Quality Review Bulletin, 8*, 7–15.

Slomczynski, K., Miller, J., & Kohn, M. (1981). Stratification, work, and values: A Polish–United States comparison. *American Sociological Review, 46*, 720–744.

Snyder, R., & Morris, J. (1984). Organizational communication and performance. *Journal of Applied Psychology, 69*, 461–465.

Staines, G. (1980). Spillover versus compensation: A review of the literature on the relationship between work and nonwork. *Human Relations, 33*, 111–129.

Staw, B. (1984). Organizational behavior: A review and reformulation of the fields outcome variables. *Annual Review of Psychology, 35*, 627–666.

Stern, G. (1970). *People in context: Measuring person–environment congruence in education and industry.* New York: Wiley.

Tjosvold, D. (1984). Effects of leader warmth and directiveness of subordinate performance on a subsequent task. *Journal of Applied Psychology, 69*, 422–427.

Tziner, A. (1983). Correspondence between occupational rewards and occupational needs and work satisfaction: A canonical redundancy analysis. *Journal of Occupational Psychology, 56*, 49–56.

Verbrugge, L. (1983). Multiple roles and physical health of women and men. *Journal of Health and Social Behavior, 24*, 16–30.

Warr, P., & Parry, G. (1982). Paid employment and women's psychological well-being. *Psychological Bulletin, 91*, 498–516.

Westman, M., Eden, D., & Shirom, A. (1985). Job stress, cigarette smoking and cessation: The conditioning effects of peer support. *Social Science and Medicine, 20*, 637–644.

Wilderman, R., & Mezzelo, J. (1984). Paving the road to financial security: The direct service model. *Administration in Mental Health, 2*, 184–194.

Wilensky, H. (1981). Family life cycle, work, and the quality of life: Reflections on the roots of happiness, despair, and indifference in modern society. In B. Gardell & G. Johansson (Eds.), *Working life* (pp. 235–265). New York: Wiley.

Wineman, J. (1982). The office environment as a source of stress. In G. W. Evans (Ed.), *Environmental stress* (pp. 256–285). New York: Cambridge University Press.

LOUIS G. TORNATZKY

TECHNOLOGICAL CHANGE AND THE STRUCTURE OF WORK

LOUIS G. TORNATZKY

L ouis G. Tornatzky has a PhD in social/personality psychology from Stanford University and a BA (cum laude) in psychology from Ohio State University. He currently is director of the Center for Social and Economic Issues, at the Industrial Technology Institute, Ann Arbor, Michigan. Prior to this position, he was head of Productivity Improvement Research, National Science Foundation, and before that, a professor of urban studies and psychology at Michigan State University. He directed the MSU-NIMH Innovation Diffusion Project while at Michigan State.

Tornatzky's research interests for the past 15 years have been focused on problems of innovation, organization change, and technology transfer. He has published seven books and written numerous articles and presented papers. His work has addressed topics as disparate as university–industry relations, organization development, management of academic research, program evaluation, and graduate training. Currently, his research is concentrated on the social and behavioral implications of computerized automation.

He resides in Ann Arbor with his wife Ann, his four children, ranging in age from 9 to 22, and two unruly dogs. When not preoccupied by problems of technological change, Tornatzky is likely to get as far as possible from the reaches of technology, by going particularly to northern Michigan trout streams and cross-country ski trails.

LOUIS G. TORNATZKY

TECHNOLOGICAL CHANGE AND THE STRUCTURE OF WORK

An Introduction to the New Technologies

The purpose of this chapter is to review the computer-assisted production or process technologies that pervade the American work place, to describe the social processes involved in their implementation, to review their impacts on work and work organization, and to suggest some research issues that might be of interest to psychologists. I should note at the outset that the body of knowledge that I review does not represent a traditional area of psychological inquiry. In fact, it would be stretching credulity to portray that literature as a research literature at all. It is confusingly interdisciplinary, rife with speculation and advocacy, and is best described as a set of observations in search of some coherent themes. However, the societal significance of the events that I describe, juxtaposed against the conceptual and methodological strengths of psychology, is proof that computer-assisted technology well ought to be a major priority for psychologists over the next decade.

The purpose of any technology is to extend human capability. Technologies can be conceived of as being tools to expand the physical, perceptual, and intellectual reach of humankind; they enable us to be stronger, see farther, and think better. To a large extent, intellectual history is a chronology of the development of increasingly sophisticated and helpful tools or technologies. It should be noted, however, that technologies differ in terms of which human capacities they extend and which functions they perform. For example, much of the technology that has been invented since the beginning of the industrial age has been designed to reduce or eliminate the labor component of work. The mechanical typewriter eliminated the hand scribing of documents; the gasoline-powered chainsaw replaced the cross-cut saw; the precision drill press eliminated the hand boring of holes. Similarly, technologies have been created to extend perceptual and sensory aspects of human behavior. These include the optic or electronic microscope and electronic communications systems.

This is not to imply that higher order intellectual functioning has not been mimicked by various technologies. In a sense, all technologies have knowledge embedded in them in one form or another (Pelz & Munson, 1980). For example, the mechanical adding machine had certain mathematical relationships built into it through various gears and levers. However, it is only within the last two to three decades that we have been able to embody in machines more extensive intellectual functions such as memory, performing complex relational tasks, and abstract learning and re-learning.

These latter developments have been closely tied to the revolution in microelectronics from the development of the transistor in the 1950s to successive generations of electronic devices, each more miniaturized and more powerful than the last, which have permitted computer-assisted technologies for the execution of work. It has now become economically and technically feasible to have microelectronic devices aiding us in our lives: controlling the ignition system in our cars; driving a desk-top PC in our homes; and, of course, as integral parts of the machines in the work place.

I will not attempt to provide a detailed description or complete catalog of the computer-assisted work place technologies that are currently available. However, let me briefly describe some technologies that are changing the world of work on both shop floor and in white collar settings.

This bare-bones description of a few core technologies is by no means a comprehensive description of the array of equipment available. The heterogeny of hardware and software available is mind-boggling (Goodman, 1985), and it is an analytic error to a priori assume that there are generic effects on social structure, job design, and the like. However, this snapshot can provide some shared nomenclature with which to discuss other aspects of computer-assisted technologies, such as their advantages and their abilities to be knit together into comprehensive production systems.

Computer-Assisted Design (CAD)

Many of us have a visual image of how product design and engineering occurs. That image is particularly acute for those of us who are familiar with mechanical drawing; we can readily see an engineer or draftsperson huddled over precise but complicated drawings and blueprints as a new product evolves. We also have a notion of products being produced as prototypes, tested in labs, and so on.

Now consider the emerging reality: A design engineer sits in front of a cathode ray tube, touching and manipulating with a light pen. He or she may sum up various geometric shapes from a computerized repertoire and glue them together electronically. The object might be rotated on the screen through various axes, to see how it looks from different perspectives. One might apply various load or stress tests to the emerging design and see how it might react in its real world application. Finally, the designed part could be converted into mathematically derived instructions for a machine tool to actually cut a piece of metal.

Numerically Controlled Machining

That machine tool is at the heart of the durable goods, particularly metal-working, industry. Machine tool is a generic term, but includes the mills, grinders, drill presses, lathes, and so on, which take raw material and convert it into finished parts. By grinding, cutting, and drilling, the general-purpose machine tool can in fact re-create itself, in addition to the wide variety of precision parts that are its normal output.

Machine tools were a particularly important focus of labor-saving technological advances during the late 19th and early 20th centuries. Much of this technology development was basic mechanical engineering, and through the use of gears, cams, and various control devices the machine tool reached its apex in mechanical development by the middle of the 20th century. Effective utilization of the general purpose machine tool is heavily contingent upon the skill and knowledge of trained machinists. Machining a part demands considerable skill in setting up the job, planning the sequence of cuts, and attending to cutting bit wear and breakage. It is not particularly adapted to high production runs, although it is uniquely appropriate for one-of-a-kind part production.

Even the skill of a journey machinist is pushed beyond its limits, however, in making parts of complex geometry. Literally hundreds of precise cuts might be necessary to produce some parts. Twenty-five years ago, with subsidization by the U.S. Air Force (Noble, 1979), a major research effort was undertaken to convert the operation and control of machine tools to digital instruction. That is, rather than the machine being guided by a set of levers and cranks under the control of a machinist, it would be manipulated by a series of instructions written in binary code. Initially, the first numerically controlled machines were directed by instructions punched on a paper tape. As the miniaturization and economies of microelectronics has emerged, this is being replaced by electronic computers, which can control the cutting operations of the machine.

The parallel evolution of computer-assisted design and engineering, as well as of computerized machine tools, permitted at least at a conceptual level the direct joining of design and engineering to manufacturing processes. The intent was to have digitalized machining instructions emerge directly from computerized design and engineering, and then be loaded on to a computerized numerically controlled machine ("Computer-Integrated Manufacturing," 1983).

Programmable Robotics

Most people have some science-fiction notion of robots, as might be judged from the immense popularity of *Star Wars* a few years ago. Industrial robots might seem more mundane than *Star Wars* robots, but they are actually more wondrous in the tasks that they can perform. Robots can be small and simple devices that merely pick up a single part, move it a few feet, and put it down; they can also be complex electric or hydraulic systems that have arms capable of moving in several axes of rotation.

One can get a finer appreciation of the capabilities of programmable robotics by considering the operation of a robotic paint line. Anyone who has wielded a can of spray paint knows that a delicate hand and arm motion is necessary to avoid drips and to ensure a uniform finish on a product. At a John Deere factory in Iowa, you can see a $150,000 tractor being painted green by a set of robots. Watching them, one gets the uncanny experience of seeing a robotic arm moving a spray paint nozzle through the air in a way that mimics a human operator. In fact, the motions of the robotic arm were programmed by playing back the actual motions of a human operator who first guided the arm through its movements. It should also be realized that the robotic paint station could be reprogrammed to paint vehicles of other sizes and shapes, and once reprogrammed would replicate that set of painting commands ad infinitum, right down to the last drip mark.

Office Automation

The origins of office automation lie perhaps in the mag-card typewriters in the mid-70s. On these machines, standard format letters or memorandums could be recorded on magnetic tape and then duplicated at will when needed. This very primitive technology was rapidly supplanted by dedicated word processing stations, which enabled the operator to summon up boilerplate phrases and paragraphs, preprogrammed structures for reports, and various routines to automatically correct spelling and grammar. Currently, office automation is moving in the direction of personal computers with which operators can do word processing and can perform a variety of other tasks, such as creating data bases, scheduling work activities, and so on.

The Advantages of Using Computer-Assisted Technologies

The term *automation* conjures up to the average individual a vision of huge machines punching or spewing out an endless progression of identical products. That is not an inappropriate metaphor for what I refer to as *hard automation,* or dedicated production technology. Up until the last 10 to 15 years, that in fact is what automation was. Its goal was to produce a single item over and over again, cheaply and reliably.

It should also be realized that there are distinct limits to the application of hard automation. Hard automation is only appropriate for mass production. In short, if one is going to produce a zillion replications of product X, then one should use hard automation. However, if one is likely to be producing from a dozen to several hundred units of part X, then convert to making part Y, and then come back to part X, then other alternatives need to be explored.

It should also be realized that batch or small lot production is the norm for most jobs. Whether machining a pulley from a casting, or sending out letters of rejection to graduate school applicants, the range of output is usually limited, with a large portion of $N=1$ situations. Most products are not truly mass produced. A great deal of effort is expended in work settings to set up jobs, and much of the time that is dedicated to making a product is actually spent in inventory waiting for the next operation to be performed. (One trade press estimate is that 95% of the time a part remains in a manufacturing shop is in in-process inventory.)

Until the advent of computer-assisted technologies, there was no alternative for batch production other than the use of general-purpose machines operated by skilled operators. This was the case on both the factory floor and in the office setting. The skilled typist with an IBM Selectric was a wonderful general-purpose production unit, as was the skilled machinist operating a lathe. The use of general purpose machines and skilled operators introduced great sources of variability into the production process, however—particularly in product quality. Too many uncertainties, particularly those introduced by inherently unpredictable human operators, exacerbated the efforts of management to rationalize and control costs.

The benefits of programmable automation are that it permits both the flexibility of general purpose machines and skilled operators and approaches the quality control and lower production costs of mass production. For example, once a well planned and formatted form letter had been entered into the memory of a computerized word processor, it could be reproduced with the same uniform quality as if it were typeset and printed in quantities of several thousand; once the programmed instructions for machine tool path had been debugged, it could then produce lots of five, a dozen, or a hundred of the same quality level (at least theoretically). The time dedicated to set-up, formatting, and design of the work task was eliminated once the first item had been made.

The discussion thus far has treated computer-assisted technologies individually and, by implication, as stand-alone machines or tools. However, one of the most significant aspects of the new technologies (particularly from a social and organizational perspective) is the ability to link them together electronically for the execution of work. In fact, it has been argued that stand-alone programmable automation, and integrated systems, are qualitatively different technologies, particularly as they influence job demands and organizational structure (Majchrzak, 1985). As computer-assisted technologies are knit together into computer-integrated systems, they begin to mimic the features of a continuous process production facility, such as an oil refinery or a nuclear reactor. As systems become integrated, the benefits of computer-assisted technologies become more apparent (National Research Council, 1984).

Consider the following scenario: Assume that a CAD workstation had created a design for a part, a process that included performing various engineering tests via computerized simulation. The digitalized production instructions would be sent to a numerically controlled machining center, with other electronic messages going to an automated warehouse, to request a steel billet for the part. Programmable robots with specially designed grippers would move the piece of steel from different sections of the production line and would also automatically change machine tool bits when sensing devices would register excessive toolware. Once the part had been machined, it would be automatically transferred to the shipping area.

Consider another scenario: Mr. X walks into a car dealership, plunks down his money and orders a new 1991 Saturn (from General Motors), including his choices on various options of accessories, trim, and color. The order is entered into the Saturn computer system, and immediately a date for production and delivery of Mr. X's car is determined. At the same time, digitalized commands are sent to hundreds or perhaps thousands of supplier companies, which build components of various types and variety for the Saturn vehicle. These commands and orders are entered on each of the suppliers' computerized production control systems, and through a cascading architecture of computer control, get down to the materials ordering and machine control level. The parts from which Mr. X's car is to be assembled at the Saturn assembly facility arrive in the correct, precoded just-in-time sequence at the loading dock and are delivered to the assembly area in the plant.

The purpose of these thumbnail descriptions is to illustrate one of the more significant characteristics of computer-assisted technologies when they are configured as integrated systems. That is, they tend to have an implosive effect on interorganizational and intraorganizational structural relations. They tend to supplant the boundaries between and within organizations. A computer-integrated work setting is not only a hard technology, it also represents a theory of organizing.

Whether one is producing reports or bumper guards, production systems tend to be rife with redundant information. Organizations tend to be organized along functional lines (lathe operators are situated in one place, and the typing pool is located in another), and the articles that are being worked on spend most of their time in an organization waiting in queues (otherwise known as inventory) to be worked on. Monitoring this sequential process in a traditional organization demands a plethora of checklists, clip boards, monitoring systems, and the like, all of which largely exist in parallel and in duplication of one another. Computer-assisted technologies significantly eliminate that situation.

Computer-Assisted Technologies as Innovations

It should be apparent from this discussion that computer-assisted technologies represent a dramatic and qualitative shift from the technologies that they replace. They disrupt functional and hierarchical organizational structure, change the nature of specific jobs, dislocate people from their prior jobs, and permit dramatic advantages in product flexibility and quality control. Moreover, the impacts of these technologies tend to be systemic rather than isolated. If one were to map these technologies against the innovation characteristics that are known to be related to ease of adoption (Tornatzky & Klein, 1982), one could predict the difficulty with which they might be utilized. These are technologies that are extremely complex, they are costly, their relative advantages are sometimes obscure, and they are often incompatible with past ways of doing business.

This implies that the deployment of these technologies is not merely a capital investment problem. The process by which computer-assisted technologies are considered, adopted, implemented, and routinized involves phenomena that are likely to take at least months and more often years to play themselves out (Yin, 1979). The most frequently needed new job that is created by introducing these technologies is that of change agent or process champion (Gerwin, 1982), a position that is rarely given official sanction. This suggests, in turn, that one cannot merely consider the features of these technologies in the abstract and then look at their effects, apart from the innovation process that is triggered when one departs along the path of programmable automation. The installation of these technologies constitutes a major technical and social innovation.

It is also difficult to think about the "steady state" effects of computer-assisted technologies because the technologies themselves are rapidly changing and evolving. It is difficult to talk about effects when the technologies themselves are moving targets. It can be argued that computer-assisted technology will always be reinverting itself, particularly in its software aspects, given the negligible capital barriers to entry. I argue that the company environment should be examined during the process of deploying these technologies, and because that process is so lengthy, perhaps never ending, it provides a good vision of the future.

Adopting and Implementing
Computer-Assisted Technologies

Most conceptions of the process of technological innovation are based on the idea that activities move through a set of stages or phases as the organization moves from initial technological awakening to full utilization of an innovation. Early work in the diffusion-of-innovation tradition (Rogers, 1962) focused primarily on the preliminary stages, such as becoming aware of a new technology and then proceeding to adopt it. Gradually, it became clearer that adoption is not a single event, but rather the start of a longitudinal process of organizational adaptation and implementation. More recently, Yin (1979) has argued that it is necessary to attend to the way in which an innovation becomes stabilized or routinized into the ongoing activities of the organization through standardized procedures, protocols, permanent staffing, and the like.

Based on a previous review of the technological innovation literature (Tornatzky, et al., 1983), I will follow a stage-specific approach in discussing the problems confronting users of computer-assisted technologies. For example, the issues and decisions involved in choosing equipment may be fundamentally different from those necessary to get it running. Additionally, it is worth emphasizing that the process of technological innovation is not confined to a single locus in the organization, nor to an unchanging set of players. Rather, different constituencies are involved at different stages, as well as different functions of the organization and different social aggregations.

The Process of Decision Making

The nature of these technologies tends to affect the work environment by changing the ways in which corporate decisions are made about whether and what technologies are to be adopted. The sources of influence include (a) the amount and sources of information about the new technologies, (b) the cross-functional nature of decisions, (c) the multilevel nature of decisions, and (d) the uncertain criteria for decisions. In contrast to other more obscure innovations, there is no lack of technical information about the new computer-assisted technologies for the potential user. The problem is trying to sort out the plethora of information available and to make rational and defensible choices among alternative technologies.

One issue is that users of the new technologies, whether on the shop floor or in the office, rely on equipment vendors as their major source of information about the technologies (Swanson, 1984). Although vendors are usually considered to be highly credible (Kozlowski, 1985; Rolland & Smith, 1984), the nature of these technologies is such that the information is inherently bound to be incomplete. For example, the productivity-enhancing advantages of computer-assisted technologies can best be realized in systemic applications rather than in stand-alone installations. This means that the potential users of these technologies need to realize how different types of machines can connect with one another. Can the programming features of this robot be utilized in conjunction with that machine tool or that automatic guided vehicle? By analogy, visualize the problems of putting together a home stereo system and choosing equipment from several companies, and then expand the choice options to several thousand uniquely configured systems; then one can realize the difficulties being confronted by users in this field. Information overload has maximized decision uncertainty.

The systemic potential of these technologies also creates problems regarding the breadth and complexity of the adoption decision process: It expands the constituencies involved. Because the technologies have the capability of linking together different functions of the organization, adoption decisions become likewise cross-functional. For example, with the old technologies it would be perfectly understandable for manufacturing to go off by itself and consider specifications for a drill press and to make a justification for that stand-alone use on the shop floor on the basis of direct labor reduction, expected machine life, and so on. However, with the computer-assisted technologies, the choice of production equipment also has implications for the kinds of products that can be sold and marketed, with how orders can be filled, and for what kinds of products ought and could be designed. As a result, it is difficult to deal out other functions of the organization during the evaluation period. A variety of functional units and stakeholder groups will need to be involved in the adoption decision-making process.

A third aspect of the planning and selection process is a de facto reduction of organizational hierarchy. Although the number of operators may be reduced, their importance for system success is usually enhanced. For example, not involving maintenance people in system planning may ultimately result in more downtime (Foulkes & Hirsch, 1984). Not forewarning or involving organized labor in new technology decisions increases the prospects of opposition. As a result, technology agreements in union contracts call for prior notification of impending technology change and, in a few cases, active involvement in the planning process. Managers in nonunion settings are also realizing the benefits of participative planning, perhaps more so.

It should be realized that abundant empirical literature exists to support participative decision making as a way to increase acceptance of new technology (e.g., Tornatzky, Fergus, Avellar, & Fairweather, 1980). For example, in a study of 55 work groups adopting office automation, user participation in planning work organization was a strong predictor of implementation success (Bikson, Gutek, & Mankin, 1985). To the extent that planning and deciding about new technology becomes an ongoing process, it will probably yield permanent changes in the organizational influence structure. It is difficult to see how the current planning process for the 1991 Saturn will not permanently change General Motors–United Auto Workers labor relations.

Finally, in attempting to cost-justify or make economic comparisons between alternative types of equipment adopting organizations are beset with problems (Kaplan, 1984). The criteria historically used are simply less appropriate. Traditional capital budgeting and accounting techniques assume some continuity in product line and manufacturing processes. However, as already noted, the programmability of computer-assisted production technologies permits replicating small batches or custom job lots economically. Computer-assisted technologies also permit the exploiting of new untested market opportunities that will have unpredictable consequences for the company. In one case, the installation of a computer-assisted manufacturing system and related business systems permitted a small company to produce custom products at nearly the same cost as it did to produce standard products (Roitman, 1985). Its business went from being primarily a catalog company to producing custom orders.

A variety of responses to this state of affairs have emerged. There is anecdotal evidence that companies have in effect thrown the baby out with the bath water, and sailed headlong into major capital investment efforts in flexible manufacturing and justified their actions on strategic grounds. However, this scenario may be overblown. A recent content analytic study was performed with five companies (Dean, 1985) that were deciding whether to adopt computer-aided manufacturing. The results indicated that the decision model that was most clearly confirmed was a rational approach. The limitations of retrospective small N studies notwithstanding, the results are interesting. Attempts have also been made to model and simulate the economic affects of advanced automation and to build more comprehensive decision models.

The Process of Implementation

Once the decision has been made to adopt computer-assisted technology, it is a lengthy and laborious process to implement the technologies. Recent innovation research has shown that getting the technologies installed, running, and working to full potential is a major source of organizational upset. I commented earlier about the dependence of purchasers on equipment vendors for information about alternative technologies; this dependence continues after their purchase. Early in the history of computer-assisted technologies there was great hope that users could in effect make turnkey procurements from vendors. That is, a complete system could be purchased, installed, debugged, and brought up to full productive capacity (including the training of employees) all by the vendors themselves. Recent research by Ettlie (in press) indicates that the user/vendor relationship is indeed crucial in successful implementation.

There are some interesting interorganizational, sociological issues involved here. To be successful, an implementing organization must be established that includes personnel from both the purchasing and the vending organization. This group must continue to exist over time, be able to work together satisfactorily, and must approach the implementation process as a continuous redesign and reperfecting activity. In short, implementers do not merely bolt down the equipment and start it up.

Similarly, an implementing company does not merely introduce its employees to a newly purchased system and expect them to operate it to full capacity. The major hidden cost in implementation lies in training employees and upgrading their skills. Technical training in computer-assisted technologies is a major and booming industry in the United States. In a survey of 300 human resource executives of Fortune 1500 firms (ITT, 1984), 76 percent of the companies reported that operations are being influenced by technological and economic change, and of these, 57 percent report that employees are consistently being put into positions that require additional training. Another industry survey (Rolland & Smith, 1984) identified lack of staff knowledge as the major obstacle to implementing advanced technology. As might be guessed, much of the formal technical training is provided by vendor organizations (Majchrzak, Nieva, & Newmann, 1985), but as also might be guessed, the quality and scope of the vendor training varies widely. In a study of managers using office automation (Fleischer & Morell, 1985) managers reported great dissatisfaction with vendor-provided training, as did a sample of general users (Johnson, 1985).

Experience and some emerging research findings (e.g., Johnson, 1985), suggest that training in the new technologies may be a misnomer; narrow skills training may be necessary but insufficient. It appears that to successfully utilize computer-assisted technologies, employees not only need to know how to operate machines in a narrow technical sense, but they also need to understand the principles behind their use and the larger systems of which they are more often a part. For example, in her study of office automation systems, Johnson (1985) identified four levels of increasingly sophisticated and innovative uses of the technology. The first level approximated a horseless carriage level of application, in which operators merely used office systems as typewriters with lights. In contrast, the highest level of implementation involved programming, greater uses of software menus, non-word-processing applications, and the like. Differences between the Level 1 type of applications and a Level 4 type of application, was not in the technology itself. Instead, the operators and users in the Level 4 organizations were much more aware of the principles involved in office systems, and understanding how the machines think.

Complementary findings emerge from a study of 34 British companies implementing CAD (Arnold & Bessant, 1984). Training was crucial in successful implementation, particularly training the manager in the systemic aspects of the technology. If not acquired, the technology was used in a "writing with light" approach, which yielded only minimal productivity-enhancing benefits. For example, to use the technology as a complete system, the operators needed to spend most of their working day on the terminal. If management did not appreciate this fact, they would not buy enough work stations.

These vignettes about CAD and office systems lead naturally to another principle of effective implementation practice. The participative decision making that began during planning must continue during implementation and must extend to the lowest levels of the organizational hierarchy, as well as across functional groups. Engineering fantasies to the contrary, direct labor and first-line operators will not be eliminated from the work place of the future. Moreover, because the technology tends to knit together different functional groups—marketing, financial, design, manufacturing—the planning of its implementation tends to involve those same groups. Cross-functional participative processes tend to become stabilized.

On the basis of experience and research thus far, there appears to be no best way or identifiable structure in which to facilitate the participation process. Some organizations have put their faith in the use of "skunk works," which is a temporary group whose defined life and single purpose is to facilitate implementation. In some organizations, the implementation process has been allocated to established and legitimated functions, particularly training. Training is seen not only as a vehicle to provide knowledge and skills; it is also seen as a need to facilitate organizational change processes and technology transfer efforts.

Although I have suggested that permanent social and organizational changes emerge as an unplanned residue of the innovation process, there is also evidence that planned administrative and social–organizational changes are paralleling technology implementation. Ettlie (1985) has reported a synchronicity between the implementation of advanced manufacturing and the implementation of innovative administrative structures. In a sample of 39 companies implementing computer-assisted manufacturing, he found a correlation of .46 between the introduction of administrative innovations and technology system radicalness and a correlation of .54 between administrative innovation and success of the implementation.

The Effects of New Technologies in the Work Place

It should again be emphasized that considering these widely heterogenous technologies as "technology variables" is a grave error conceptually and in point of fact (Goodman, 1985). A better approach is to consider technology clusters, such as numerical control, CAD, and so forth. This qualification noted, and realizing that most companies are still in the throes of changeover, there is some accumulating experience on how these technologies affect employment, work, and the organization more permanently. The growth of these technologies will have affects on the numbers of jobs, types of jobs, and the nature of organization structure and processes.

Job Displacement

It is clear that computer-assisted technologies, on both the shop floor and in the office setting, will displace workers from their jobs. How many jobs will be displaced, and at what rate, remains in some dispute. This issue has been addressed in several labor economic studies (Hunt, 1983; Leontief & Duchin, 1983; Levin & Rumberger, 1983; Rumberger & Levin, 1984). In order to qualify what follows, it should be understood that these are macroeconomic studies with differing assumptions and sometimes using different data bases. Past history suggests that they are better at predicting in terms of large job or industry categories and subject to considerable variability in making finer estimates.

Most researchers agree that the implementation of computer-assisted technologies will produce job loss or decreased job gain in these settings or industries in which they are heavily deployed. For example, there is a consensus that they will accelerate the decline of jobs in manufacturing that has been occurring for several years now. It is also clear that job displacement effects will be technology-specific or will manifest themselves via technology-industry or technology-industry job interactions. For example, a study on robotics (Hunt, 1983) estimates that over 100,000 U.S. jobs will be eliminated by the technology by 1990, although some 12,000 to 25,000 new robotics technician jobs will be created, as well as 4,000 to 5,300 new engineer positions.

Two investigators (Levin & Rumberger, 1983; Rumberger & Levin, 1984) argue that the new technologies are heavily involved in the "deskilling" of the economy—more low-skilled jobs are being created than are high-tech jobs. Citing data on the high absolute growth (computer-related jobs are clearly in the top 20 of job growth rate) of jobs in service industries and in job categories that are nontechnical, such as secretarial, these investigators implicate computer-assisted technologies as the villain.

I will treat the deskilling issue in more detail later, but I should note that the relation between job growth and technology implementation, in the near term at least, is nowhere that clear. In a highly provocative paper, Adler (1986) cited data between 1966 and 1981 from 19 manufacturing industries on productivity growth (seen as a proxy for technology) and job growth. The relationship was negligible (r=.10) albeit positive. Macroeconomic considerations, such as trade policy, were seen as being much more important.

Moreover, it is relatively clear that the job displacement effects of computer-assisted technologies will have wide geographic variability in their impact and will be particularly concentrated in certain types of jobs. For example, major displacement has already taken place in the industrial midwest, where manufacturing tends to be concentrated, and where short-term macroeconomic pressures have been the greatest. Additionally, certain technologies will have dramatic effects on certain jobs. For example, it is estimated that up to 20 percent of welding jobs will be eliminated in the automobile industry by the year

1990, as well as up to 37 percent of spray painting jobs (Hunt, 1983): These are particularly fruitful areas for the application of computer-controlled robotics. Another technology-specific estimate (Leontief & Duchin, 1983), suggests that all drafting jobs will be eliminated by the year 2000 due to computer-aided design.

It should also be realized that displacement in the form of dismissal is not inevitable, but dependent on human resources policies and whether the technologies are introduced at a gradual, manageable pace or in an effort to play technological catch-up. For example, a study of Japanese technology by Mine (1985) suggests that most workers keep their jobs and at a similar or greater skill level.

It is important to get a historical perspective on these issues. One interesting historical analogue is the experience of the agricultural sector over the past 100 years (Leontief & Duchin, 1983). As late as the year 1870, 53 percent of the U.S. labor force was tied up in farming. Over a period of 100 years, this was reduced through a series of labor-saving technology to the present level of 3 percent. For the most part this was accomplished without major social dislocations. The reason, of course, is that this transition in the agricultural sector was largely achieved through attrition of the farming population, and it played itself out over a period of decades. Sons of farmers tended not to become farmers themselves but moved into other parts of the economy.

To the extent that the transition in American manufacturing is less than optimal, it will largely be attributable to international economics. Since WWII, the United States is increasingly part of a world economy and subject to the intense price and quality competition from Japan and western Europe. In short, the computer-assisted technologies have necessarily been implemented in a relatively rapid timeframe, particularly in the automobile industry. This is essentially the argument that Adler (1986) makes; we can thank the Reagan dollar and trade policies more for job displacement than the new technologies. It is imperative, however, that implementation of the new technologies *does* occur so that the United States does not lose further market share thus causing major social dislocations among displaced industrial workers.

Redistribution of Responsibility

What will be the permanent social system in the work place confronted by workers not displaced, and what will their jobs be like? I have stated repeatedly that computer-assisted technologies tend to blend organizational functions and to relax hierarchical structures. Advanced manufacturing technology has enabled manufacturers to organize plants according to products rather than to function (Kolodny & Armstrong, 1985). Thus, all the machining and processing functions pertaining to an individual product can be linked together by computer and located in a single area of the shop. This has also enabled workers in that production area to have responsibility over a larger portion of the total work task, which is compatible with social technical design considerations (Davis & Taylor, 1976): A single operator might have control, aided by computer, over a sequence of machining operations, just as an engineer, by the use of computer-aided design, has control over a greater portion of the design process (Majchrzak, Collins, & Mandeville, 1985).

Not only has the new technology tended to link together different organizational functions, it has also tended to disrupt the nominal status hierarchy of those functions. In recent history the business functions—marketing, sales, and finance—have tended to be the road to influence in the corporate world. This is all being changed by the product flexibility and quality enabled by the new production technologies. For example, product design can no longer be considered as an autonomous function but one that is linked into a larger system (Liker, Hancock, Lowy, & Tornatzky, in press) that includes information and resources from manufacturing, post-sales service, and so forth. Manufacturing engineering is driving corporate strategy and decision-making to a greater extent (Goldhar & Jellinek, 1984). Thus, the extended capabilities of the manufacturing function are driving what ought or could be designed, as well as what ought and could be marketed.

The growth of computer-assisted technologies might also alter the distribution of power in future organizations. To the extent that computer-assisted technologies are knowledge-embedded technologies, they also tend to bring the center of gravity of corporate knowledge down to the shop floor or office workstation. As has been noted many years ago, knowledge is a source of social power (French & Raven, 1959). As such, computer-assisted technologies, in their full flowering, represent a potent source of increasing overall organizational influence. Knowledge is embedded in these technologies to a degree unparalleled in the history of humankind. The issue becomes how that power is distributed, and that distribution decision is a sociotechnical one. Different sociotechnical solutions might yield different types of influence patterns such as described by Tannenbaum (1968). Systems can be "wired" such that operators really cannot utilize the technology in a way that expands their organizational influence; others could redistribute influence. In fact, in one study of end-use computing by managers it was found that the locus of influence tended to move down in the organization, whereas senior managers retained their ability to monitor and control (Fleischer & Morell, 1985).

As Shaiken (1985) has pointed out, the extent to which numerical control is used to increase control over and monitoring of employees or to extend an employee's creativity rests on the management's choice of whether operators will make modifications to machining programs or are locked out. Whether office automation becomes merely routine and mechanical or an expansive, creative process is largely a question of managerial choice. For example, Johnson (1985) found that providing office workers the opportunity to regularly participate in decisions about hardware, software, work roles, procedures, and training was a significant predictor of an innovative use of office automation.

The Effects of Technology on Skill

Now let us consider the question of skill. There has been much controversy about whether the technologies under consideration are used to deskill employees or to enhance the repertoires of skills that they employ. The skilling–deskilling controversy, once separated from the control–ownership issue, becomes much more complicated. The most comprehensive review of the empirical literature on the relation between technology and skill indicates that historically technology has yielded no net changes, or perhaps a small increase in workers' skills (Spenner, 1983). However, the relationships are not that strong, and for a variety of conceptual and methodological reasons the issue is unresolved. Managers have always run the gamut from wisdom to ignorance in utilizing the full potential of their workforce. So will it be with computer-assisted technologies.

Research on technology and skill has employed a variety of approaches (Spenner, 1983). Aggregate-level studies have used nonmeasurement or indirect measurement approaches to data collection, such as assuming that people in certain job categories or with certain levels of formal education are more or less skilled. More direct measurements of skill have focused on job content per se, but have measured skill along several dimensions, clustering around "substantive complexity" or "autonomy–control." The ideal approach is to vigorously define the job content of occupations, assess the composition of the work force in terms of distribution of workers to occupations, and then monitor both longitudinally as well as assessing the utilization of technology in certain settings.

Empirical data on job skill content with computer-assisted technology are negligible. One direct comparative study (Huber & Hyer, 1984) showed no differences in workers' perceptions of autonomy, identity, satisfaction, or significance as a result of cellular manufacturing. In contrast, in a study of Communication Workers of America (CWA) members, Adler (1986) reported that workers felt that technology had increased their skills. One neglected group in the skilling–deskilling debate has been managers. Fleischer and Morell (1985) reported enhanced information, greater decision-making authority, and the ability to address more complex problems, as a result of end-use computing by managers.

The multidimensional aspects of skill have particular relevance for computer-assisted technologies. My previous comments on training suggest that significant learning is being achieved by operators; how much skill and what kinds are being manifested in job performance is another issue. It is clear, for example, that a perceptual–motor skill will be in less demand as a result of these new technologies. On the basis of observation, analysis, and the few comparative empirical studies (e.g., Hazlehurst, Bradbury, & Corlett, 1969), it appears that operators will have less need to manipulate the work, exhibit motor dexterity, or work fast, while at the same time they will be asked to exhibit considerable cognitive skill and judgment. Although the qualitative mix changes, the net amount of skill remains the same or perhaps increases. The new technologies do move the worker into a button-pushing, dial-watching mode of work, and in effect, the operator will assume a white collar role in a blue collar setting. The operator will need to do less but will need to observe and monitor more, and will assume greater responsibility over more operations and more capital equipment. It would be useful to examine the current jobs of nuclear reactor operators (e.g., Hirschorn, 1984) to understand the future jobs of factory workers.

In order to effectively perform these monitoring tasks, the worker will have to have an extensively expanded knowledge of underlying principles and processes. Is that skill? Yes, but it is skill of a cognitive, conceptual sort. In the case of office automation this means that workers will have to understand how computers think, how to program them, and how to select among various software packages and relate them creatively. From this perspective, the evidence (i.e., Johnson, 1985) is that skill requirements for clerical workers in settings where the technology is effectively utilized have been increased. Similarly, the worker on the shop floor who is responsible for several machines in a machining cell will need to have a greater appreciation of how work moves from one workstation to the next, how to maintain system up-time, and how to anticipate breakdowns. The evidence from Japan (Mine, 1985), which has a longer history with computer-assisted technologies, indicates that worker skills are generally increased.

Admittedly these are different types of skills. From the perspective of the traditional machinist, the work is being deskilled. From another perspective skills may be construed as involving either substantive complexity or autonomy–control. Most of the deskilling advocates (Noble, 1979; Shaiken, 1985) seem to be emphasizing the latter, with a particular concern about whether automation has reduced the power of organized labor. However, if one considers that skills are not unitary or homogeneous activities, it is difficult to argue that overall skill levels are being reduced.

It should be emphasized that the skill repertoires of workers are dependent on the workers' level of responsibility and whether workers use stand-alone technology or integrated systems (Majchrzak, 1985). Operators of stand-alone equipment will be performing less-skilled tasks if they are confined to monitoring and excluded from programming; in contrast, maintenance workers may have an increased need for knowledge. Integration of systems probably increases the need to have communication skills and to be able to work interdependently with other workers. In one sense the whole skilling–deskilling controversy may be employing the wrong focus of analysis in the single-person job. To the extent that autonomous work groups, cross-training, and job rotation become the norm, what will define the skill level for an individual—the job done on Tuesday or the one done on Thursday?

Although, as Majchrzak et al. (1985) have pointed out, the extent of cross-occupancy, cross-skill training in U.S. industry is quite limited (approximately 11 percent in a national sample), it is likely to increase. Interestingly, the extent to which multilevel, multiskilling was pursued was related to the adoption of integrated systems. Since the technology is moving toward integrated systems, perhaps the skill controversy will become the multiskill debate.

The nature of job tasks and worker skills also has implications for how workers are rewarded. As the nature of production tasks has moved away from physical activities and toward perceptual–conceptual tasks, there have been two results. On the one hand, jobs are designed so that workers have control over a greater portion of the overall task. (From the sociotechnical design perspective this is a healthy departure.) On the other hand, workers have less direct contact with the materials being worked on, and it is difficult to relate any single act that the worker engages in to overall levels of productivity. The latter development creates interesting problems regarding compensation systems.

It has been difficult to design compensation systems that reflect the new roles of workers in computer-assisted technology environments. To a significant degree, the new plant revolution (Lawler, 1978) has evolved in parallel with the implementation of computer-assisted technologies. Many of Ettlie's (1985) administrative innovations that accompanied implementation of advanced technology involved compensation systems. Pay-for-knowledge systems, group-compensation, salary for shop floor personnel, and rewards for system maintenance and product quality have increased. As I have noted, these technologies change the nature of the product and change what can and should be produced. The use of relatively mindless quantitative measures of output will have decreasing relevance to the new settings.

In turn, the nature of compensation systems has implications for the explicit or implicit labor contract. Labor relations, whether in the context of union-organized or nonunion settings, have been changed by the advent of computer-assisted technologies. A variety of factors have influenced a movement toward a more cooperative, less confrontative, and more interactive mode of labor–management relations. For example, the complexities and problems of the implementation process demand a significant degree of worker participation in planning, design, and implementation. This could only be accomplished in the context of more benign labor relations. Similarly, the sheer cost and complexity of these systems argues for nonadversarial labor relations. In addition, the greater emphasis of technical skills and training that accompanies the computer-assisted technologies tends to elevate the stature of human resources in adopting organizations. Rather than viewing labor as a commodity that can be bought and sold at will, it tends to be perceived as a resource that must be nurtured and effectively utilized.

Despite the advent of technology agreements in organized labor contracts, the changes in labor relations that have just been described have developed largely in parallel to, and independent of, the organized labor movement. Only a few unions, especially ones in industries being rapidly automated, have become aware of the sociotechnical issues of new technology. The United Auto Workers and the Communication Workers of America are notable here. Although technology agreements in labor contracts have become increasingly common (Fadem, 1982), for the past part they have been used solely for giving advance notice of technology changes and for making provisions to handle the transition of workers. (The recently established UAW "nickel funds" with the major automobile makers now total almost $100 million.) In the future one can expect labor–management negotiating activity to be more focused on who controls training than on simple bread-and-butter issues.

Whether the technology agreements that have been written into union contracts have achieved real changes on the shop floor in terms of participative planning and decision-making is an empirical question. The labor–management cooperation that is being epitomized by General Motors' Saturn, is an exception. There has been little explicit emphasis on cooperative design and planning for new technology.

Research Issues

Sociotechnical Design: The Unfulfilled Promise

Given the plethora of conceptual and empirical issues that I have raised thus far, what are the possibilities for social science, and psychology in particular, of making a contribution to this area of inquiry? Unfortunately, there have been no contributions to date. For example, for more than 30 years the social sciences have been living with the intellectual residue of the sociotechnical movement. It would seem that this field would have clear relevance to the understanding of, and intervening in, systems incorporating computer-assisted technologies. Many of us are familiar with the classic and fascinating studies of longwall coal mining (Trist & Bamforth, 1951), Indian textile mills (Rice, 1958), and, more recently, the tales of autonomous work group organization at Volvo, Saab, and other western European companies. This tradition has led to a body of both empirical and theoretical knowledge (Cherns, 1976; Davis & Taylor, 1976), and the vigorous growth of a practitioner industry (Cummings, 1976). However, there have been two major failings of this tradition regarding computer-assisted technologies.

For one, much of the sociotechnical design field has diverted itself from one of the major premises of sociotechnical design. That is, that *both* the social and technical aspects of jobs and work settings need to be jointly optimized. This implies that neither the social system nor the technical system is to be taken as given in any design problem. Unfortunately, the fact is that sociotechnical design has increasingly focused on social interventions, as opposed to technical interventions, or even more rarely, on social and technical changes together (Pasmore, Francis, & Haldeman, 1982). Perhaps the reason for this is that for the most part practitioners of sociotechnical design are psychologists, sociologists, or social scientists of one stripe or another, who have not become sufficiently technologically knowledgeable to address technical issues. There are some examples in which technology processes have been altered (Taylor, Gustavson, & Carter, 1983), but for the most part, sociotechnical design has become social design. In effect, the field has evolved to a mode of dealing with the effects of technology on work in which advanced technology is implemented first and figuring out what to do with it comes after the fact.

The divorcement of sociotechnical design from the principle of joint optimization has been even more acute with the modern technologies. There are few instances of interventions in settings involving CAD, robotics, or numerically controlled machining. One exception to this general state of affairs is the role of sociotechnical design in office automation. Perhaps reflecting the different organizational culture of the electronics industry, equipment vendors in this area have been much more sensitive to expanding the job roles and designs of individuals involved in word processing and related technologies (Johnson, 1985).

More important to the further evolution of the field, sociotechnical theory has not responded to the qualitatively different computer-assisted technologies. In a recent review (Fadem, 1982) of sociotechnical designs conducted in the context of computer-assisted manufacturing, it is not clear how the peculiar characteristics of computer-assisted technology drove the designs or whether tried-and-true solutions (autonomous work groups, participative decision-making) were blindly applied. Just because the "new plant revolution" (Lawler, 1978) has occurred at the same time as the emergence of computer-assisted technologies, it is not clear what causal relationship there is between the two. The most cogent argument (Taylor, 1985) linking sociotechnical systems to computer-assisted technology is that the latter will be more dependent on skilled and committed workers than on traditional production systems. In effect, increased quality-of-worklife will leverage more productivity gains with computer-assisted technologies. This presents an interesting empirical question, and a possible comparative study, for anyone who wants to pursue it.

The Problem of Definition

Throughout this chapter, computer-assisted technologies have been treated as a homogeneous entity. In fact, this is inaccurate, and further research is needed to develop a meaningful way of typologizing both the new and the old technologies. In an earlier review by Davis and Taylor (1976), it was difficult for the authors to make definitive conclusions about the relationship between technology and social structure, because the former was usually defined along fairly gross dimensions. A more recent analysis by Goodman (1985) of the relationship between technology and group performance, similarly bemoans the limited descriptions of technology and the equating of a technology with simple sets of dimensions. He argues for a more extensive and intensive set of descriptions, for considering technology as a main effect variable, and for considering a task as a subcomponent of technology.

What research is needed? First researchers need to understand at an observational and phenomenological level what a given technology entails in getting work done. Then the elements need to be separated out using multidimensional coding or rating schemes. These would need to significantly extend, in variable domains and data elements, anything that currently exists. Finally, researchers need to determine empirically what technologies can justifiably be grouped together for analytic purposes. Only then can substantive statements be made about the relationship between technologies—I emphasize the plural—and work.

Interdisciplinary Problems and the Role of Psychology

What is the role for psychology in this problem area? There is, of course, the potential of traditional subspecialties of social science becoming involved in work aspects of computer-assisted technology. Many of the issues that I have described seem to lie in the bailiwick of social psychology, community psychology, organizational behavior, or behavior modification. The problem, of course, is that the matching is by no means perfect. To a significant degree, the problems and issues that I have described are interdisciplinary and involve different conceptual and methodological traditions. As I have noted, most problems of technology implementation involve phenomena operating at the individual, group, and organizational levels, all interacting at the same time. The relevant processes can only be understood longitudinally and probably only through a mixture of qualitative case studies, surveys, and experimentation. Not surprisingly, such an omnibus approach slashes across various theoretical domains, academic disciplines, and subdisciplines. Groups and organizations are rarely the units of analysis in psychological research.

The result is that it is very difficult to involve research-oriented psychologists in these issues. As some of you may know, before my most recent incarnation as a technology innovation guru, I had some visibility and influence in the community psychology field (Tornatzky, 1982). One of the premises of that field, of course, is that psychological concepts and robust methodologies (particularly experimentation) could be applied to problems of society, in field settings. Unfortunately I have been singularly unsuccessful in persuading my colleagues in that subdiscipline to become involved in technology. The problem seems to be a mismatch in unit and level of analysis, as well as an ideological misunderstanding.

It must be realized that much of community psychology, or applied social psychology, is premised on a 60s and 70s view of social policy issues. This often translates itself into a fairly naive, knee-jerk liberal view of refusing to have anything to do with private sector settings. It is acceptable to work with clients and problems in community mental health centers or hospitals, but somehow reprehensible to ease the plight of people who are already working, but threatened by a technological revolution. A review by Lounsbury, Leader, Meaves, and Cook (1980) of the community psychology literature indicated that it was largely preoccupied with health and mental health, with the individual as the unit of analysis. I find this state of affairs intellectually unacceptable. Although I have no data to support this, I wonder how much psychology's estrangement from problems of the work setting reflects the demographics of the profession. How many psychologists are middle-class liberals, largely devoid of any experiential contact with ordinary working people or blue collar problems?

I see no near-term solution to this state of affairs. The financial support for psychology is for the most part derived from health and mental health institutions, and the result has been that the payer of the piper has called the tune. There is no defensible reason why psychologists are not heavily involved in problems of work and technology.

References

Adler, P. (1986, January–February) Technology and us. *Socialist Review* (*85*), 67–95.

Arnold, E., & Bessant, J. (1984). Oiling the wheels of technical change: Skills, training, and the adoption of computer-aided design. In J. E. Rignsdorp & T. Plomp (Eds.), *Training for tomorrow* (pp. 123–128). New York: Pergamon Press.

Bikson, T. K., Gutek, B. A., & Mankin, D. A. (1985). *Implementing computerized procedures in office settings: Influences and outcomes* (R-3104-NSF). Santa Monica, CA: The Rand Corporation.

Cherns, A. (1976). The principles of socio-technical design. *Human Relations, 29* (8), 783–792.

Computer-integrated manufacturing: Firm vision to reality. (1983, November). *Production Engineering*, pp. 46–53.

Cummings, T. G. (1976). Socio-technical systems: An intervention strategy. In W. W. Burke (Ed.), *Current issues and strategies in organizational development* (pp. 187–213). New York: Human Sciences Press.

Davis, L., & Taylor, J. C. (1976). Technology, organization, and job structure. In R. Dubin (Ed.), *Handbook of work, organization and society* (pp. 379–419). Chicago: Rand-McNally.

Dean, J. W. (1985, August). *Decision processes in the adoption of advanced technology.* Paper presented at the meeting of the Academy of Management, San Diego, CA.

Ettlie, J. E. (in press). The implementation of programmable manufacturing innovations. In D. Davis (Ed.), *Implementing advanced technology.* New York: Jossey-Bass.

Ettlie, J. E. (1985, August) *Organizational adaptations for radical process innovations.* Paper presented at the meeting of the Academy of Management, San Diego, CA.

Fadem, J. A. (1982). *Automation and work design in the United States* (Working Paper No. 43). Los Angeles, CA: University of California, Institute of Industrial Relations.

Fleischer, M., & Morell, J. (1985). The organizational and managerial consequences of computer technology. *Computers in Human Behavior, 1* (1), 83–93.

Foulkes, F. K., & Hirsch, J. L. (1984, January/February). People make robots work. *Harvard Business Review*, pp. 94–102.

French, J. B., & Raven, B. R. (1959). The bases of social power. In D. Cartwright (Ed.), *Studies in social power* (pp. 607–623). Ann Arbor, MI: Institute for Social Research.

Gerwin, D. (1982, March/April). Do's and don'ts of computerized manufacturing. *Harvard Business Review*, pp. 107–116.

Goldhar, J. D., & Jellinek, M. (1984, November/December). Plan for economics of scope. *Harvard Business Review,* pp. 141–148.

Goodman, P. S. (1985). *Task, technology, and group performance.* Unpublished manuscript, Carnegie-Mellon University, Pittsburgh, PA.

Hazlehurst, R. J., Bradbury, R. J., & Corlett, E. N. (1969). A comparison of the skills of machinists or numerically controlled and conventional machines. *Occupational Psychology, 43*(3,4), 169–182.

Hirschorn, L. (1984). *Beyond mechanization.* Cambridge, MA: MIT Press.

Huber, V. L., & Hyer, N. L. (1984). *The human factor in group technology: An analysis of the effects of job redesign.* Unpublished manuscript, Cornell University, Department of Personnel and Human Resources Studies, Ithaca, NY.

Hunt, T. L. (1983, May) *Impact of automation and robotics on jobs.* Paper presented at the Conference on State Strategies for Economic Revitalization in the Northeast and Midwest, Council of State Governments, Boston, MA.

ITT Educational Services (1984). *America at work: The management perspective of training for business* (Unpublished report). Washington, DC: Author.

Johnson, B. M. (1985). *Innovation in office systems implementation* (NSF Report No. 811-0791). Norman, OK: University of Oklahoma, Department of Communication.

Kaplan, R. S. (1984, July/August). Yesterday's accounting undermines production. *Harvard Business Review,* pp. 95–101.

Kolodny, H. F., & Armstrong, A. (1985). *Three bases for QWL improvements: Structure, technology, and philosophy.* Unpublished manuscript, University of Toronto, Faculty of Management Studies, Toronto, Canada.

Kozlowski, W. F. (1985, March) *U.S. manufacturers' five-year industrial automation plans for automation machinery and plant communication systems* (Unpublished report). Washington, DC: National Electrical Manufacturers Association.

Lawler, E. E. (1978, Winter). The new plant revolution. *Organizational Dynamics,* pp. 8–12.

Leontief, W., & Duchin, F. (1983, September). *The impacts of automation employment, 1963–2000.* Draft Final Report to the National Science Foundation, New York University, Institute for Economic Analysis.

Levin, H., & Rumberger, R. W. (1983, February). *The educational implications of high technology* (Unpublished Project Report No. 83-A4). Stanford University, Institute for Research on Educational Finance and Governance.

Liker, J., Hancock, W., Lowy, A., & Tornatzky, L. (in press). Organizing for quality design engineering. In *Handbook of technology management.* New York: Wiley.

Lounsbury, J. W., Leader, D. S., Meaves, E. P., & Cook, M. P. (1980). An analytic review of research in community psychology. *American Journal of Community Psychology, 8* (4), 415–441.

Majchrzak, A. (1985, November). *Effects of computerized integration of shopfloor human resources and structures.* Paper presented at the Society of Manufacturing Engineers AUTOFACT Conference, Detroit, MI.

Majchrzak, A., Collins, P., & Mandeville, D. (1985, November). *A quantitative assessment of changes in work activities resulting from computer-assisted design.* Paper presented at the annual convention of the American Institute of Decision Sciences, Las Vegas, NV.

Majchrzak, A., Nieva, V. F., & Newmann, P. D. (1985). *CAD/CAM adoption and training in three manufacturing industries.* Final Report for the National Science Foundation, Division of Industrial Science and Technological Innovation.

Mine, M. (1985, March). The impact of microelectronic technology and the related policies in Japan. In *Monthly report of research materials.* Japan: Hosei University, Research Center on Resources and Social Problems.

National Research Council. (1984). *Computer integration of engineering design and production: A national opportunity.* Washington, DC: Author.

Noble, D. (1979). Social choice in machine design: The case of automatically controlled machine tools. In A. Zimbalist (Ed.), *Case studies on the labor process* (pp. 18–50). New York: Monthly Review Press.

Pasmore, W., Francis, C., & Haldeman, J. (1982). Sociotechnical systems: A North American reflection on empirical studies of the seventies. *Human Relations, 35*(12), 1179–1204.

Pelz, D., & Munson, D. (1980). *The innovating process: A conceptual framework.* Unpublished manuscript, University of Michigan, Institute for Social Research, Ann Arbor.

Rice, A. K. (1958). *Productivity and social organization: The Ahmedabad experiment.* London: Tavistock Publications, Ltd.

Rogers, E. M. (1962). *Diffusion of innovations.* New York: Free Press.

Roitman, D. (1985, March). *Organizational development: Midwife to the factory of the future?* Paper presented at the meeting of the Southeastern Industrial/Organizational Psychological Association, Atlanta, GA.

Rolland, W. C., & Smith, L. Y. (1984, January 10) *Summary report for the automated systems user survey of NEMA membership* (Unpublished report). Washington, DC: Electrical Manufacturers Association.

Rumberger, R. W., & Levin, H. M. (1984, February). *Forecasting the impact of new technologies on the future job market* (Unpublished Report No. 84-A4). Stanford University, Institute for Research on Educational Finance and Governance.

Shaiken, H. (1985). *Work transformed: Automation and labor in the computer age.* New York: Holt, Rinehart & Winston.

Spenner, K. I. (1983). Deciphering Prometheus: Temporal change in the skill level of work. *American Sociological Review, 48*, 824–837.

Swanson, P. H. (1984). Research needs of industry. *Journal of Technology Transfer 1*, 39–55.

Tannenbaum, A. S. (1968). *Control in organizations.* New York: McGraw-Hill.

Taylor, J. C. (1985, January). *The human element and socio-technical interaction in the effective use of information technology.* Unpublished manuscript.

Taylor, J. C., Gustavson, P. W., & Carter, W. S. (1983). *Socio-technical design and the adoption of computer-aided design processes.* Paper presented at the Conference on the Adoption and Implementation of Advanced Manufacturing Processes, Dominican University, Norfolk, VA.

Tornatzky, L. G. (1982). Educating professionals for social systems interventions: A ten-year retrospective. In A. M. Jeger & R. S. Slotnick (Eds.), *Community mental health and behavioral ecology: A handbook of theory, research, and practice.* New York: Plenum Press.

Tornatzky, L. G., Eveland, J. D., Boylan, M. G., Hetzner, W. A., Johnson, E. C., Roitman, D., & Schneider, J. (1983, May). *The process of technological innovation: Reviewing the literature.* Washington, DC: National Science Foundation.

Tornatzky, L. G., Fergus, E. O., Avellar, J. W., & Fairweather, G. W. (1980). *Innovation and social process.* New York: Pergamon Press.

Tornatzky, L. G., & Klein, K. (1982). Innovation characteristics and innovation adoption-implementation: A meta-analysis of findings. *IEEE Transactions on Engineering Management, 29,* 28–45.

Trist, E., & Bamforth, K. (1951). Some social and psychological consequences of the long wall method of coal-getting. *Human Relations, 4,* 3–38.

Yin, R. (1979). *Changing urban bureaucracies.* Lexington, MA: Lexington Books.

J. RICHARD HACKMAN

THE PSYCHOLOGY OF SELF-MANAGEMENT IN ORGANIZATIONS

J. RICHARD HACKMAN

J. Richard Hackman is Professor of Organizational Behavior and of Psychology at Yale University. He received his undergraduate degree in mathematics from MacMurray College in 1962 and his doctorate in social psychology from the University of Illinois in 1966. He has been at Yale since then.

Hackman conducts research on a variety of topics in social and organizational psychology, including the design of work, the task effectiveness of work groups, and social influences on individual behavior. He is on the editorial board of several professional journals and has consulted with a number of organizations on quality of worklife issues.

He is the author or editor of five books (the most recent being *Work Redesign*, co-authored with Greg R. Oldham and published in 1980) and more than 50 chapters and articles. He was winner of the sixth annual American Institute for Research Creative Talent Award in the field of "Measurement and Evaluation: Individual and Group Behavior," and co-winner of the 1972 Cattell Award of the American Psychological Association. He is a Fellow of APA both in the Division of Industrial and Organizational Psychology and in the Division of Personality and Social Psychology.

J. RICHARD HACKMAN

THE PSYCHOLOGY OF SELF-MANAGEMENT IN ORGANIZATIONS

A couple of years ago a senior manager at Cummins Engine corporation visited my class on organizational design to talk with students about the company's innovative plant in Jamestown, New York. One of the students asked, quite reasonably, for the visitor's views about the circumstances under which a self-managing organizational design, such as the one at Jamestown, would be preferred over a traditional organizational structure. "I'm not going to answer," he responded, "because that's last year's question. The question for today's managers is not *whether* to design organizations for high involvement and self-management, but *how* to do it, and how to do it well."

In 1984, the Harvard Business School celebrated its 75th anniversary by hosting a series of symposia on management. At the symposium on productivity and technology, Richard E. Walton, a senior professor at Harvard, took the occasion of the celebration to suggest that we may be in the midst of some revolutionary changes in how people are managed in work organizations. He pointed out that the major

Support for the preparation of this chapter was provided in part by the Organizational Effectiveness Research Program, Office of Naval Research, through Contract Number N00014-80-C-0555 to Yale University. The material in the "Leadership in Self-Managing Units" section of this chapter is adapted from Hackman and Walton (1986).

premise underlying work force management traditionally has been that efficiency can be achieved best by imposing management control over workers' behavior. Today, in response to massive evidence that control-oriented management models can produce outcomes that subvert the interests of both organizations and the people who work in them, a new work force management model is appearing. The premise of the emerging model is that organizations must elicit the commitment of their employees if they are to achieve a sustainable competitive advantage in contemporary markets. The change from a control to a commitment organizational model, Walton argued, portends a fundamental change in how organizations are designed and managed. Rather than relying on top-down management controls to elicit and enforce desired behavior, organizations in the future will rely heavily on member self-management in pursuing collective objectives.

What we have here is a senior corporate manager and a distinguished organizational scholar agreeing that something significant is afoot in the design and management of work organizations. And although the changes they foresee may not turn out to be as powerful or widespread as they suggest, it behooves organizational psychologists to understand as much as they can about the manifestations, precursors, and implications of organizational self-management. That is what this chapter is about.

I begin by exploring the key features of self-managing performing units, with special attention to how authority is distributed between those who execute work and those whose responsibilities are mainly managerial. I then identify the key behaviors that distinguish self-managing from traditional organizations, and review evidence on the relative effectiveness of self-managing organizational units. Next I turn to the major conceptual question of this chapter: What conditions foster and support a kind of self-management that will contribute both to personal well-being and to the achievement of collective objectives? Existing research and theory suggest five such conditions, each of which is described and discussed. I conclude with an exploration of the implications of the material for organizational leadership and for research and theory on the psychology of work behavior.

Varieties of Organizational Self-Management

The Allocation of Organizational Authority

Four different functions must be fulfilled when work is done in an organization. First, of course, someone must actually *execute* the work—applying personal energy (physical or mental) to accomplish tasks.

Second, someone must *monitor and manage* the work process—collecting and interpreting data about how the work is proceeding and initiating corrective action as needed. Third, someone must *design* the performing unit and arrange for needed organizational supports for the work—structuring tasks, deciding who will perform them, establishing core norms of conduct in the work setting, and making sure people have the resources and supports they need to carry out the work. And finally, someone must *set direction* for the organizational unit—determining the collective objectives and aspirations that spawn the myriad of smaller tasks that pervade any organization.[1]

Self-managing organizations (or organizational units) can be defined in terms of how authority for these four functions is distributed. To do this, three terms must be clarified. The term *manager* refers to individuals whose responsibilities have primarily to do with directing and structuring the work of others; the term *member* refers to individuals whose primary responsibilities are to perform that work.[2] And the term *performing unit* refers to the people who have been assigned responsibility for accomplishing some specified task or set of tasks. Generally, I will speak of performing units as if they consisted of several individuals working interdependently on a common task—an organizational form that is common in organizations that aspire to self-management (Walton & Hackman, 1986). It should be kept in mind, however, that a performing unit can be as small as a single individual, or it can consist of a large number of people who share responsibility for a major piece of organizational work.

Four types of performing units are identified in Figure 1. In a *manager-led* unit, members have authority only for actually executing the task; managers monitor and manage performance processes, structure the unit and its context, and set overall directions. This type of unit has been common in U.S. industry since the "scientific management" ideas of Taylor (1911) took hold early in the century. Managers

---

[1]These functions deal specifically with the management of work performance, and they define the domain of coverage for this lecture. Matters having mainly to do with organizational governance (e.g., the mechanisms used to determine major organizational policies) are not specifically addressed here. The performance and governance systems of an organization are, nonetheless, interdependent in many respects, and the direction-setting function is a key point of linkage between them.

[2]Managers often are viewed as "bosses" or "executives" who spend much of their time in offices—planning, deciding, and issuing orders. Organization members (commonly called "rank-and-file employees" or "workers") are thought to spend most of their time actually generating the products or delivering the services that the organization exists to provide. These views are too restrictive. A plant manager in industry, or an agency director in government, may simultaneously function as a manager (vis-à-vis his or her subordinates) and as a member (vis-à-vis more senior executives). This chapter presents a way of understanding self-management that is applicable to all organization members, not just those who perform front-line tasks.

manage, workers work, and the two functions should never be confused.

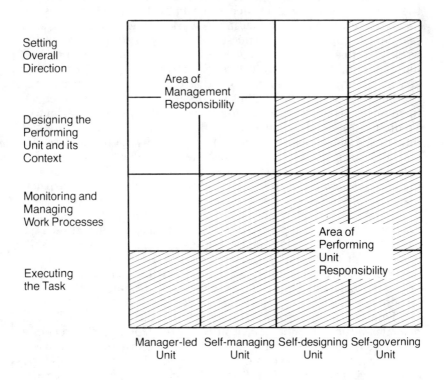

Manager-led Self-managing Self-designing Self-governing
Unit   Unit   Unit   Unit

Figure 1. The Authority Matrix: Four characteristic types of performing units.

In a *self-managing* unit, members have responsibility not only for executing the task but also for monitoring and managing their own performance. This type of unit is often seen in new plants designed in accord with what Walton calls the commitment model (see, for example, Lawler, 1978) and is commonplace in managerial and professional work (e.g., a team of research assistants who share responsibility for collecting a set of interviews and observations).

Members of *self-designing* units have the authority to modify the design of the unit itself or aspects of the organizational context in which the unit functions. Managers set the direction for such units but assign to members full authority to do what needs to be done to get the work accomplished. Examples of self-designing units include some top management task forces (e.g., a team created to develop a new program and given free reign in determining how the design work will be structured, supported, and carried out) or an individual who is given autonomous responsibility for some task (e.g., "find 10,000 square feet of additional office space within two miles of headquarters, and get it ready for occupancy by June") with the right to corral helpers and call on organizational resources as needed to accomplish that task.

Finally, members of *self-governing* units have responsibility for all four of the major functions listed in Figure 1: They decide what is to be done, structure the unit and its context, manage their own performance, and actually carry out the work. Examples of self-governing units include certain legislative bodies, corporate boards of directors, advisory councils of community service agencies, worker cooperatives, and sole proprietorships.

Figure 1 is presented as if the columns represent distinct types of performing units, but that is merely a convenience. In fact, the horizontal axis of the figure is a continuum reflecting increasing amounts of authority held by unit members relative to managers. In practice, units often fall on the column boundaries or have responsibility for only parts of certain functions. This chapter is concerned mainly with units in the "self-managing" column; however, I will speculate occasionally about the implications of the material for self-designing and self-governing units.

Behavioral Signs of Self-Management

How would one know if members of a performing unit were behaving as self-managers? What behaviors would one expect to see there that might be absent, or less frequent, in a manager-led unit? I list five behavioral signs, which are arranged from the most basic self-managing behaviors to those that one would find only in relatively mature self-managing units. I also provide some examples of positive and negative instances of each behavior, taken from a relatively new airline whose top management has a thorough-going commitment to self-management. These examples were generated by airline managers in seminars on the topic. The diversity of behavior seen in the company illustrates the varieties and vagaries of the concept and suggests that it can be difficult to elicit and sustain self-management, even when starting an organization from scratch.

1. People take *personal responsibility* for the outcomes of their work and show in their behavior that they feel personally accountable for the results of what they do.

One instance of individuals accepting personal responsibility for outcomes occurred during peak travel season, when a developing weather system raised the possibility that a jumbo jet on an overnight transcontinental trip might be seriously delayed or diverted to an alternate airport. If that occurred, hundreds of customers would be inconvenienced. Two individuals decided to remain in the airline's offices overnight (even though they had already completed a regular work day) to track the aircraft as it flew through the night and to call others to work if problems developed that would require special arrangements to get customers to their destinations. It turned out that the flight arrived nearly on time, and the passengers never knew that two people had spent the night standing by in case their assistance was needed.

A negative instance involved a flight that did experience weather and air traffic control delays. The cockpit and cabin crews on this aircraft had completed six hours of flying (which is what the schedule originally had called for), but there was still one round trip to be made. Although all crew members were still permitted by Federal Aviation Administration regulations to continue flying, they departed the aircraft, leaving others to figure out how to find a crew to fly the last trip.

If personal responsibility for outcomes has been accepted by an organization member, one often observes expressions of pride and overt celebration when the work turns out well—and overt dismay and self-criticism when it goes poorly. Self-management probably cannot be sustained unless reasonably intense feelings of personal responsibility for outcomes are present; without them, the temptation to "self-manage myself home" on a bad day may be nearly impossible to resist.

2. People *monitor* their own performance continuously, actively seeking data and feedback to learn how well they are accomplishing their tasks.

Cockpit crews enjoy a feedback-rich environment: Aircraft instrumentation, air traffic control, and company operations together keep crew members very well informed about how they are doing with the technical aspects of their flying task. Less feedback is available to pilots about their contributions to other organizational objectives, and one crew I observed decided to do something about that. After the aircraft had reached cruising altitude, all systems had been checked, and the crew was in a relatively relaxed attitude with the autopilot engaged, the co-pilot turned to the captain and said, "Okay, let's figure out how we're doing on this one." The crew members then calculated an estimate of the total cost of the flight, multiplied the number of customers on board by the fare for the trip, subtracted the first number from the second, and found that they were losing about $4,500 on the trip. At that point, the captain got on the public address system and told the customers that, although the company really liked flying people to the destination city, there were not quite enough of them on this flight to break even. He asked the customers to tell him or the cabin crew about anything that was unsatisfactory in the service they were providing, so they could improve their performance and attract more people from that city to the airline. This crew was obviously paying attention to available data about performance; beyond that, members took an initiative to obtain additional information that could be used to improve it.

A negative instance involves a situation where performance-relevant data were already collected, summarized, and available—but people systematically ignored them. One group in the airline is charged with selecting the correct number of reservations to accept for each flight, using a set of standard formulas to estimate the number of people who will "no show" for flights. Early in the airline's history, flights originating in one city on a certain day of the week were sometimes being oversold, resulting in people with confirmed reservations being denied boarding. Although company reports documented this problem, the planning group did not examine those data. Only after staff in that city (who had to deal with the angry customers who were left on the ground) complained to a member of senior management did the problem come to the attention of planning group members.

3. People *manage* their own performance, taking corrective action at their own initiative to improve their performance.

When a flight is delayed, customers typically crowd around the check-in counter listening for news, seeking help or advice, or complaining about what is happening. Under these conditions, it is difficult for staff members to deal with whatever is causing the problem. One organization member decided that the crowding problem had to be solved in order to serve the customers well and convened an informal group of colleagues to consider ways of dealing with it. The group decided that the best solution was to get inconvenienced customers away from the counter and give them special attention. Members found some unused space nearby, got some chairs and a telephone put in the space, and revised the counter operating plan so that one or more team members could give full attention to customers' questions and complaints in the holding area during irregular operations— thereby allowing the rest of the counter team to work on the cause of the difficulty. No senior managers were involved in either the diagnosis of the problem or in the action planning.

A negative instance also involves on-ground service, this time at a city distant from the airline's hub of operations. Flights often departed from this city without all customers' bags on board. That happens occasionally in the airline business, but it was happening at this city more frequently than at others in the system. It was clear that responsibility for the problem lay with the staff in the city, and they were aware that they were not doing well with bags (customers are quick to complain when their bags do not arrive at their destination, and those complaints find their way back to the city staff). Yet no action to correct the problem was taken by staff members, and when queried about the problem, one response was "I don't know what the trouble is. We're following standard bag handling procedures." That individual showed no inclination to investigate and attempt to find a solution to the problem.

4. When people do not have what they need to perform well, they actively *seek from the organization* the guidance, help, or resources they need for excellent performance—and they do so assertively and constructively.

Sometimes people feel responsible for work outcomes, have data showing that performance is substandard, and are eager to take corrective action; but they find that they do not have the authority to fix whatever is at the root of the performance problem. How do self-managers behave in such circumstances?

In one instance, a manager who was responsible for certain operational matters found, as the airline grew, that he was unable to handle personally the significant increases in his day-to-day workload. He concluded (after trying various alternative strategies for managing the work) that he needed some additional people to help coordinate his part of the operation, but he did not have the authority to make staff assignments. Moreover, the president of the company was deeply and publicly committed to a flat, lean organization with as few people as possible assigned to staff support activities.

The manager first sought the advice of his colleagues and an outside consultant. Some new ideas developed in these discussions, which he tried but which did not solve the problem. He then developed a plan for creating a small staff support group, tested it against the overall values and aspirations of the company, and finally proposed it to the president. The president had serious concerns about the idea and refused to approve it. The manager then sought further counsel from his colleagues, redesigned the plan to take account of the president's objections, and brought it once again to the president. Eventually he succeeded in obtaining the staff support he needed to accomplish the work for which he was responsible.

By contrast, a group in the financial area of the airline found, as the company grew, that its office was increasingly inadequate for the volume of work that flowed in. Paper was everywhere, there were no file cabinets in which to organize and store it, and people were sitting in every available space (including the floor) trying to process the work. Perhaps because of the president's stated opposition to large support groups and plush offices, or perhaps because of the "can do" attitude that permeated the airline, no one took an initiative to secure the physical space and equipment that was needed to get the work done accurately and on time. Only when complaints from senior managers about the performance of the unit became numerous and painful did the group raise the issue of its inadequate work environment.

Whereas the financial group tolerated less-than-acceptable performance rather than initiating action to secure needed resources, others in the organization have responded by letting their feelings of frustration build to an explosive level. One person, who had struggled for months with inadequate equipment, finally charged into the president's office unannounced, laying out all his frustrations and complaints angrily and in vivid detail. The president initially was speechless (he was hearing about the problems for the first time), but when he recovered he responded in kind—resulting in an interaction that was constructive neither for the two parties nor for the organization as a whole. Because of the ambivalence many people have about dealing with organizational authorities, it is often difficult for organization members, even those in units that are committed to self-management, to seek absent and needed resources from senior managers in a way that is both assertive and constructive.

5. People take initiatives to *help people in other areas* improve their performance, thereby strengthening the policies and performance of the organization as a whole. And they make sure that their own responsibilities are being met before reaching out to help others.

Each employee of the airline I have been discussing is expected to work in more than one functional area—people who fly also work in accounting or marketing, and so on. When a pilot came into the reservations office to help out, he discovered that it took much of the time he had available merely to get through the reservations manual (the document that explains reservations policies and procedures). Because he assumed that the same would be true for other pilots taking a turn in the reservations office, he undertook (on his own time) to write a brief summary of the manual, covering only the essentials of reservation practice and using language he referred to as "pilot talk." This mini-manual increased the amount of productive time relative to preparation time for others who assisted with reservations.

The ideal of helping out in other areas also can be a trap. One individual whose primary staff work was in training determined that he could lend a valuable hand in corporate recruiting. So he volunteered to go on a number of road trips to solicit employment applications and screen candidates. The problem was not that recruiting did not need or appreciate his help; in fact, he provided valuable assistance to that area. The problem was that his own major area, training, was not in good shape when he left it temporarily to help out the recruiters. Whether knowingly or not, this individual used a relatively high-order self-management value (helping other areas) to escape the imperatives of more basic values (taking responsibility for the outcomes of one's own work, and monitoring and managing one's performance to ensure that the work is accomplished well).

Self-Management and Unit Effectiveness

The previous section identifies and illustrates the behaviors that operationalize self-management. Do organizations perform better or worse when these behaviors are commonplace within them? Do people fare better or worse in self-managing organizational units? To address these questions, I must first define what is meant by "better" and "worse."

Unit effectiveness defined. There are, of course, many dimensions on which one could assess the effectiveness of a self-managing performing unit, and one's choice of dimensions is, implicitly but necessarily, a statement of what one values. My view is that the effectiveness of a performing unit depends on its standing on the following three dimensions (adapted from Hackman, 1986; Hackman & Walton, 1986):

1. The degree to which the unit's productive output (that is, its product or service) meets the standards of quantity, quality, and timeliness of the people who receive, review, or use that output. If, for example, a self-managing unit generated a product that was wholly unacceptable to its legitimate client, it would be hard to argue that the unit was effective—no matter how unit members evaluated their product, or how it scored on some objective performance index. Although it is uncommon for researchers to rely on system-defined (rather than objective) performance assessments, reliable objective performance measures are actually quite rare in work organizations—and even when they do exist, what happens to a unit usually depends far more on others' assessments of its output than on those measures.

2. The degree to which the process of carrying out the work enhances the capability of organization members to work together interdependently in the future. Consider, for example, a self-managing team that functions in a way that makes it impossible for members to work together again—perhaps because mutual antagonism becomes so high that members would choose to accept collective failure rather than share knowledge and information with one another. Alternatively, members of a team can become extraordinarily skilled at working together, ever increasing the unit's performance capability (for example, a string quartet or athletic team whose members learn to anticipate one another's next moves and initiate appropriate responses to those moves even as they occur). Even when a unit is temporary (such as a one-shot task force), one would examine changes in its performance capability over time in judging its overall effectiveness.

3. The degree to which work experiences contribute to the growth and personal well-being of unit members. Some jobs, and some teams, block individuals' development and frustrate satisfaction of their personal needs; others provide many opportunities for learn-

ing and need satisfaction. Even when the official purpose of an organizational unit has nothing to do with personal development, the impact of the work experience on individual members would be included in an assessment of its effectiveness.

In summary, measuring the performance of a self-managing unit always involves much more than simply counting outputs. Not only must social and personal criteria be considered, but even assessments of task outcomes are complex because they depend on system-specified (rather than researcher-specified) standards. Although these three dimensions could be used in judging effectiveness in any organization, they are particularly salient for organizations that aspire to self-management. If a unit is poor on the second and third dimensions, for example, both the ability and the willingness of unit members to engage in self-managing behaviors surely would diminish over time. On the other hand, a unit that stands high on all three criteria has at least a chance of entering a self-reinforcing cycle of improved task performance, unit capability, and member learning and satisfaction.

The relative weight given each of the three dimensions will vary across circumstances. If, for example, a temporary self-managing team were formed to perform a single task of extraordinary importance, then the second and third dimensions would be of little relevance in judging the team's effectiveness. On the other hand, tasks sometimes are created mainly to help members gain experience, learn some things, and become competent as a performing unit (see, for example, Eisenstat's [1984] analysis of a "core skills" production unit that was created during the start-up of an industrial plant specifically to build employees' skill and experience as members of self-managing metal-working teams). The task of such units may be more an excuse for the unit than the reason for it, and assessments of effectiveness in such cases would depend far more on the second and third dimensions than on the first.

The relative effectiveness of self-managing units. Does self-management enhance or depress unit performance on the three criterion dimensions? For a sampling of research evaluating the efficacy of self-management in work organizations, see Gunn (1984); Poza and Marcus (1980); Wall, Kemp, Jackson, and Clegg (n.d.); Walton (1980); and collections of cases edited by Lindenfeld and Rothschild-Whitt (1982) and by Zwerdling (1980). There is also a growing body of evidence on self-management in nonwork settings. Kanfer (1984), in assessing self-management as a clinical tool, has shown how social system variables affect the success of such applications. Even in medicine, where physicians traditionally have controlled all aspects of patient treatment, there is increasing interest in patient self-management. For example, Check (1982) reported that when patients directly control the amount of morphine they receive after an operation, pain relief is improved, and far less of the drug is used than when it is administered by medical staff. Despite the fact that numerous research reports describe and analyze self-management successes and failures, evidence bearing directly on the question is scant. In fact, the question is probably unanswerable. Comparative studies of existing self-managing and traditional organizations inevitably invite numerous alternative interpretations of whatever is found (because of inescapable confounds involving labor markets, technologies, senior managers, organizational histories, and so on). And there will never be trustworthy findings from true experiments comparing self-managing and manager-led units in real work organizations. For one thing, the level of experimenter control required in such studies (e.g., to randomly assign people to units and units to conditions) will not be tolerated by most managers who have work to get out. Moreover, if an organization were found in which managers would relinquish such control to experimenters, there would be serious questions about the external validity of any findings obtained there (Hackman, 1985).

My observations of self-managing units suggest that they frequently are found at both ends of the effectiveness continuum. That is, poorly designed self-managing units are easily outperformed by smoothly functioning traditional units—in part because there are no organizational controllers around to provide early warning that problems are developing or to mandate corrective action. On the other hand, self-managing units that function well can achieve a level of synergy and agility that never could be preprogrammed by organization planners or enforced by external managers. Members of such units respond to their clients and to each other quickly and creatively, resulting in both superb task performance and ever-increasing personal and collective capability. Self-managing units, then, are somewhat akin to audio amplifiers: Whatever passes through the device—be it signal or noise—comes out louder.

Thus, a question of potentially greater practical and conceptual interest presents itself: What factors account for the difference between those self-managing units that perform superbly and those whose performance is abysmal? As I explore this more tractable question, it quickly will become apparent that creating, maintaining, and working in self-managing units generally requires more expertise and commitment than are needed in traditional units. The skills required to get along in a traditional organization, whether as a manager or a rank-and-file member, are relatively well learned by most people in the U.S. work force. Moreover, commonly held expectations about how one should behave at work generally are more congruent with life in manager-led units than with what is required of self-managers.

As the founding members of many cooperative organizations have learned through painful experience, effective self-managing units cannot be created simply by exhorting democratic ideals, by tearing down organizational hierarchies, or by instituting one-person-one-vote decision-making processes. Instead, it appears that certain conditions must be in place for a self-managing unit to have a real chance of achieving a high standing on the three criterion dimensions discussed previously.

I examine those conditions next. In doing so, I will give more attention to the first criterion dimension (i.e., acceptable task outcomes) than to the latter two (improved unit capability, and individual growth and well-being). This is because one of the best ways to help a unit achieve a high standing on the social and personal criteria is to foster its task-performance effectiveness. Indeed, it may be next to impossible for a unit to succeed on the social and personal criteria while it is failing on its task.

Conditions That Foster and Support Effective Self-Management

Existing research, theory, and organizational practice identify five general conditions that appear to foster and support unit effectiveness through self-management: (a) clear, engaging direction, (b) an enabling performing unit structure, (c) a supportive organizational context, (d) available, expert coaching, and (e) adequate material resources. As will be seen, the conditions are not direct, proximal causes of performance outcomes, but rather they serve to increase the likelihood that self-managing units will perform effectively. One must be careful not to think of them in traditional cause-effect terms.

Each of the conditions consists of a number of successively more detailed conditions, which represent the means by which it is operationalized (in research) or enacted (in practice). Although I discuss some of these subconditions here (particularly to illustrate differences in how the conditions apply to individual self-managers versus self-managing teams and larger organizational units), I focus on the general processes by which the conditions shape self-management and performance effectiveness.

Clear, Engaging Direction

Effective self-management is not possible unless someone exercises authority to set direction for the performing unit. This assertion may sound a bit strange, in that self-management and the exercise of authority often are seen as being competing and inconsistent control strategies. I hope to show that the opposite is true, that the appropriate use of authority is essential in creating conditions for self-management.

Except in self-governing performing units (see Figure 1), the overall directions for performance are established by representatives of the larger organization in which a performing unit operates. Those who own an enterprise for example, or who act on their behalf, have the right to determine organizational objectives—to say, in effect, "This is the mountain we will climb. Not that one, this one. And while many aspects of our collective endeavor are open for discussion, choice of mountain is not among them."

Will such an assertion de-power and alienate organization members? On the contrary, having a clear statement of direction tends to be empowering, for three related reasons. First, it *orients* organization members toward common objectives, thereby facilitating coordinated action in pursuing them. Ambiguity about what the collectivity exists to achieve is lessened, which reduces the amount of time and energy people spend arguing about questions of purpose or wallowing around trying to figure out what is supposed to be accomplished. When direction is made clear, some people may discover that it is not to their liking—a stressful state of affairs, but one that ultimately is constructive. As some people decide not to join the unit and others decide to leave, the unit should be populated increasingly by individuals who are interested in aligning themselves with collective directions. A far more difficult situation exists when organizational directions are distasteful or alienating to the majority of members and potential members. There is no real possibility for effective self-management in such a situation, and organizational control of member behavior is likely to be a continuing problem that may never be satisfactorily resolved (Walton & Hackman, 1986).

Second, clear direction *energizes* people, even when the goals that are articulated may not rank highest on members' personal lists of aspirations. People seek purpose in their lives and are energized when an attractive purpose is articulated for them. Consider, for example, the impact of President John F. Kennedy's statement "We will go to the moon," or that of Reverend Martin Luther King's "I have a dream" speech. On a less grand scale, but for similar reasons, a clear statement of organizational direction can energize people by adding to the meaning and purpose they find in their work. Some purposes are, of course, more engaging than others. Research suggests that engagement is enhanced when aspirations have three attributes: (a) they are consequential—i.e., what is to be accomplished has a visible and substantial impact on others, be they customers, co-workers, or other unit members (Hackman & Oldham, 1980; Manz, in press); (b) they stretch members' energy and talent—i.e., achieving them is neither routine nor impossible (Atkinson, 1958; Locke, Soari, Shaw, & Latham, 1981; Walton, 1985; Zander, 1980); and (c) they are simultaneously rich in imagery and incomplete in detail, thereby providing room for members to add their own meanings to the aspirations (Bennis & Nanus, 1985; Berlew, 1979; Cohen, 1985; House, 1977).

Finally, a clear statement of direction *provides a criterion* for unit members to use in testing and comparing alternative possibilities for their behavior at work. Because self-managers are not given detailed, step-by-step behavioral prescriptions, it is imperative that they have some clear set of values or aspirations to use in evaluating ways they might proceed. Without clear direction, there will be high variation in work behavior as people rely mainly on trial and error to identify appropriate work strategies. The result, in many cases, will be heightened frustration, loss of efficiency, and poor coordination among individuals and units.

Setting a clear and engaging direction for self-managers is a more difficult and risky business than one might expect. Because it necessarily involves the exercise of authority, ambivalence and anxiety typically are aroused for both those who give direction and those who receive it. A common strategy for managing ambivalence and anxiety is to wholly embrace one or the other side of the difficult issue. So, in traditional organizations, managers sometimes are observed making decisions and giving orders in ways that make it completely clear to everyone who is in charge, even when that turns out to close off the ideas and involvement of others.

In organizations that aspire to self-management, on the other hand, managers sometimes decline to take a position on anything, even if that turns out to blur the direction of the enterprise and withhold from its members the guidance they need to manage their own behavior. It is clear that the order-giving syndrome is inappropriate for the management of self-managers. Perhaps less obvious is the fact that a managerial style in which consensus is relentlessly pursued is just as inappropriate. To chart a course between the Scylla of authoritarian behavior and the Charybdis of abdication is a significant intellectual and emotional challenge for many managers of self-managers.

A second pitfall in setting direction has to do with the focus of managerial authority. Although it is fully appropriate for people in positions of legitimate authority to be insistent about ends, they must take care not to exercise their authority regarding the specific means by which those ends are to be sought. To do so will compromise members' feelings of personal control over their life at work, with predictable and negative motivational consequences (Langer, 1983; Seligman, 1975). So, to return to the mountain-climbing metaphor, an effective direction setter will be clear and unapologetic about the choice of mountain to be climbed and about the broad limits on the behavioral latitude of individual climbers on the team. On the other hand, he or she will suppress any inclination to dictate how each stream should be crossed on the way up the mountain, or to ask individuals to await instructions at each fork in the trail. Making this distinction, and behaving in accord with it, also turns out to be a considerable challenge for many managers of self-managers.

The voluminous literature on leadership and management includes little research that specifically examines the direction-setting function of leaders. Although authoritative (not authoritarian) direction setting is a potent device for orienting and energizing self-managers toward the achievement of collective objectives, not much is known about how those activities actually take place in work organizations.

As important as clear, engaging direction is in creating conditions for effective self-management, it is far from the whole story. I turn now to ways that the structure of a self-managing unit can either undermine good direction or exploit its positive potential.

An Enabling Performing-Unit Structure

Individuals or teams that know where they are supposed to be going have three hurdles to surmount in order to get there. They must (a) exert sufficient *effort* to get the task accomplished at acceptable levels of performance, (b) bring adequate levels of *knowledge and skill* to bear on the task work, and (c) employ *task performance strategies* that are appropriate to the work and to the setting in which it is being performed (Hackman, 1986).

To illustrate the idea of a performance strategy, consider an individual self-manager who decides to free associate about task solutions in his or her first encounter with the task, reflect for a week about the ideas that came up, and then do a rough draft of the product. Or he or she might decide to spend considerable time checking and rechecking for errors after learning that the client cares a great deal about product quality. If the performing unit were a team, it might decide to divide into two subgroups, each of which would do part of the overall task, with the final product to be assembled later. All of these choices involve task performance strategy.

I refer to the three hurdles as the "process criteria of effectiveness." They are not the ultimate test of how well a group has done (I addressed that earlier), but they turn out to be of great use both in assessing how a performing unit is doing as it proceeds with its work and in diagnosing the nature of the problem if things are not going well. One can readily ask, for example, whether observed difficulties are rooted in an effort problem, a talent problem, or a strategy problem. And, as I will show later, the answers that emerge can be useful in determining what might remedy the problem and thereby improve unit effectiveness.

Although valuable as indicators, the process criteria do not provide useful points of intervention for improving unit effectiveness. For one thing, direct managerial interventions aimed at increasing effort, improving the utilization of talent, or making performance strategies more task-appropriate may undermine the self-managing character of the performing unit. Moreover, existing evidence suggests that direct process interventions have little or no reliable impact on unit performance (Kaplan, 1979; Woodman & Sherwood, 1980). There are, however, certain structural features of performing units that can increase the chances that the unit will achieve a high standing on the process criteria. Three such features (task design, unit composition, and sent expectations about member behavior), have special relevance to the process criteria.

Task design. Existing research and theory on self-management (e.g., Cummings, 1978; Hackman, 1986; Hackman & Oldham, 1980) suggests that the effort an individual self-manager (or members of a self-managing team) will apply to the work depends significantly on the design of the task that is being performed. Specifically, people try hard to perform well when the following three task-induced states are present:

• Performers experience the task as *meaningful,* a state that is fostered when (a) the task requires use of a variety of relatively high-level skills; (b) the task is a whole piece of work with a beginning, end, and readily-discerned outcomes; and/or (c) the task has outcomes that are consequential for other people (be they other organization members or external clients).

• Performers experience *personal responsibility* for the outcomes of the work, a state that is fostered when the task provides substantial autonomy for performers to decide how the work will be carried out (in effect, allowing them to personally or collectively own the work, rather than merely execute work on behalf of someone else).

• Performers experience *knowledge of the results* of their work, a state that is fostered when executing the task generates trustworthy and informative feedback about work progress and outcomes.

When a task has these properties, performers are more likely to engage in self-rewarding behaviors when they find that they have done well (and in self-punishing behaviors when they do poorly), a state of affairs that has been referred to as "internal work motivation" (Hackman & Oldham, 1980, Ch. 4). Internal motivation is a means for sustaining task-focused effort in the absence of external controls and direct supervision, and contributes to one's overall perceptions of self-efficacy (Bandura, 1977). It is, therefore, a key ingredient in a self-managing performing unit.

This emphasis on task design runs counter to traditional wisdom about motivated work behavior. One often hears managers report that some person is "lazy" or "hard-working" or that members of some team "have a norm of not working very hard" or of "always giving their best." It is true that people have different chronic energy levels, but there is not much one can do about that. And although norms do emerge in groups that encourage especially high or low effort, such norms usually develop as a reaction to how things are set up, as a means of coping with the group task and work situation. Thus, if the work is routine and unchallenging, of dubious importance, and wholly preprogrammed with no opportunity for feedback, it is likely that individuals will slack off and that groups will develop antiproductivity norms. Improving the design of the work is usually a better way to deal with such a state of affairs than attempting directly to modify individual motivation or group norms.

The task dimensions discussed are applicable both to work designed for individual self-managers and for self-managing teams. The different referent of those dimensions in the two cases is critical. In the first instance, one is dealing with the properties of a task intended to be performed by one person, whereas in the second the focus is on a (usually larger) piece of work that is assigned to an intact team—or, possibly, to an even larger unit such as a department or division. Care must be taken to make sure the dimensions that are used to characterize the work are applied at a level of analysis consistent with the unit that is performing the work.

In promoting effort by creating conditions for self-motivation, task design reinforces the benefits of clear, engaging direction; indeed, the two conditions serve partially redundant functions and have effects that in many instances cannot be clearly distinguished from one another. Although this may seem to be a problem (at least for those who seek unitary, independent causes of phenomena), it will become increasingly evident that social systems do not follow the rules of experimental design: Many of the more interesting and important things that happen in social systems are the result of multiple, redundant, nonindependent forces.

Unit composition. The first of the process criteria (effort) depends significantly on how the work itself is designed; the second (knowledge and skill) depends primarily on the people who are assigned to that work. The basic assertion is obvious: The best way to increase the knowledge and skill brought to bear on a piece of work is to have one or more highly talented people perform that work. Some complications arise, however, when that general proposition is applied to work done by individual self-managers and by self-managing teams.

First, knowledge and skill are more consequential in self-managing units than in traditional units. Self-managers have responsibility for decision making about the work, not just executing it, which means that what people know (and know how to do) has high leverage on unit outcomes. In addition, consequences are higher for the performers themselves if organizational conditions fostering self-management are in place. Assume, for the moment, that a performer understands and is engaged by the direction for the enterprise and that the task he or she is performing is well designed. The person should have high internal work motivation—feeling pleased when the work goes well, and unhappy when it does not. Now, if the performer does not have the talent required to perform the task well, he or she will be unhappy most of the time—more unhappy than if self-managing conditions were not present. Because feeling bad about one's self is not a state of affairs that most people choose to maintain, the eventual result is likely to be psychological or behavioral withdrawal from the work or the organization.

Second, some people are more responsive to opportunities for self-management at work than others. It has proven difficult to isolate specific individual characteristics that empirically distinguish those who respond eagerly to motivationally engaging tasks from those who balk at them. (O'Connor, Rudolf, & Peters, 1980; White, 1978), and little is known about the dynamics by which individual differences in readiness for self-managing work emerge developmentally and change over time as a function of work experiences. Nonetheless, organizations that aspire to self-management generally do take the selection and placement of members extremely seriously—attending to their apparent interest in and psychological readiness for such work as well as to more traditional measures of task-relevant knowledge and skill. Although such organizations have been criticized (e.g., by Fein, 1974) on the grounds that their success may be due more to their favorable selection ratio than to any organizational innovations, evidence to date suggests that careful assessment of the readiness of people for work in self-managing units is a well-warranted organizational practice (Walton, 1980).

Additional complexities arise when individuals are being selected for membership on self-managing teams. When work is assigned to a team, one must attend not merely to the qualities and qualifications of individual members, but also to the composition of the team *qua* team. Although there has been relatively little research in recent years on issues in team composition (for reviews of early work on the topic, see Haythorn, 1968, and Schutz, 1961), existing evidence suggests that the following factors are significant in considering the composition of a self-managing team:

- team size (many teams in organizations are far larger than they need to be and, for effectiveness, should be)
- the balance between homogeneity and heterogeneity of members' skills (when people are either too similar to one another or too different from one another, performance problems often develop)
- members' competence in working cooperatively with other

people (some minimum level of social skill is required to accomplish tasks that require coordination among members and to manage the interplay between individual desires and group goals).

Sent expectations about behavior. A performing unit's standing on the third process criterion (appropriateness of task performance strategies) is perhaps most powerfully shaped by the expectations that senior managers communicate to unit members. Two expectations are critical. First, unit members must understand that they are responsible for regulating their own behavior. This is, of course, the core expectation for any self-managing unit. Unless members accept it, they will be unlikely to adjust their performance strategies as circumstances change—perhaps persisting too long with whatever strategy they began with or waiting too long for instructions from someone else about what behaviors are appropriate. The second critical expectation is that unit members are obligated to continuously assess the performance situation (with particular attention to changes in the task or environment) and to actively plan how they will proceed with the work based on those assessments.

These expectations, even when accepted and acted upon by unit members, do not directly cause performance strategies to become more appropriate. As with the other conditions I have discussed, they merely increase the chances that unit members will discover and implement ways of proceeding with the work that fit well with the requirements and opportunities in the task and situation—a better fit, perhaps, than otherwise would be the case.

Expectations that encourage active scanning and planning usually must be communicated vigorously to the performing unit, because it is far from a sure thing that they will occur naturally. Many individuals and teams operate under the assumption that they are the mere executors of work, that others are responsible for decision making about how and when their behaviors should be adjusted. This assumption may make sense given members' previous organizational experiences, but the result is that situation scanning and strategy planning rarely occur spontaneously (Hackman & Morris, 1975).

For individual self-managers, these sent expectations are part of his or her work role and therefore are viewed as a structural feature of the organizational system (Kahn, Wolfe, Quinn, Snoek, & Rosenthal, 1964). Researchers are increasingly interested in the processes by which individuals regulate behavior within their work roles (e.g., Luthans & Davis, 1979; Manz, Mossholder, & Luthans, in press; Manz & Sims, 1980). Although research on self-regulation has provided many ideas about *how* a person can control his or her behavior, it has less to say about the conditions under which people actually *do* engage in behavioral self-management—an issue informed by a recent study by Brief and Hollenbeck (1985). These researchers assessed the extent of self-regulation by a group of insurance agents in order to determine its effect on job performance. They found a low incidence of the activities posited by social learning theorists as critical to self-regulation. This finding further supports the view that self-regulatory behaviors are likely to occur only when they are specifically encouraged. In organizations, one of the most powerful and efficient ways to accomplish this is to structure an explicit expectation of self-management into individuals' formal work roles.[3]

For self-managing teams, the issue is once again more complex. Here there must be collective self-regulation, not just the creation of a set of individual role expectations. Groups regulate collective and member behavior through norms about behavior, that is, shared expectations about what will and will not be done in the group that are enforced by behaviorally contingent approval and disapproval (Jackson, 1965). Key norms tend to form very early in the life of a group and are sustained until something fairly drastic occurs that forces team members to reconsider what are and are not appropriate behaviors. Thus, expectations sent to a group early in its life (for example, when members first meet) can create a relatively enduring group structure. In the present instance, of course, those expectations would have to do with the team's responsibility for self-regulation and for ongoing situational scanning and strategy planning.

As an example of how such norms can contribute to performance effectiveness, consider a team of cabin attendants from the airline I discussed earlier. This team had been sent and had accepted expectations that members were to manage themselves within broad constraints (primarily having to do with safety procedures) and that they were to tailor the way they provided cabin service as necessary to achieve a set of clear corporate objectives. I observed this crew on two very different flights. The first was a flight to Florida on a sunny day. The plane was only half full of people, most of whom appeared to be on holiday. As people were boarding the plane, the crew got a sense of its clientele, had a brief conversation, and decided to have some fun. The cooperation of the cockpit crew was secured, and all the way to Florida various games were played (such as guessing the city over which the plane was flying) and service was provided in a light-hearted way with lots of informal conversation between crew and customers.

The second flight was a much shorter trip to an industrial city on a stormy day. The plane departed late because of the weather, and every seat was taken. Instead of vacation garb, there were newspapers, attache cases, and people who looked preoccupied and distinctly impatient. On this flight, the crew was fast, efficient, and altogether

---

[3]Organizations where this is done would seem to be especially good sites for research on the psychological dynamics of self-regulation because the phenomena of interest should be more abundant there than in traditional, manager-led units.

businesslike. The crew, in each case, took a look at the performance situation and adapted its strategy for carrying out its work to be as appropriate as possible to that situation, given overall corporate objectives. It provides a sharp contrast with cabin attendants in some other airlines, where crews are required to behave strictly in accord with standard, management-specified service routines.

Summary. A summary of three structural features that foster achievement of the process criteria of effectiveness is provided in Figure 2. When these features are present—a motivating task, a well-composed unit, and sent expectations that support proactive self-regulation—then the chances increase that self-managers will exert sufficient effort on the task, bring sufficient knowledge and skill to bear on it, and choose or develop a performance strategy that is appropriate to the task and the situation.

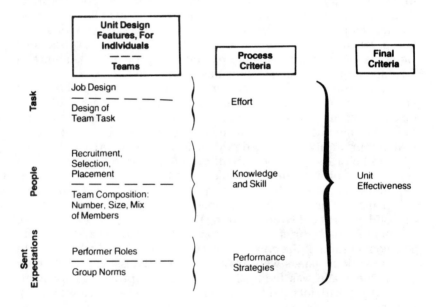

Figure 2. Design features that foster achievement of the process criteria.

Achieving a high standing on the process criteria, in turn, increases the chances that a unit ultimately will be effective—that is, that clients will judge its work satisfactory, that the performance capability of the unit will improve over time, and that individual members will learn from their work experiences and find them personally satisfying.

When the two ingredients I have discussed so far are present (that is, the performing unit has clear, engaging direction and an enabling structure), a solid basis for effective self-management is established. That is not, however, the whole story, because performing units do not operate in an organizational vacuum. There are two kinds of support that can help a unit exploit the potential provided by good direction and structure: those provided by formal organizational systems and those provided through hands-on coaching and consultation. I will discuss them in turn.

A Supportive Organizational Context

Although organizational supports may seem mundane, their presence (or absence) can dramatically foster (or limit) the effectiveness of a self-managing performance unit. Three specific features of the organizational context are particularly significant in supporting self-managing units. It will be no surprise that the first of the three has mainly to do with the effort self-managers apply to the work, the second with the knowledge and skill they bring to bear on it, and the third with the appropriateness of the task performance strategies they use in executing it.

The reward system. A reward system that recognizes and reinforces excellent unit performance can complement and amplify the motivational incentives of a well-designed task. Which specific rewards will work best, of course, depends on what the unit members value. Sometimes simple recognition of excellence will suffice; in other cases, more tangible rewards will be required. But whatever the rewards, their impact on effort will be greater if they are contingent on performance, that is, if they are provided only when they are earned.

Two other features of supportive reward systems in self-managing organizations merit special mention. First, the rewards must preserve performers' "line of sight" (Lawler, 1981). It is not sufficient for performance–reward contingencies simply to exist; performers must perceive that their behavior makes a difference in the outcomes they receive. Devices such as stock ownership and profit sharing, common in organizations that aspire to self-management and organizational democracy, may have limited impact in larger organizations, where the link between what an individual does on a day-to-day basis and his or her eventual financial benefits is so remote as to be difficult to discern. Just as a citizen may ask "What difference does my one vote make?" so may a self-manager in a large enterprise wonder how much of a difference coming to work today or persevering with a difficult customer will make in his or her share of the profits. It usually is necessary, therefore, either to break large self-managing units down into smaller groups that serve as the basis for member rewards or to install multiple-level reward systems that provide immediate as well as long-term rewards and recognition.

Second, the system must be appropriate to the self-managing unit. When the work is designed for individual self-managers, an individually focused reward system may be fully appropriate. But when the performing unit is a self-managing team, consequences should focus on the performance of the team as a whole. When this principle is violated (for example, by providing rewards to individual team members based on managers' judgments of their relative contributions to the group product), dissension and conflict often develop within the group. This is the dilemma of the athletic coach, who must try to motivate the team as a whole while simultaneously cultivating and reinforcing individual performance. And it is a problem routinely faced by managers of work teams in organizations where the reward system traditionally has focused on identifying and recognizing excellent individual performers.

When the performing unit is a team, the destructive effects of rewarding individual contributions rather than unit performance can be substantial. Therefore, if it is not feasible to provide performance-contingent rewards to the group as a whole, it may be better to base rewards on the performance of the next-larger unit (such as a department or division) or not to use contingent rewards at all rather than to invite the divisiveness that can develop when members of a team are put into competition with one another for scarce and valued rewards (Lawler, 1981).

The education system. Sometimes members of a performing unit collectively have all the knowledge and skill they need for optimum task performance. More commonly, there are aspects of the work for which outside expertise would be helpful. The education system of the organization can help fill in gaps in member talent and contribute to the development of members' own knowledge and skill.

For this potential to be realized, two conditions must be met. First, relevant educational resources, which can include technical consultation as well as training, must exist somewhere in the organization. Second, a delivery system must be in place to make those resources accessible to the unit. This may sound like a straightforward organizational design problem, but it often turns out to be a thorny political issue, particularly when unit members are rank-and-file members who never have had the right to call on staff resources. In effect, staff experts become the providers of service to clients whom they previously may have viewed as subordinate to them. Such reversals of traditional roles are never easy to negotiate.

The particular kind of assistance required depends on both task requirements and specific unit needs, and the appropriate form of the assistance varies as well. Sometimes a one-shot technical consultation will suffice; sometimes a continuing consulting relationship will be needed; and sometimes a formal training program will be more appropriate. Whatever the content of the assistance provided and the vehicle used to deliver it, the objective of the education system is the same: to help units that do not have the full complement of knowledge and skill required for excellent task performance obtain it.

The information system. The information system of an organization is critical to a performing unit's ability to plan and execute a task-appropriate performance strategy. If a unit cannot obtain clear information about its performance situation, or if it does not have access to data about the likely results of alternative approaches to the task, it may develop a way of proceeding that seems reasonable to group members but that turns out to be grossly inappropriate when executed.

To develop a good performance strategy, unit members need a clear map of the performance situation. It is especially important for members to have information about (a) task requirements, constraints, and opportunities that may limit or channel strategic options; (b) the resources that are available for use; and (c) the people who will receive, review, or use the group product, including the standards they are likely to employ in assessing its adequacy. Consider, for example, a self-managing manufacturing team that is deciding how to approach a complex assembly task. One possibility might be a cyclic strategy, in which all members build components for a period of time, then assemble final products (producing a relative flood of output), followed by another component-building period, and so on. How would this strategy compare to one in which some members build components continuously while others are dedicated to final assembly? To choose between these strategies, the group needs information about the timing of demand for their product, the availability of space for storing components and completed products, and the cost of obtaining and holding parts for use in batch production. It would be quite risky to choose a strategy without this information.

As was the case for educational resources, the delivery of information often turns out to be a major roadblock in supporting self-managers. In many organizations, information is shared only on a "need to know" basis. If rank-and-file members traditionally have been merely executors of the work with no responsibility for monitoring and managing their own performance, then historically they had no legitimate need for strategy-relevant information. Even when member roles are redefined to include self-managing responsibilities, senior managers may persist in a view that it is unnecessary (or too risky) to share confidential strategy-relevant information with them—a stance that can compromise unit effectiveness, particularly in a fluid and competitive environment, but one that also can be difficult to change.

Expert Coaching and Consultation

The organizational supports I have discussed so far typically are provided relatively impersonally, through the normal operation of organizational systems. Additional support can be provided to self-managers directly, through hands-on coaching and consultation by their leaders (Fournies, 1978; Thomas, 1979). Coaching is an especially critical support for self-managers, who must learn how to regulate their behavior in often uncertain work situations (Mills, 1983).

Consistent with the general framework I have been using, I will focus on ways that coaching and consultation can affect the standing of a performing unit on the three process criteria. How, for example, can a leader or consultant help members avoid unnecessary losses of effort, misapplications of talent, or implementation of flawed performance strategy? And, on the positive side, how can members be helped to strengthen their commitment to hard, effective work on the task, increase their task-relevant knowledge and skill, and invent uniquely appropriate strategies for proceeding with the work? Although the objectives of coaching are the same whether the work is done by an individual self-manager or by a self-managing team, the nature of the consultation will vary substantially in the two cases.

Consider first individual self-managers. Earlier I discussed individual differences in psychological readiness for self-managing work, and in capability to do the work well, as two factors to be considered in recruiting, selecting, and placing self-managers. No matter how good those practices are, there always will be a less-than-perfect match between the person and the work. Direct coaching can help an initially skeptical or confused self-manager become aware of opportunities for personal satisfaction and growth present in the work and provide support and assistance as the individual learns how to exploit those opportunities. Moreover, a coach can help a self-manager hone and develop his or her task-relevant knowledge and skill, thereby shrinking any gap between a person's talents and the requirements of the task. Helping people accept their roles as self-managers has particularly high leverage for individuals who have worked mainly in traditional enterprises. These people may not know how to monitor and adjust their behavior in response to a changing task or situation or how to go about inventing and testing alternative work strategies. These skills are key to effective self-management, and a good coach can significantly assist people in acquiring them.

Teams, like individuals, often need coaching in self-management skills, particularly when team members have relatively little (or predominantly negative) experience with collaborative work. Too often a task is tossed to group members with the assumption that "they'll work it out among themselves." And too often members do not know how to do that. A leader or consultant can do much to promote team effectiveness by helping members learn how to work together as self-managers.

The role of the help-provider is not to dictate to group members the "one right way" to go about their collaborative work, but rather to help members learn (a) how to minimize the "process losses" that invariably occur in groups (Steiner, 1972) and (b) how they might work together in ways that generate synergistic process gains (for a detailed discussion of process losses and gains, see Hackman & Morris, 1975, or Hackman, 1986). Specific kinds of help that might be provided include the following:

• *Effort:* helping members minimize coordination and motivation decrements (process losses that can waste effort) and helping them build commitment to the group and its task (a process gain that can build effort).

• *Knowledge and skill:* helping members avoid inappropriate weighting of members' ideas and contributions (a process loss) and helping them share expertise and learn from one another (a process gain).

• *Performance strategies:* helping members avoid flawed implementation of performance plans (a process loss) and helping them invent creative ways of proceeding with the work (a process gain).

This focus on process losses and gains that are specifically relevant to task accomplishment contrasts with group process consultations that seek to minimize intermember disagreement and promote harmonious group relations. There is no consistent evidence that group performance is facilitated by smooth, conflict-free relations among members; indeed, research suggests that working through conflicts over ideas promotes both group creativity and member satisfaction (Hoffman, 1978, p. 85). So, despite the fact that turbulent intermember relations may appear to impede performance, it often is wiser to let such turbulence run its course. Rather than help members resolve their disagreements as quickly as possible, then, a consultant might encourage them to stay engaged with their ideational conflicts and to attempt to remedy only those process issues that are compromising the team's level of effort, its utilization of member talent, or its management of performance strategy.

In summary, coaching can help both individual self-managers and self-managing teams become more effective, but it is neither a cure-all nor an always-appropriate activity. If, for example, the direction provided to performers is poorly articulated or alienating, if the performing unit has serious structural flaws, or if the organizational context undermines rather than reinforces excellence, then it is highly unlikely that direct, hands-on coaching will be of much help. The leader's attention, in such cases, might more appropriately focus on getting the overall performance situation squared away, thereby creating a setting in which coaching can have a real chance of improving unit effectiveness.

Even when performance conditions are positive, self-managing units are not always receptive to coaching interventions. For example, in charting the life cycles of a number of self-managing task forces, Gersick (1984) found that there were certain times in teams' lives when they were receptive to consultation and coaching from outsiders (for example, around the midpoint of the work) and other times when they were not (for example, in the period between the first meeting and the midpoint, when members were almost wholly preoccupied with internal matters and seemingly uninterested in outside help). It appears that the timing of coaching interventions can sometimes be as important as their content in determining their impact.

The kind of coaching contemplated here has little in common with traditional performance appraisal programs in organizations. Such programs are structured organizational devices for assessing on a regular basis the acceptability of the work people do. Although assessment results may prompt training and development activities, they usually have direct consequences for individuals' compensation and advancement as well. By contrast, I have been discussing a coaching role in which performers are helped, on line, to learn how to behave so as to accomplish their work at high levels of excellence—and to improve their own skills and capabilities in the process. The term *coach* was selected deliberately, to suggest behaviors intended to help others perform as well as they can, in an enterprise to which both the coach and the performer are committed. In this view, coaching involves persistence, repetition, and constant vigilance for opportunities to help self-managers improve themselves and their performance. It is a cooperative venture between performers and leaders that is always unfinished, and it is an activity of great potential benefit to all parties—albeit one that may be impossible to do well if the performing unit and its organizational context are not properly set up in the first place.

Adequate Material Resources

I have now discussed four conditions that are critical to the effectiveness of self-managing performing units: direction, structure, context, and coaching. The fifth and final condition is also the simplest: having the wherewithal required to get the work done, such as money, space, staff time, tools, and so on. This condition is not particularly interesting conceptually, and until relatively recently it has been almost wholly overlooked by organizational researchers. Yet insufficient material resources often are a major roadblock to performance effectiveness in self-managing units (see, for example, Peters & O'Connor, 1980). Even units that have a clear and engaging direction, and whose performance situation promotes the process criteria, eventually will fail if they do not have (and cannot get) the resources they need to do their work. Among the saddest kinds of failures are those experienced by well-designed and well-supported self-managing units whose members understand their objectives and are committed to achieving them, but who cannot obtain the resources they need to fulfill their promise.

Conclusion: Five Conditions That Support Effective Self-Management

To summarize, here are the five conditions that together promote the effectiveness of self-managing units:

1. The overall direction for the work is clear and engaging.

2. The structure of the performing unit fosters competent performance, through the design of the task, the composition of the unit, and sent expectations regarding the management of performance processes.

3. The organizational context supports competent work, through the reward, education, and information systems.

4. Expert coaching and consultation are available and are provided at appropriate times.

5. Material resources are adequate and available.

The first condition provides the overall frame within which the unit operates and, when present, amplifies the constructive impact of the remaining conditions. The final condition provides the means for getting the work done. If it is present, execution can proceed smoothly and according to plan; if it is not, performance will be undermined even when all the other conditions are in place.

The middle three conditions—structure, context, and coaching—together increase the chances that a self-managing unit will achieve the three process criteria of effectiveness. The relationship between these conditions and the process criteria is illustrated in Figure 3. For each of the process criteria, some aspect of unit structure, some feature of the organizational context, and some type of process assistance is identified as having particular relevance.

For *effort*-related issues, one would consider (a) the motivational structure of the task, (b) the reward system of the organization, and (c) individual and group dynamics having to do with motivation, commitment, and coordination.

Points of Leverage

	Unit Structure	Organizational Context	Coaching and Consultation
Ample Effort	Motivational Properties of the Unit Task	Organizational Reward System	Help with Motivation, Commitment, and Coordination Issues
Sufficient Knowledge and Skill	Composition of the Unit	Organizational Education System	Help with the Use and Development of Members' Talents
Task-Appropriate Performance Strategies	Sent Expectations About Scanning/ Planning	Organizational Information System	Help with the Invention and Implementation of Strategic Plans

Process Criteria of Effectiveness

Figure 3. Points of leverage for creating a favorable performance situation.

For *talent*-related issues, one would consider (a) unit composition, (b) the education system of the organization, and (c) individual and group dynamics having to do with the development and use of members' talents.

For *strategy*-related issues, one would consider (a) roles and norms relevant to the management of performance processes, (b) the information system of the organization (i.e., whether the unit gets the data it needs to design and implement an appropriate strategy), and (c) individual and group dynamics having to do with the invention and implementation of new ways of proceeding with the work.

The view of self-management I have sketched here is broad and encompassing. Rather than focus on the immediate causes of specific self-managing behaviors, I have attempted to identify a set of general conditions that, taken together, foster effective self-management. When these conditions are present, one should find good alignment between individual and collective objectives, autonomous monitoring and managing of work activities by unit members in pursuit of those objectives, and a high level of satisfaction (by both unit members and their clients) with what transpires and what is achieved. By contrast, most existing research and theory on self-management in organizations is based on the principles of social learning theory (Bandura, 1971) as applied to shaping up one's own behavior (Mahoney, 1974; Watson & Tharp, 1977). The emphasis in that work is on strategies people can use to increase the frequency of constructive behaviors that they rarely exhibit or to decrease the frequency of dysfunctional behaviors that they often exhibit (see, for example, Brief & Hollenbeck, 1985; Luthans & Davis, 1979; Manz and Sims, 1980).

The two approaches, heretofore distinct in the literature, complement one another (see for example, Manz, in press). Recognition of the importance of social system conditions can enrich the design and interpretation of research on the psychology of self-regulation, for example, by identifying circumstances when self-regulation is likely to be observed and when it is likely to be associated with effective work performance. The social learning theorists' research on the dynamics of self-regulation, on the other hand, can illuminate in detail the psychological and behavioral processes that occur within the broad orienting and enabling conditions I have set forth here. I hope that future research and theory on self-management will exploit the complementarities of the two approaches in ways that both deepen conceptual understanding of the phenomena and advance practical knowledge about how to create and maintain effective self-managing units.

Leadership in Self-Managing Units

According to Manz and Sims (1984, p. 410), there is an inherent contradiction in thinking about the leadership of self-managers. "How," they ask, "does one lead employees who are supposed to lead themselves?" In working through the dilemma they set for themselves, Manz and Sims have proposed the concept of the "unleader"—someone who "leads others to lead themselves" (p. 411). Although the idea of the unleader is novel, it is common for those who write about self-management to take the view that there is relatively little need for leadership in such units, that leaders should help unit members get the work under way and then fade into the background as quickly as possible. I take a contrary view and argue that leadership is both more important and a more demanding undertaking in self-managing units than it is in traditional organizations.

The approach to self-management that I have been discussing lends itself rather naturally to a functional analysis of leader roles and behavior. As articulated by McGrath (1962), the key assertion in the functional approach to leadership is this: "[The leader's] main job is to do, or get done, whatever is not being adequately handled for group needs" (p. 5). If a leader manages, by whatever means, to ensure that all functions critical to both task accomplishment and group maintenance are adequately taken care of, then the leader has done his or her job well. By leaving room for an indefinite number of specific ways to get a critical function accomplished, the functional approach avoids the need to delineate the specific behaviors that a leader should exhibit in given circumstances—a trap into which it is all too easy for leadership theorists to fall.

Yet the functional approach is generic almost to a fault: It could apply to virtually anybody leading virtually anything. To apply the approach, one needs a theory that specifies what is critical to the effectiveness of the group or organization being led. I have attempted to provide such a specification for self-managing units (that is, in terms of the five enabling conditions I have been discussing) and will now draw on that material to explore what is required of those who lead self-managers.

Critical Leadership Function

The critical leadership functions for a self-managing unit are *those activities that contribute to the establishment and maintenance of favorable performance conditions.* Following the framework proposed by McGrath (1962, p. 17), this involves two types of behavior: (a) monitoring—obtaining and interpreting data about performance conditions and events that might affect them—and (b) taking action to create or maintain favorable performance conditions.

For the monitoring function, a leader would ask the following. Does the unit have clear and engaging direction? Is it well structured? Does it have a supportive organizational context? Are ample coaching and process assistance available? Does it have adequate material resources? Although I have framed these questions in the present tense, the monitoring function includes not only assessments of the present state of affairs (diagnosis), but also projections about how things are changing and what deleterious or fortunate events may be about to occur (forecasting).

Action-taking follows these assessments of the group and situation and involves behaviors intended to create favorable performance conditions or to remedy problems (or exploit opportunities) in existing conditions. Sometimes the focus of such actions will be within the unit (as when the leader works with members to help them understand the significance of their task or learn better ways of coordinating their activities). Other times external action will be required (as when the leader negotiates a change in the organization's compensation system to provide rewards for excellent performance or when he or she helps establish a relationship between the unit and a consultant from elsewhere in the organization).

These leadership functions can be arranged in a matrix, as in Figure 4. There are two types of functions (monitoring and action-taking) for each of the five enabling conditions (direction, structure, context, coaching, and resources). For the monitoring function, both diagnosis and forecasting are specified; for the action-taking function, both internal and external targets are specified.

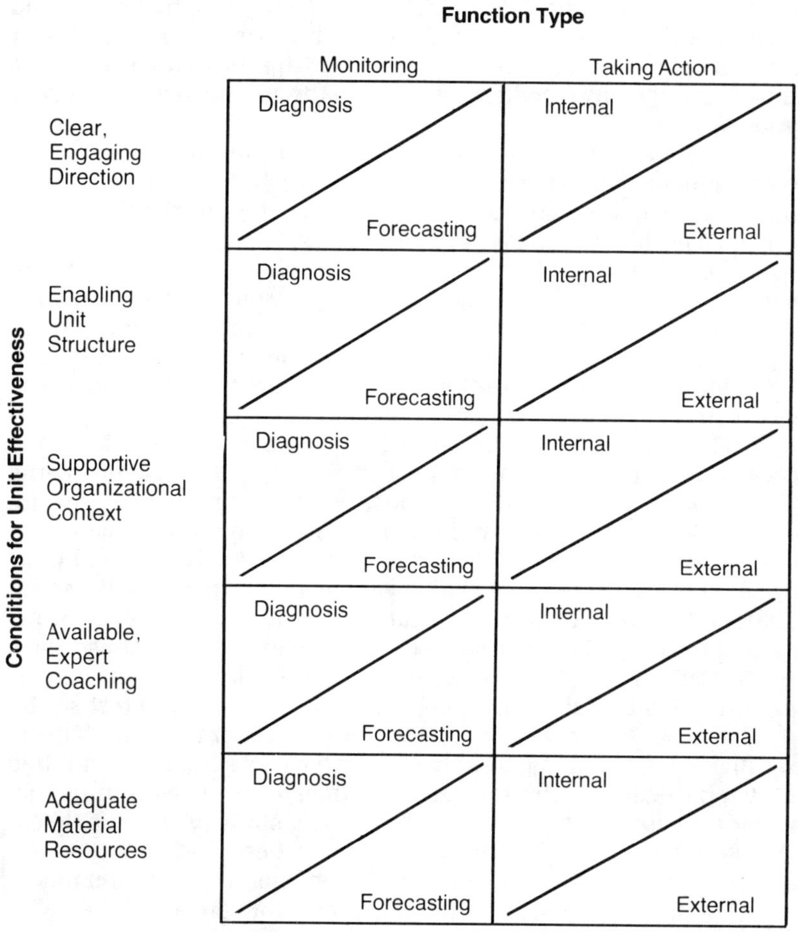

Figure 4. Summary of critical leadership functions for self-managing units.

Although the leader's responsibility is to ensure that these functions are fulfilled, this does not mean that he or she must handle them personally. Leadership is appropriately shared in self-managing units, and as such units mature unit members typically assume responsibility for an increasing number of leadership functions (Walton & Schlesinger, 1979). Thus, there is no single set of leader behaviors that is always desirable and appropriate, nor will any single style of leadership be generally effective.

Does this view of leadership invite the development of a complex table of contingencies that explicate the specific leader behaviors that should be exhibited in various circumstances? On the contrary, the five enabling conditions provide a relatively straightforward and theory-specified set of tests that a leader can use in managing his or her own behavior. Figure 5, by highlighting the substantive focus of a leader's monitoring activities, shows how the approach would work in practice.

First a leader would assess the outcome states at the right of the figure, and then work backwards to identify (and ultimately do something about) performance conditions that may be contributing to performance problems or missed opportunities. "How is the unit doing?" the leader would ask. "Are there signs of problems in the task work, in members' ability to work together interdependently, or in the quality of individuals' experiences in the unit?" When problems, unexploited opportunities, or negative trends are noted, he or she would examine the process indicators in the center of the figure to learn more about what may be going on.

Then, guided by the answers to the diagnostic questions, the leader's attention would turn to the conditions at the left of the figure. "Which performance conditions most need strengthening? How are we doing in direction, in structure, in context supports, in hands-on assistance, in resources?" If it turns out that performance conditions are suboptimal, the leader's challenge is to invent (the word is chosen deliberately) ways of behaving that may remedy a deficiency or exploit an unrealized opportunity. The five enabling conditions I have been discussing would serve as criteria for a leader to use in comparing and evaluating alternative behaviors. This invent-and-test strategy is far easier to use than one that requires a leader to learn a table of contingencies specifying exactly what behaviors should be exhibited in what particular circumstances—and then to regulate his or her behavior in accord with that table. The present strategy also should encourage innovation and creativity in leader behavior.

Leaders always act in accord with some model (even if implicit, and even if wrong) that specifies what behaviors are associated with what outcomes. Typically, the models used by leaders (and studied by researchers) focus on interactions that take place between leaders and unit members. In the model I have proposed here, only two of the

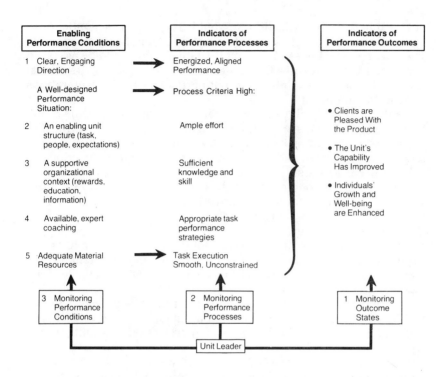

Figure 5. The unit leader's monitoring function: A summary.

five key conditions (setting direction, and coaching/consultation) involve leader–unit relations centrally; the other three (structuring the unit, tuning the organizational context, and providing material resources) are oriented toward the situation in which the unit functions. If this model has validity, then effective leaders would be observed to spend at least as much of their time and energy working with peers and senior managers as they do with unit members, monitoring and taking action vis-a-vis all five of the performance conditions. A leader who attempts to foster unit effectiveness primarily through hands-on work with unit members when the surrounding performance situation is flawed and unsupportive would be predicted to fail.

Designing Leader Roles

Should the leader roles be designed to foster competent leadership in self-managing units? The logic for addressing this question is the same as that used in considering the design of performing units. The major difference is that this time the focus is on the role of the leader, not the unit itself. Specifically, one would first generate a number of alternative ways to structure leader roles for the unit being considered. Then, with several possibilities on the table, each would be assessed to determine which show the greatest promise of getting the critical leadership functions fulfilled for that particular unit. Considerations include the following:

• From what perch would a leader be best able to provide direction to the unit? Will he or she be setting direction, or merely translating and communicating it? How much authority needs to be built into the role to legitimize and support the direction-setting function?

• How can leadership roles be designed so as to foster rather than undermine the autonomy a unit has in managing its own affairs? Would designating a formal leader within the unit make it harder or easier to maintain an appropriate balance between collective direction and unit autonomy?

• How much external influence will the leader require to create supportive structural and contextual conditions and to marshall needed resources? How can the role be designed to strengthen the leader's influence outward and upward?

• What information will the leader require, and with whom will he or she need to coordinate on a regular basis? Can access to critical information and contact with key co-workers be built into the role?

Once questions such as these are reviewed, it is likely that one or another of the alternative designs under consideration will emerge as dominant (or, perhaps, a new and better alternative will come up in the testing process). It often turns out in practice that leadership functions can best be fulfilled when a unit has both a defined internal leader (who is also a working unit member) and an external manager who may have responsibility for several units. There is, however, no generally best design for leadership roles in self-managing units. As was the case for the design of performing units, the right answer is to have a design process that will generate an answer that is right for particular organizational circumstances.

Training Leaders of Self-Managers

How can leaders of self-managing units develop the knowledge and skill they need to perform their roles well? Once again, McGrath's (1962) paper on leadership functions is helpful. He suggests that one can develop a matrix, with the critical functions as rows and the knowledge and skills required to fulfill those functions as columns. For leaders of self-managers, the matrix is as follows:

Critical Leadership Functions	Required Knowledge	Required Skills
Monitoring and Taking Action Regarding:		
1. Setting Direction		
2. Designing the Unit		
3. Tuning the Context		
4. Coaching and Consulting		
5. Providing Resources		

In designing a leadership training program, then, one first would determine which functions have the greatest leverage for the work to be done, and then proceed to fill in the cells with the actual knowledge and skills that are required to fulfill those functions. The specific content of the cells will necessarily depend on the properties of the work to be done and the organization in which it will be done. In some organizations, for example, political skills will be needed to obtain organizational supports and resources; in others, those supports may be abundantly available or obtainable simply by asking. As another example, consider the support leaders provide unit members through on-line coaching and process assistance. In some organizations, there will be great need for such help and no one available to provide it but the leader; in others, members may be experienced and expert in self-management (and therefore less in need of assistance) and, moreover, there may be a staff of organization development professionals on call to lend a hand if asked. Obviously, the need for leader training in process skills will vary as a function of such circumstances.

There are, nonetheless, some knowledge and skills that may be of general value in leading self-managers. Here are some ideas about what these might be, presented separately for the leader's monitoring and action-taking functions.

Monitoring. To effectively diagnose the state of a performing unit and forecast likely future problems and opportunities, a leader needs *knowledge* about the key conditions for effective performance. In addition, he or she must understand how these conditions are linked to the process criteria and to unit effectiveness. I have attempted to provide some guidance about such matters in this lecture, and I suspect that it would be a reasonably straightforward task to develop a training course for unit leaders based on this material.

Leadership *skills* that may help leaders of self-managers perform well include the following:
- Data gathering skill: the ability to collect data about social systems that are reliable and valid.
- Diagnostic and forecasting skill: the ability to apprehend complexity and make sense of it, drawing on both data and existing knowledge in shaping one's conclusions.
- Hypothesis testing skill: the ability to use data to conduct assessments of the relative validity of alternative hypotheses about the state of a social system (or, for forecasting, about its likely future state).

Action-taking. In taking action to help a self-managing unit perform well, a leaders needs knowledge about both (a) the key levers that are available (or can be made so) to improve performance conditions, and (b) timing considerations that condition when various interventions are likely to "take" (versus when they may fall on barren ground and have little effect).

Among the skills required for competent action-taking by leaders of self-managers may be the following:

Envisioning skill: the ability to envision desired end-states and to articulate and communicate them to others.

Inventive skill: the ability to think of numerous nonobvious ways of getting something done.

Negotiation skill: the ability to work persistently and constructively with peers and superiors to secure resources or assistance needed to support one's subordinates.

Decision-making skill: the ability to choose among various courses of action under uncertainty, using all perspectives and data that can be efficiently obtained to inform the decision.

Teaching skill: the ability to help others learn both experientially and didactically.

Interpersonal skill: the ability to communicate, listen, confront, persuade, and generally to work constructively with other people, particularly when people's anxieties are high.

Implementation skill: the ability to get things done. At the simplest level, knowing how to make lists, attend to mundane details, check and re-check for omitted items or people, and follow plans through to completion. At a more sophisticated level, the ability to constructively and assertively manage power, political relationships, and symbols to get things accomplished in social systems.

It is, I suspect, entirely feasible to develop training that will help leaders develop the knowledge and skill they need to fulfill the critical leadership functions. Yet there are some individuals for whom such training would be a waste of time—individuals who, perhaps, should not be invited to serve as leaders of self-managers. With that possibility in mind, let me turn finally to the problem of selecting people for leadership roles in self-managing units.

Selecting Leaders of Self-Managers

Are there general qualities or traits that can be used to differentiate people who are likely to develop into first-rate leaders of self-managers from those who will never be effective in such roles? Although I am mindful of the pessimistic conclusions that have emerged from decades of research on leadership effectiveness traits, I believe that relatively stable individual differences in potential for leading self-managers do exist, and that these differences can be assessed.

There are three qualities that might be measured when people are being considered for leadership roles—qualities that probably are not trainable in the short term. These qualities have little in common with those that have been studied in trait-oriented leadership research, and I offer them in a speculative spirit.

Courage: a willingness to buck the tide (and social norms) when necessary to create conditions required for effectiveness. To help a unit address and modify dysfunctional dynamics, a leader may need to challenge group norms and disrupt established routines—and may risk incurring some anger in doing so. To improve a unit's contextual supports or to increase the resources available to it, a leader may need to rock the organizational boat—and may risk a loss of esteem with his or her peers and superiors in doing so. Such behaviors require courage.

Emotional maturity: the ability to move toward anxiety-arousing states of affairs in the interest of learning about them and doing something about them (rather than moving away to get the anxiety reduced as quickly as possible).

Clear and appropriate personal values: an internalized commitment to both organizational effectiveness and human well-being. Leaders who are confused about what they personally value find it difficult to choose among competing options for action. Although almost any clear set of values can be used as the basis for managing one's own behavior, one cannot be agnostic about the content of those values in considering how to select leaders of self-managers. Only individuals who genuinely value both collective outcomes and the growth and satisfaction of unit members are likely to invent and implement conditions that promote the two values simultaneously—something that surely is necessary if a self-managing unit is to be effective over the long term.

This list may seem a bit strange to organizational scientists who typically do not deal with things such as courage, emotions, and values. But stranger still, perhaps, is the fact that excellent leaders in self-managing units tend to have many, if not all, of these very qualities. It would appear to be well worthwhile to give new thought to old questions about how candidates for leadership positions might be assessed on such difficult-to-measure but potentially significant attributes.

Conclusion

The model of self-management that I have presented in this chapter emphasizes the creation of conditions that direct, enable, and support effective performance, but that also leave a great deal of behavioral latitude for unit members and their leaders. It deals with multiple, nonindependent factors that have redundant influences on a set of outcomes that also are not independent.

This kind of approach can jar scientific sensibilities. Scientists are trained to look for the true causes of phenomena in which they have interest. When a performing unit performs particularly well or poorly, for example, a scientist would attempt to rule out as many explanations as possible and eventually pin down the real causal agent. Standard scientific methods are appropriate for many purposes, but there are at least three reasons why they can mislead researchers who are interested in social system effectiveness.

First, influences on performance effectiveness do not come in separate, easily distinguishable packages. They come, instead, in complex tangles that often are as difficult to straighten out as a backlash on a fishing reel. Trying to partial out the effects of each possible determinant of unit effectiveness, then, can lead one to the conclusion that no single factor has a very powerful effect—a conclusion reached by more than one reviewer of the literature on work performance. Each possible cause loses its potency when studied in isolation from other conditions also in place for the units under study.

Second, there are many different ways unit members can behave and still perform work well and even more ways to be nonproductive. Systems theorists call this aspect of organized endeavor "equifinality" (Katz & Kahn, 1978, p. 30). According to this principle, a performing unit can achieve the same outcome from various initial conditions and by a variety of means. Equifinality supports the view that leading self-managers centrally involves creating conditions that amply support effective performance—but in a way that leaves plenty of room for unit members to develop and implement their own idiosyncratic strategies for accomplishing the work. There is no single strategy that will work equally well for different units, even units that have nearly identical official tasks.

Third, social systems develop and enact their own versions of reality and then act in accord with the environment they have helped create. A unit's redefinition of reality, which cannot be prevented, can either blunt or enhance the impact of specific actions taken by a researcher or manager to influence it. This issue is especially salient for self-managing units because of the latitude self-managers have in making sense of their performance situation and in deciding how they will behave within it.

Together, these difficulties suggest that traditional scientific models in which specific external causes are tightly linked to specific, well-defined effects may have to give way to an alternative kind of theorizing—one that is more congruent with the facts of life in social systems. I have attempted in this lecture to describe one such an approach. I conclude by discussing the implications of that approach for practice, for theory, and for research methodology.

Implications for Practice

Working in a self-managing unit is somewhat akin to driving from New York to Chicago rather than taking a train. When driving, you have many alternative routes; if one of them is blocked, there are still many ways to get to Chicago. A train, however, has only one set of tracks; if there is an obstruction on them, you cannot proceed until it is removed. As long as organizational structures and policies provide self-managers with enough room to maneuver around whatever obstacles they encounter, unit performance can be fully acceptable even in the face of management errors and suboptimal organizational conditions.

Those who design self-managing units also enjoy maneuvering room. The conditions I have been discussing can take multiple forms, and there are multiple ways to create and install them. For example, one can think of many ways a piece of work could be designed and still foster internal work motivation; so are there many ways a reward system could be structured and still provide positive consequences contingent on unit performance. The same is true for the other conditions we have considered. This feature of self-managing work systems both invites managerial creativity in organizational design, and allows specific design features to be adapted to idiosyncratic realities of the work place.

Because the five enabling conditions are in many ways redundant, they can to some presently unknown extent substitute for one another. Rather than attempting to optimize a design, then, those who are setting up a self-managing unit would be well-advised to deliberately foster redundancy and interdependence among positive performance conditions, thereby creating an over-determined performance system that can continue to function satisfactorily even if some of its components fail.

It is, of course, far easier to create a self-managing unit from scratch than to change over an existing system. Moreover, there is reason for skepticism about the viability of converting a performing unit from manager-led to self-managing using the planned change strategy traditionally favored by organization development professionals. Such programs typically involve sequential chains of activity, with each successive step depending on successful completion of the prior one—and the truth about the strength of chains is well known.

An alternative strategy for moving an existing organization toward self-management involves waiting for, and then vigorously exploiting, naturally occurring opportunities for change. This approach (which is described in more detail by Hackman & Oldham, 1980, Ch. 10), requires three things of change advocates. First, they must know where they want to go, that is, they must be clear about their organizational and human resource values and aspirations. Second, they must understand the conditions that are required to promote effective self-management, a matter about which I hope this lecture has been helpful, and one that is critical in focusing one's change activities on the highest-leverage targets. And finally, they must be sensitive to realities of timing and politics—factors that, perhaps more than any other, determine when one should take action and when it is wiser to lie in wait for a more favorable opportunity.

Implications for Theory

Throughout this lecture, I have argued that behavior and performance in self-managing units are overdetermined. That is, they are shaped by multiple, nonindependent factors whose influence depends in part on the fact that they are redundant. Standard cause–effect models obviously are inappropriate for construing such phenomena, as are contingency models of the "X is a cause of Y, but their relationship is moderated by Z" variety. Multivariate models, designed specifically for analyzing causally complex phenomena, would seem a reasonable alternative. Yet if self-managing systems do operate as suggested here, so many key assumptions of these models would be violated so severely that they would be of little use (cf. James, Mulaik, & Brett, 1982). One could, of course, select variables and structure research situations to make sure that these assumptions are not violated, but then one would be in the unfortunate situation of altering the phenomena to make them more suitable for study with the tools that happen to be available. Somehow, the substantive horse must be put back in front of the methodological cart. First better ways of theorizing about influences on work performance must be found, and then appropriate ways of gathering and analyzing data to test those ideas can be located or invented.

What kinds of conceptual models would be most useful in furthering an understanding of performance in self-managing organizational units? One intriguing lead is provided in the theory of multiple possibilities set forth by Tyler (1983). Whereas contingency theory assumes that if one knew the right moderating variables it would be possible to predict and control behavior in virtually any situation, multiple possibility theory holds that such an aspiration is ill-conceived. Instead, the theory maintains, there are many possible outcomes that can emerge in any situation, and the particular outcome that is actualized is not completely determined by the causal factors that precede it. Thus, multiple possibility theory envisions a world with some "play" in the system, and it encourages attention to human choice as a factor that transforms multiple possibilities into single courses of action.

Multiple possibility theory fits nicely with the phenomenon of self-management and also complements the systems theorists' notion of equifinality discussed earlier. Where equifinality asserts that the same outcome can occur in response to many different causes, multiple possibility theory posits that the same cause can generate a variety of different outcomes. Taken together, the two notions provide an alternative to stimulus–response models in which situational causes are tightly linked to behavioral effects—whether directly ("Introduce this management practice and performance will improve") or contingently ("Performance will improve, but only for certain kinds of people under certain circumstances").

If the notions of equifinality and multiple possibilities were taken seriously, would that signal an abandonment of "scientific" approaches to understanding work behavior? Not at all. But it would require that scholars of organizations generate qualitatively different kinds of models to deal with performance in social systems and that they also invent some new methods for assessing the validity and usefulness of those models.

Implications for Method

The methodological challenges posed by the approach to understanding work behavior and performance I have been discussing are considerable. How, for example, can one study nonindependent influences on performance in ways that will yield more than mere descriptions of what has transpired—that will, instead, offer insight into the dynamics of organizational conditions that foster and support effective self-management? What methods can be used to learn about factors that have powerful cumulative influences on work behavior, but whose effects are almost impossible to discern at any given moment in time? How can one tap into self-reinforcing cycles of increasingly good or poor performance in ways that reveal how those cycles feed themselves?

One strategy for approaching such questions would be to bring the case study out of the management school classroom and put it to work in scholarly pursuits. It is true that case studies, as traditionally prepared, often give too much credence to the interpretations favored by their authors. Selective emphasis of material, and decision making about what data to include and exclude are real problems (although these problems are shared by writers of quantitative empirical studies to a far greater extent than is usually admitted). Are there ways to present case studies that invite disconfirmation and tests of alternative interpretations? Would it be possible, for example, to carry out competing analyses for each interpretation of a given case—one that seeks to support the interpretation as convincingly as possible and one that attempts to cast the greatest possible doubt on it? Would such an approach to case analysis and presentation foster learning by other scholars and contribute to the accumulation of knowledge across cases?

Another possibility, heretofore used more by coroners, detectives, and aircraft accident investigators than by scholars of organizations, is the "modus operandi" method (Scriven, 1974). If one can generate a list of the *possible* causes of some outcome or event and has some knowledge about the special "signature" of each one, then it often is possible to use logical, historical, and microexperimental techniques to identify the *probable* causes of that outcome—even when it is complexly determined or overdetermined. The modus operandi approach, which as far as I know has not been used in the study of work performance, provides an interesting alternative to standard quasi-experimental and correlational designs for organizational studies.

Whatever new devices are developed for use in studying self-managing social systems, I suspect that they will require careful, systematic descriptions of the phenomena under study, interpretations that cross traditional levels of analysis (that is, that link individual, group, organizational, and environmental variables), and renegotiation of the turf boundaries that presently keep psychologists from having to worry about contextual and structural influences on behavior (and that free scholars in other disciplines from worries about psychological dynamics that affect the phenomena in which they have special interest). Eventually, there may even be greater recognition of the value of multiple perspectives on the same data from people in different groups with different stakes in how those data are interpreted. What will be seen less and less, I hope, are analyses of the causes of performance outcomes that isolate causal agents from the social systems in which they operate and research strategies that require the phenomena to accommodate to the methodology rather than vice versa.

The practical, conceptual, and methodological challenges that have emerged from this exploration of the psychology of self-management are substantial—and obviously are not ones for which I have ready answers. I am optimistic, nonetheless, that in these challenges lies the potential for developing scholarly models of work performance that are considerably more congruent with the realities of social systems than are the deterministic contingency models presently in favor in organizational psychology. Moreover, as the challenges are confronted, I have hope that some guidelines for managerial action will emerge, guidelines that will be both powerful in affecting work performance and usable by people who design and manage purposive social systems of many varieties—including, but certainly not limited to, organizations that aspire to self-management.

References

Atkinson, J. W. (1958). Towards experimental analysis of human motivation in terms of motives, expectancies, and incentives. In J. W. Atkinson (Ed.), *Motives in fantasy, action, and society.* Princeton, NJ: Van Nostrand.

Bandura, A. (1971). *Social learning theory.* Morristown, NJ: General Learning Press.

Bandura, A. (1977). Self-efficacy: Towards a unifying theory of behavioral change. *Psychological Review, 84,* 191–215.

Bennis, W., & Nanus, B. (1985). *Leaders: The strategies for taking charge.* New York: Harper & Row.

Berlew, D. E. (1979). Leadership and organizational excitement. In D. A. Kolb, I. M. Rubin, & J. M. McIntyre (Eds.), *Organizational Psychology* (3rd ed.). Englewood Cliffs, NJ: Prentice-Hall.

Brief, A. P., & Hollenbeck, J. R. (1985). An exploratory study of self-regulating activities and their effects on job performance. *Journal of Occupational Behavior, 6,* 197–208.

Check, W. A. (1982). Results are better when patients control their own analgesia. *Journal of the American Medical Association, 247*(7), 945–947.

Cohen, S. G. (1985). *The beginnings of a model of group empowerment.* Unpublished manuscript, Yale University, School of Organization and Management, New Haven, CT.

Cummings, T. G. (1978). Self-regulating work groups: A socio-technical synthesis. *Academy of Management Review, 3,* 625–634.

Eisenstat, R. A. (1984). *Organizational learning in the creation of an industrial setting.* Unpublished doctoral dissertation, Yale University, New Haven, CT.

Fein, M. (1974). Job enrichment: A reevaluation. *Sloan Management Review, 15,* 69–88.

Fournies, F. F. (1978). *Coaching for improved work performance.* New York: Van Nostrand Reinhold.

Gersick, C. J. G. (1984). *The life cycles of ad hoc task groups: Time, transitions, and learning in teams.* Unpublished doctoral dissertation, Yale University, New Haven, CT.

Gunn, C. E. (1984). *Workers' self-management in the United States.* Ithaca, NY: Cornell University Press.

Hackman, J. R. (1985). Doing research that makes a difference. In E. E. Lawler, A. M. Mohrman, S. A. Mohrman, G. E. Ledford, & T. G. Cummings (Eds.), *Doing research that is useful for theory and practice.* San Francisco: Jossey-Bass.

Hackman, J. R. (1986). The design of work teams. In J. W. Lorsch (Ed.), *Handbook of organizational behavior.* Englewood Cliffs, NJ: Prentice-Hall.

Hackman, J. R., & Morris, C. G. (1975). Group tasks, group interaction process, and group performance effectiveness: A review and proposed integration. In L. Berkowitz (Ed.), *Advances in experimental social psychology* (Vol. 8). New York: Academic Press.

Hackman, J. R., & Oldham, G. R. (1980). *Work redesign.* Reading, MA: Addison-Wesley.

Hackman, J. R., & Walton, R. E. (1986). Leading groups in organizations. In P. S. Goodman (Ed.), *Designing effective work groups.* San Francisco: Jossey-Bass.

Haythorn, W. W. (1968). The composition of groups: A review of the literature. *Acta Psychologica, 28,* 97–128.

Hoffman, L. R. (1978). Group problem solving. In L. Berkowitz (Ed.), *Group processes.* New York: Academic Press.

House, R. J. (1977). A 1976 theory of charismatic leadership. In J. G. Hunt & L. L. Larson (Eds.), *Leadership: The cutting edge.* Carbondale: Southern Illinois University Press.

Jackson, J. (1965). Structural characteristics of norms. In I. D. Steiner & M. Fishbein (Eds.), *Current studies in social psychology.* New York: Holt.

James, L. R., Mulaik, S. A., & Brett, J. M. (1982). *Causal analysis: Assumptions, models, and data.* Beverly Hills, CA: Sage.

Kahn, R. L., Wolfe, D. M., Quinn, R. P., Snoek, J. D., & Rosenthal, R. A. (1964). *Organizational stress: Studies in role conflict and ambiguity.* New York: Wiley.

Kanfer, F. H. (1984). Self-management in clinical and social interventions. In R. P. McGlynn, J. E. Maddux, C. D. Stoltenberg, & J. H. Harvey (Eds.), *Interfaces in psychology: Social perception in clinical and counseling psychology.* Lubbock, TX: Texas Tech Press.

Kaplan, R. E. (1979). The conspicuous absence of evidence that process consultation enhances task performance. *Journal of Applied Behavioral Science, 15,* 346–360.

Katz, D., & Kahn, R. L. (1978). *The social psychology of organizations* (2nd ed.). New York: Wiley.

Langer, E. J. (1983). *The psychology of control.* Beverly Hills, CA: Sage.

Lawler, E. E. (1978). The new plant revolution. *Organizational Dynamics, Winter,* 31–39.

Lawler, E. E. (1981). *Pay and organization development.* Reading, MA: Addison-Wesley.

Lindenfeld, F., & Rothschild-Whitt, J. (Eds.). (1982). *Workplace democracy and social change*. Boston: Porter Sargent.

Locke, E. A., Soari, L. M., Shaw, K. N., & Latham, G. D. (1981). Goal setting and task performance: 1969-1980. *Psychological Bulletin, 90,* 125–152.

Luthans, F., & Davis, T. R. V. (1979). Behavioral self-management: The missing link in managerial effectiveness. *Organizational Dynamics, Summer,* 42–60.

Mahoney, M. J. (1974). *Cognition and behavior modification*. Cambridge, MA: Ballinger Publishing.

Manz, C. C. (in press). Self-leadership: Toward an expanded theory of self-influence processes in organizations. *Academy of Management Review*.

Manz, C. C. , Mossholder, K. W., & Luthans, F. (in press). An integrated perspective of self-control in organizations. *Administration and Society*.

Manz, C. C., & Sims, H. P. (1980). Self-management as a substitute for leadership: A social learning theory perspective. *Academy of Management Review, 5,* 361–367.

Manz, C. C., & Sims, H. P. (1984). Searching for the "unleader": Organizational member views on leading self-managed groups. *Human Relations, 37,* 409–424.

McGrath, J. E. (1962). *Leadership behavior: Some requirements for leadership training*. Washington, DC: U.S. Civil Service Commission.

Mills, P. K. (1983). Self-management: Its control and relationship to other organizational properties. *Academy of Management Review, 8,* 445–453.

O'Connor, E. J., Rudolf, C. J., & Peters, L. H. (1980). Individual differences and job design reconsidered: Where do we go from here? *Academy of Management Review, 5,* 249–254.

Peters, L. H., & O'Connor, E. J. (1980). Situational constraints and work outcomes: The influences of a frequently overlooked construct. *Academy of Management Review, 5,* 391–397.

Poza, E. J., & Marcus, M. L. (1980). Success story: The team approach to work restructuring. *Organizational Dynamics, Winter,* 3–25.

Schutz, W. C. (1961). On group composition. *Journal of Abnormal and Social Psychology, 62,* 275–281.

Scriven, M. (1974). Maximizing the power of causal investigations: The modus operandi method. In W. J. Popham (Ed.), *Evaluation in education: Current applications*. Washington, DC: American Educational Research Association.

Seligman, M. (1975). *Helplessness: On depression, development, and death*. San Francisco: W. H. Freeman.

Steiner, I.D. (1972). *Group process and productivity*. New York: Academic Press.

Taylor, F. W. (1911). *The principles of scientific management*. New York: Harper.

Thomas, G. (1979). *The advisor: Emissary from Teachers' Center to classroom* (Teachers' Centers Exchange Occasional Paper No. 6). San Francisco: Far West Laboratory for Educational Research and Development.

Tyler, L. E. (1983). *Thinking creatively*. San Francisco: Jossey-Bass.

Wall, T. D., Kemp, N. J., Jackson, P. R., & Clegg, C. W. (n.d.). *An outcome evalua-*

tion of autonomous work groups: A long-term field experiment (Memo No. 649). Sheffield, UK: University of Sheffield, MRC/ESRC Social and Applied Psychology Unit.

Walton, R. E. (1980). Establishing and maintaining high commitment work systems. In J. R. Kimberly & R. H. Miles (Eds.), *The organizational life cycle.* San Francisco: Jossey-Bass.

Walton, R. E. (1985). From control to commitment: Transformation of workforce management strategies in the United States. In K. B. Clark, R. H. Hayes, & C. Lorenz (Eds.), *The uneasy alliance: Managing the productivity-technology dilemma.* Boston: Harvard Business School Press.

Walton, R. E., & Hackman, J. R. (1986). Groups under contrasting management strategies. In P. S. Goodman (Ed.), *Designing effective work groups.* San Francisco: Jossey-Bass.

Walton, R. E., & Schlesinger, L.S. (1979). Do supervisors thrive in participative work systems? *Organizational Dynamics, Winter,* 24–38.

Watson, D. L., & Tharp, R. G. (1977). *Self-directed behavior.* Belmont, CA: Brooks/Cole.

White, J. K. (1978). Individual differences and the job quality-worker response relationship: Review, integration, and comments. *Academy of Management Review, 3,* 267–280.

Woodman, R. W., & Sherwood, J. J. (1980). The role of team development in organizational effectiveness: A critical review. *Psychological Bulletin, 88,* 166–186.

Zander, A. (1980). The origins and consequences of group goals. In L. Festinger (Ed.), *Retrospections on social psychology.* New York: Oxford University Press.

Zwerdling, D. (1980). *Workplace democracy.* New York: Harper Colophon.

SAMUEL H. OSIPOW

CAREER ISSUES THROUGH THE LIFE SPAN

SAMUEL H. OSIPOW

S amuel H. Osipow earned his PhD in psychology at Syracuse University in 1959, specializing in counseling psychology. This work was built on an earlier master's degree in experimental psychology at Columbia University. He has held positions in the U.S. Army, at the Pennsylvania State University, and at the Ohio State University, where he has chaired the Department of Psychology since 1973. He has also had brief appointments at the University of Wisconsin, Harvard University, the University of Tel Aviv, and the University of Maryland.

Osipow's research has focused on the psychology of career development. In his early work he examined career entry and career decision making, whereas more recently he has studied career adjustment during the adult years. His work has had implications for interventions to enhance career satisfaction and effectiveness. In addition, Osipow has tested and extended the theoretical understanding of career behavior.

Osipow has authored, co-authored, edited, or co-edited numerous books and monographs, all dealing with some aspect of careers or counseling. Most notable among these are *Theories of Career Development,* now in its third edition, and the two-volume *Handbook of Vocational Psychology,* co-edited with W. Bruce Walsh. He has also co-developed measures of career indecision and of occupational stress, strain, and adjustment. From 1970 to 1975, he was the founding editor of the *Journal of Vocational Behavior,* and from 1975 to 1981 he was editor of the *Journal of Counseling Psychology.* Osipow has authored more than 70 articles in journals.

Osipow is a past-president of APA's Division 17, and has served on numerous boards and committees. He is currently serving on the APA Board of Directors.

SAMUEL H. OSIPOW

CAREER ISSUES THROUGH THE LIFE SPAN

Introduction

One of the attractions of the invitation to present in the Master Lecture series was the opportunity to popularize the active research and practice field of the psychology of work. Although my own fascination with the study of work is long standing, going back to my early school days, I have found relatively few people seriously interested in the field beyond concerns about their own or their loved ones' personal adjustment to work. Most people, including psychologists, grow interested in vocational matters only at selected times in their lives: when, as youngsters, they begin planning their own careers; a little later when they initially choose career paths and implement their choices; sometimes as their career matures and issues of secondary pathways and career adjustment or advancement emerge; for a subset of people, when their work requires them to manage, evaluate, or promote others; and when they sense retirement in the offing. In addition, parents are usually concerned about children's careers, and spouses are often involved in each other's careers.

Despite these personal concerns, little systematic attention has been paid to principles of career behavior, and investigators and practitioners have often been pulled almost reluctantly into the study of work behavior and its applications. This is true, despite the wide recognition that work "occupies" all of us for significant portions of our lives and the fact that work exerts a strong influence on life style. Once enticed into the study of work, however, most professionals find that it becomes an absorbing interest.

Thus, because the study and application of career behaviors has so often been coolly received, I especially welcome the chance to entice generalists into the effort through the Master Lecture. I focus on issues of interest to the informed nonspecialist. I then discuss some commonly held assumptions about careers, some useful concepts and theories, common barriers to career development and problems that result from them, a few significant applications of career knowledge to the adult phase of life, and some topics of significance for the future.

Some years ago I had the opportunity to present a lecture on the topic of career development (Osipow, 1969). My assignment was to try to identify the solid ground, if any, that underlay principles and understandings related to how people's careers develop. The request to present the Master Lecture in 1985 reminded me of that earlier lecture given 16 years ago, because that was essentially a state-of-the-art assignment, as is this one. I thought a good place to begin would be to review what I said about "what we really know about career development" in 1969 and use it as a starting point for thinking about what we "really know about career development" in 1985. Much progress has been made in the last 16 years, but unfortunately in many respects we are no further advanced in our understandings than we were a generation ago.

In 1969 I made several assertions based on the literature. First, I stated that career development is a socially bound process, which emphasizes the importance of the impact of culture, economy, and social status on people's vocationally relevant experiences. A second idea that I derived from the literature was that there is a principle of change that occurs both within and external to the individual as well as across a temporal dimension. The third assertion I made was that for many people career development occurs in the context of emotionality, particularly anxiety. Freedom to choose leads to responsibility to choose wisely, to accept the consequences of one's choices; acceptance of consequences of choices exposes one to anxiety, lest the choices be unwise and their implementation be inadequate. Fourth, I asserted that occupations require substantially different kinds and levels of abilities for success. The fifth assertion was that there is an interaction between the individual and his or her environment that significantly influences several important dimensions of career choice. These dimensions include success, satisfaction, adequacy of implementation, and access, as examples.

Since 1969, my work in the area of career development has broadened considerably. At that time a major part of the field and I both focused on career entry and implementation. Many investigators and theorists have since broadened their activities to include adult career behavior and the study of the many important work-related variables associated with the adult part of the life span. More recently, some investigators have begun to inquire into issues related to the later phases of careers, transition to retirement, and adjustment to retirement, as retirement relates to preretirement work patterns and adjustment.

Common Assumptions About Careers

Certain assumptions are often expressed about careers that many writers use to help them cope with the complexity of the psychological aspects of careers, and certain contextual factors have been found to be important in understanding what happens to people in their career lives. The following are 14 statements that are often made about careers.

1. There is one occupation for which each individual is best fit.
2. Once a field is chosen, the choice is irreversible.
3. One can succeed at whatever interests one.
4. Effort and motivation can overcome all obstacles.
5. You know when you have chosen the right work because it is fun.
6. Intrinsic job satisfactions are better than extrinsic ones.
7. Most people dislike their work.
8. Most people would not work if they did not have to.
9. People make decisions about their occupations once, when they are young. After that most people pay little attention to their careers.
10. Educational choice and vocational choice are nearly the same.
11. Interests are more important in determining the choice of occupation than skills or aptitudes.
12. In the future, people will work less and less.
13. There are certain occupations for which men are inherently better suited than women and vice versa.
14. The younger a person is when the choice of career is made the better.

Most of these statements are usually false. Interestingly, however, for certain individuals and occupations, some of the statements are occasionally true. The first assumption is a case in point. Theoretically there might be an occupation for which one is best fit, and such a fit might become apparent for some individuals (for example, for Mozart). Practically speaking, however, this best fit rarely occurs. Ordinarily, occupational suitability reflects a wide band of activities. The assumption of best fit has caused much mischief over the years, however, as people have obsessively searched for their best match.

The second assumption, that once a field is chosen the choice is irreversible, is true in the sense that time, effort, and money invested in implementing a choice cannot be recovered, but it is not true in the sense that modifications, although at some cost, can be made once a choice and a direction are pursued. Although few people will become surgeons after age 45, a considerable number will change their field of work.

The third and fourth assumptions, that interests and effort and motivation can overcome career obstacles, are true and false, too. If interest is assumed to be analogous to motivation, it is clear that given equal capacities, a more highly motivated person will get more mileage and performance out of these capacities than will a less motivated person. This is true up to a point, however. Motivation cannot raise levels of performance beyond some absolute limits of capacities inherent in the individual. This is another assumption that has caused considerable grief, because many people have been ill advised that if they want something enough to work hard for it, it can be achieved. Not only does this assumption unnecessarily frustrate people by leading them in poorly conceived directions, but it also can lead them to feel that they failed because they did not work hard enough or want hard enough to achieve their goal.

Assumption number 5, that you know you have chosen the right work when you find your work to be "fun," has led many a person astray searching for the elusive work activity that is "fun." Work varies in its level of enjoyability over time and situations, and, even if that is not problem enough, defining what "fun" is proves to be impossible.

The assumption that intrinsic satisfactions are better than extrinsic ones is one that varies with current social mores. In times of social commitment such as the 1960s, extrinsic motives were frowned upon, and the predominant value of the time was to pursue your true self in your work. In more materialistic periods such as today, extrinsic motives seem to be more important and desirable to many people. In fact, these are individual matters that are probably not even stable in one person over a lifetime.

Assumptions 7 and 8—most people dislike their work and most people would not work if they did not have to—can also be both true and false. Most people would probably continue to work even if they became extraordinarily wealthy, but they would change what they did, and that is what makes these statements both true and false.

The assumption that people make occupational decisions once when they are young and after that pay little attention to their careers is, unfortunately, often true. People tend to pay attention to their careers only when there is some problem to be addressed, some dissatisfaction in their work life, some disruption of their work pattern. Ideally, however, people would periodically plan their career moves and take inventory of their work activities in order to prepare themselves for the next stage and the next decision demanded of them.

The 10th assumption, that educational and vocational choice are the same is, generally speaking, not true; although educational and vocational choice are often the same, they are not the same inherently. One may arrive at the same occupational activity as another person through a different educational vehicle and, conversely, one may choose the same educational device as another person yet enter a very different occupational activity. Too often people assume that what they choose to train in is identical with what they will actually be employed to do later in life. Thus people often search obsessively for educational choices that will lead to what they think will be occupationally suitable activities, even when it would be much simpler and more desirable for many people to make those decisions separately. Most people are not ready to make occupational decisions when they are 18 or 19 years old and are just embarking on educational careers.

The 11th assumption is partly true in that interests tend to determine the field of occupational activity, but skills and aptitudes determine the level of work and the access to avenues of advancement. Skills and aptitudes seem to define a floor for occupational attainment that is in some ways independent of interests. Because many people choose careers on the basis of interests independent of skills and aptitudes, many choices are poorly conceived and lead to frustration for the chooser. It might be useful for people to recognize the questionable status of this assumption so that they look at their interests together with their skills and aptitudes in making choices.

It is often assumed that people work less now than formerly and that in the future they will work even less. Actually this is not true. Before the industrial revolution, the work week was relatively short. The length of the work week increased for a time until industry became more efficient in production processes. Even now the work week is sometimes artificially shortened by work rules that determine that time worked over a certain number of hours results in pay at a different rate; thus, people are not working fewer hours; rather, they get paid differentially for work beyond a certain number of hours.

The 13th assumption is that there are certain occupations for which men are inherently better suited than women and vice versa. Fundamentally, the issue behind the assumption is one of the key factors underlying the feminist movement—that men and women should have equal access to occupations. Whether certain occupations have physical or intellectual requirements that are differential by sex is an empirical question that has not yet been answered. Because so many personal attributes are normally distributed, it is difficult to think of any attribute in which some women might not exceed some men and some men might not exceed some women. The essence of the question raised by the assumption is really what factors should determine occupational aspiration and attainment: personal attributes or stereotyped assumptions about attributes as a function of sex or of some other external variable. It is easy to recognize that this assumption has led to considerable misery for many people, both women and men, who have felt constrained to pursue occupations that conformed to a particular sex stereotype.

The final assumption, that a person should choose a career as early as possible, is a common one, and as a result, many people have made choices based on profound ignorance. Career psychology and career development programs have encouraged people to defer their career choices until later in life to permit those decisions to be made in the context of more reliable predictions about what people will be like at maturity. Most career psychologists would encourage delaying career decision making well into late adolescence and early adulthood at the least, and in some circumstances even later if possible. Institutions and organizations tend to press people to make such decisions earlier for their own convenience. Obviously, for some individuals, early choice is to be desired. Child prodigies, for example, have special attributes that, if not developed starting at an early age, may be lost or at least never fully developed.

The Influence of Culture on Career Choices

In my list of assertions, I indicated that in 1969 career development appeared to be heavily influenced by culture. Nothing has happened in the intervening 15 or 16 years to change my opinion; in fact, I think there is *more* evidence now than earlier to suggest that cultural factors may play an even more important part than has been realized.

These cultural factors include regional differences within one country that are reflected in the geographic climate or in industrial factors that shape the opportunity packages available to people. They also include national and regional political and economic conditions that have implications for education, employment services, training, and not the least of all, the job market. Cultural factors include ethnic and subethnic factors that shape attitudes not only about how to approach work tasks but also about what kind of work is most valuable, how active one should be in the selection of work, and material versus spiritual or intrinsic values in work.

Sex role is an important cultural influence on career choices. There is a considerable body of literature on sex role stereotyping (e.g., Fitzgerald & Betz, 1983), its effect on career choices, and society's differential reaction to men and women in various careers.

Several new ideas and models to explain sex role aspects of career development and behavior have recently been proposed. Astin (1984) has proposed an expectancy model based on four principles:

1. Survival, pleasure, and contribution motivate work behavior.
2. The capacity to satisfy those motives and expected access to appropriate work influence career choices.
3. Early socialization and perceived opportunity structures significantly shape expectations.
4. These expectations can be altered via opportunity structure changes which, in turn, lead to changes in career choices and behavior.

Astin's model assumes that because men and women have the same motivations, differences in career choices and behaviors result from different expectations based on sex role socialization and sex role related differences in perceived opportunity structures.

Although Fitzgerald and Crites (1980) have taken a different approach to understanding sex-related career behaviors, their conclusions anticipated Astin's model in many ways. Fitzgerald and Crites assumed that the career development processes of men and women are similar, differing primarily in complexity. They viewed women's career development as being more complex than men's; the complexities reside in differences in sex-role-socialized knowledge about work, in counselor and inventory effects on female clients and their perceived options, in the fields women choose, and in women's adaptation patterns once they are employed. Similar forces, however, seem to affect men as well as women, although in different combinations (Fitzgerald, 1980; Fitzgerald & Cherpas, 1985).

Finally, Fassinger (1985) and Farmer (1985) have developed models independently to explain women's career behavior. Fassinger used a structural equation modeling method to examine how variables such as work experience, academic success, the influence of role models, and perceived encouragement affect attitudes toward work, sex role, and self. The most promising model found that ability, achievement orientation, and feminist orientation influence family and career orientations, which in their turn influence career choice. Ability has a separate and direct effect on career choice.

Similarly, Farmer (1985) was interested in determining the sources of career motivation for women and for men. Using variables similar to those used by Astin (1984), Fassinger (1985), and Fitzgerald and Crites (1980)—that is, motivational variables, achievement and ability variables, and personal and environmental variables—Farmer found that environmental variables mediate motivational variables more for women than for men. What is especially promising about Farmer's model is its inclusion of both women and men.

Not surprisingly, these approaches have some shortcomings. Most of these models have not compared the sexes directly. Reviewing the Astin (1984) and Fassinger (1985) models, I wondered how large are the differences in women's and men's career development. Furthermore, the models focus on career entry rather than on adjustment and progress. Perhaps a shift in emphasis is in order now, because understanding what happens to women in their careers might provide a feedback loop useful to younger women. Finally, although these models correctly use many variables to explain very complex processes, conceptual integration is lacking; therefore the results are difficult to understand. Perhaps a concept such as self-efficacy is needed to drive these models (see, for example, Betz & Hackett, 1981; Hackett & Betz, 1981).

Despite these shortcomings, there is no question that the study of women's career issues has considerably increased the understanding of career development and career behavior in general.

The Occupational Adjustment of Adults

As the study of careers has itself matured, increased attention has been focused on the occupational adjustment of adults. For example, in a recent article, Super (1980) has explicated an approach to understanding how careers unfold across the life span. The approach describes settings that Super calls theaters. Some of these theaters are common to all people—for example, home, community, school, and work place; others are not universally available, such as unions, clubs, and churches. These theaters allow people to play a variety of roles throughout life. The roles are child, student, leisurite, citizen, worker (which includes the unemployed and the nonworker), spouse (although not everyone marries), homemaker, parent (although not everyone has children), and pensioner. One's life stage determines both the availability of theaters and one's roles. Even the same role changes throughout life: A person's role as child is different at age 10, 30, and 50. A person's involvement in various roles waxes and wanes, depending on life stage.

Gottfredson (1981) has proposed another life span developmental model of occupational aspirations. The major constructs include self-concept and occupational images. The model also includes a cognitive map of occupations, which relates occupations to one another in terms of levels and fields of work, as well as in terms of sex, occupational preferences, perceived accessibility of occupations, and occupational alternatives, including the range of occupations the individual considers to be acceptable. Gottfredson made a strong case for the hypothesis that occupations are perceived similarly. Given that similarity, something must account for differences in occupational preferences.

To explain those differences, Gottfredson proposed a model that describes self-concept development as being related to occupational preferences. There are four developmental stages: orientation to size and power, to sex roles, to social valuation, and to the internal, unique self. These stages describe development differentially according to thought processes; the ability to classify people, objects, and occupations; perceptions of self and others; and occupational perceptions and preferences. The model, then, should facilitate an understanding of age-stage-related cognitive processes as they pertain to careers.

Vondracek, Lerner, and Schulenberg (1983) have supported a developmental basis for understanding careers but were critical of previous efforts. They believed that most career development theorists had not developed their models with sufficient attention to the "conceptual, empirical, and methodological problems involved" (p. 179), and, furthermore, that new and significant changes in developmental theory, along with distortions or misrepresentations of important empirical results, had been ignored by career theorists. Although this view is controversial and has been criticized (e.g., Gottfredson, 1983), it cannot be ignored.

For example, Markham (1983) has criticized the truncated notions of career theory that do not pay sufficient attention to deviance from normative career behavior or to those aspects of career theories that do not explain the substantial amount of variance unaccounted for in research results. To correct this deficiency, Markham has proposed that vocational behavior be studied in the context of life-style and that researchers use Heider's (1958) psychology of action to understand career behavior. Thus, using Heider's formulation that "action is a function of trying, ability, task difficulty, and luck," (p. 75), Markham developed a model with implications for job choice strategies, adaptive processes, and career interventions. The advantages of Markham's approach lie in its emphasis on cognitive-processing variables and its orientation to applications.

Vondracek, Lerner, and Schulenberg (in press) criticized the way career psychologists use the term *developmental*. Substitution of the terms *stage* or *life cycle* or *life span* is equally controversial, because the meaning of each of these terms depends on the theory base. *Stage* may mean "a universal or invarient sequence of qualitative change through which *all* people pass" (Erikson's theory, 1959), but this meaning does not hold for other theorists (e.g., Bijou, 1976).

Vondracek, Lerner, and Schulenberg (in press) have tried to rectify the shortcomings that they identified in career development theory. They have proposed a life span developmental approach to career development that is contextually based, interactive, and multidimensional. Their approach has implications for health behavior, women's career development, and career counseling interventions.

Clearly, age differences are important in understanding psychological aspects of careers. For example, certain occupational activities are more appropriate at some ages than at others, and there are data indicating that age relationships exist regarding occupational stress, strain, and coping (Osipow, Doty, & Spokane, 1985). Much more remains to be learned, however.

Theories of Career Behavior

There are many ways to organize the analysis of occupational behavior. The one that makes the most sense to me and seems most useful is a life-stage development view that focuses on variables within the contexts of sex, occupational level, occupational field, and western industrialized technology. Any attempt to develop a universal understanding of work and its impact on behavior is likely to be far too complex and broad to be effective. In my view, career theory must be built on fragments.

Theoretical constructs that are used to understand career development have been substantially influenced by a few individuals. One of the most important researchers has been Donald E. Super, who proposed a theory of careers that is based on two factors: life-stage development and self-concept implementation in work (e.g., Super, Starishevsky, Matlin, & Jordaan, 1963). The major developmental concept arising from Super's theory is vocational maturity. Vocational maturity presumes that at each life stage, individuals are expected to master tasks that prepare them to deal competently with an age-stage-related vocational task, be it choice, implementation, or adjustment. The major self-concept factors are its development, skills in self-knowledge, and skill in implementation.

Another major career development theorist is John Holland. His theory focuses on person–environment interaction (Holland, 1985). The major concepts in Holland's theory involve six occupational environmental types and six corresponding personality types (realistic, investigative, artistic, social, enterprising, conventional). The guiding principle underlying Holland's theory is that to the degree that individuals are able to find and enter an environment that is congruent with their major personality orientation, they will be more effective and satisfied in their occupational life. The amount of research that documents this view is impressive, as a recent review by Spokane (1985) has revealed. A number of related constructs such as differentiation, crystallization, and identity have also furthered the understanding of the career development process.

Super's theory focuses on the variables that deal with the process of career selection and adjustment to work, whereas Holland's deals with the prediction of the content and level of the field. The two theories complement each other and together represent the full range of career selection and adjustment possibilities.

Two other theories have been developed that, although they have less support in empirical literature, fit well within the parameters described by Super and by Holland. One of these is the Work Adjustment Theory of Lofquist and Dawis (1969), recently revised by Dawis and Lofquist (1984). According to this trait-oriented, person–environment theory, it is assumed that certain aspects of people's personalities develop that lead them to be differentially suited for working in certain environments. This concept resembles Holland's person–environment idea, although the details differ substantially. The principal variables predicted are occupational satisfactoriness and satisfaction. The other theory is the social-learning approach to career development, best described in Mitchell, Krumboltz, and Jones (1979). This view focuses on the processes of behavior development that lead to the acquisition of occupationally related attitudes, behaviors, and skills.

Other theories about career development exist (see Osipow, 1983) and include works by Tiedeman (e.g., Tiedeman & O'Hara, 1963) and Roe (1957), as well as psychodynamic approaches (Bordin, Nachmann, & Segal, 1963). The Super, Holland, work-adjustment, and social-learning theories, however, are the most influential and promising now, and their commonalities suggest that theorizing in career development may be converging. For example, the Dawis and Lofquist theory (1984), Holland's latest exposition of his theory (1985), Super's description of self-concept development (1963), and the social-learning approaches (Mitchell, Krumboltz, & Jones, 1979), all have a striking similarity in that they identify the processes and patterns by which personality attributes develop, especially work-related attributes. Fifteen years ago these theories were not so well developed nor were they so similar in their understandings and descriptions of the work personality.

Until relatively recently these theories have been used primarily to predict career entry. Holland's theory has been used widely in counseling high school and college students about career environments that might be appropriate for them to consider on the basis of their personality types. Super's theory has been used to devise interventions designed to increase prevocational maturity so that high school and college students could develop attitudes and behaviors that would enhance their abilities to implement career choices. Social-learning approaches have been used to create programs that help high school and college students develop behaviors useful to them in learning about careers, shaping productive and useful work attitudes, and the like.

The early phase of the application of these theories and procedures is designed to facilitate career entry decisions. Certainly, the major problem related to the entry behavior of young people into the world of work involves career decision and indecision. The theories just mentioned have been useful in identifying factors associated with career indecision. Approaches have been developed to assess levels of career indecision (Harren, 1979; Holland, Daiger, & Power, 1980; Osipow, Carney, Winer, Yanico, & Koschier, 1976), to assess interests (e.g., Strong, Hansen, & Campbell, 1985), and to develop typologies to understand decision-making styles, such as the approaches proposed by Harren (1979) and Johnson (1978).

More recently, however, attention has been focused on what happens to people after they enter the labor market, how they adjust, and how they advance. In addition, increasing attention has been paid to identifying barriers in general and employment barriers for special groups. In this area, the potential contributions of the theories have not been well explored. Each theory has made some contribution to increasing the adequacy of researchers' analyses of career problems.

Barriers to Making Career Choices

As I noted earlier, individuals are faced with several kinds of changes as they grow older. Some of these changes involve internal subjective responses and cognitive processes, whereas others involve external environmental changes. Usually the changes are not synchronized, so that what might have been an appropriate occupational field of entry at one age may not be appropriate at another age, because the rates of internal and external change differ.

Thus, some of the barriers people face with respect to career implementation are internal, and others are external. Many of the internal barriers involve the process of aging, changes in capacities to perform, changes in the capacity to adapt and adjust to changes, and changes in one's own interpersonal environment. With aging there may be less energy, fatigue may occur earlier, work patterns and work rhythms may change, and individuals may not be able to perform their work at the same levels of productivity as before. One's capacities to perform may change not only through the normal aging process with its diminution of energy, loss of visual acuity, reduction in muscle tone, reduction in physical strength, and memory decline, but also as a result of physical trauma—illness and accident—which can make a person no longer able to perform adequately a formerly appropriate and acceptable occupational activity. Finally, one's ability to adapt may diminish because one's ability to learn new coping skills and strategies and to learn new occupational tasks may slow down.

Some of the external barriers concern ease of access to occupations, stereotyping and prejudicial behaviors from other people that make certain occupations less available than others to individuals of particular subgroups, family constraints, economic constraints, and temporal constraints. These external barriers are usually well recognized, understood, and accepted; most people anticipate encountering some barriers of this type in their occupational careers. Well-adjusted individuals usually develop strategies to minimize the adverse impact of these events.

A Taxonomy of Career Development Problems

Two recent approaches have been proposed that contribute to a better understanding of how these barriers operate, how they may impede vocational adaptability, and, potentially, how they may be overcome. The first of these is a taxonomy of adult career development problems proposed by Campbell, Cellini, Shaltry, Long, and Pinkos (1979). This taxonomy builds upon an analysis of vocational developmental stages that reflects the various theoretical constructs that have been used to help understand how careers unfold and, in particular, the vocational development tasks that confront people at various life stages. Heretofore, the focus has been primarily on the development of instrumentation and on concepts related to vocational maturity in adolescence. Campbell and Cellini have extended that work and built on more recent work that examines career development and vocational maturity in early adulthood, middle and later adulthood, and the preretirement and retirement years.

Table 1 is an outline of the diagnostic taxonomy that Campbell and Cellini's group developed. There are four major problem areas: (1) problems in career decision making, (2) problems in implementing career plans, (3) problems in organizational/institutional performance, and (4) problems in organizational/institutional adaptation. Furthermore, each of these four categories was subdivided. Problems in career decision making were further classified into four subcategories: 1.1. getting started; 1.2. information gathering; 1.3. generating, evaluating, and selecting alternatives; and 1.4. formulating plans for implementing decisions.

What the table does not show is that within problem category 1.1, getting started, another level of subcategories might be as follows.

1.1.a. Being unaware of a need for a decision. An example might be an employee of a company that is reorganizing, who seems unaware of the need to make a position change decision.

1.1.b. Lacking knowledge of the decision-making process. An individual who did not know the best way to approach making a decision would illustrate this point.

1.1.c. Being aware of the need to make a decision but refusing to assume the personal responsibility to do so.

Table 1
Diagnostic Taxonomy Outline:
Problem Categories and Subcategories

1.0 Problems in Career Decision Making

  1.1 Problems in Career Decision Making: Getting Started
  1.2 Problems in Career Decision Making: Information Gathering
  1.3 Problems in Career Decision Making: Generating, Evaluating, and Selecting Alternatives
  1.4 Problems in Career Decision Making: Formulating Plans for Implementing Decisions

2.0 Problems in Implementing Career Plans

  2.1 Problems in Implementing Career Plans: Characteristics of the Individual
  2.2 Problems in Implementing Career Plans: Characteristics External to the Individual

3.0 Problems in Organizational/Institutional Performance

  3.1 Problems in Performance: Deficiencies in Skills, Abilities, and Knowledge
  3.2 Problems in Performance: Personal Factors
  3.3 Problems in Performance: Conditions of the Organizational/Institutional Environment

4.0 Problems in Organizational/Institutional Adaptation

  4.1 Problems in Organizational/Institutional Adaptation: Initial Entry
  4.2 Problems in Organizational/Institutional Adaptation: Changes Over Time
  4.3 Problems in Organizational/Institutional Adaptation: Interpersonal Relationships

Adapted from Campbell, Cellini, Shaltry, Long, & Pinkos (1979) by permission.

Information gathering (subcategory 1.2) can also be further subdivided.

  1.2.a. Having inadequate, contradictory, or insufficient information with which to make a decision.
  1.2.b. Having an overload of information. Some people seem to need so much information in order to make a decision that it is virtually impossible for them ever to accumulate that much information.
  1.2.c. Lacking knowledge about how to gather information.
  1.2.d. Being unwilling to accept the validity of collected informa-

tion if it does not agree with one's preconceived notions or self-concept.

The next category, the problems involved in generating, evaluating, and selecting alternatives (1.3), can be subdivided into six more categories.

1.3.a. Having problems deciding because of too many career options.
1.3.b. Having personal limitations that create problems in generating options.
1.3.c. Having problems resulting from anxiety.
1.3.d. Making unrealistic choices.
1.3.e. Having problems resulting from interpersonal conflicts that interfere with choices.
1.3.f. Lacking knowledge of how to include the many factors that should be considered in making a decision, resulting in an inability to evaluate alternatives.

The last category of career decision-making problems, formulating plans for implementing decisions (1.4), can be subdivided into three further subcategories.

1.4.a. Lacking knowledge of the steps needed to formulate a plan.
1.4.b. Failing to utilize appropriate time in planning.
1.4.c. Being unable or unwilling to get the information needed to formulate a plan.

In Table 1, the problems in implementing career plans (2.0) are divided into problems that result from individual characteristics (2.1) and problems that involve characteristics that are external to the individual (2.2). Each of these categories can be further subdivided.

2.1.Individual characteristics.
2.1.a. Having motivational problems.
2.1.b. Having incomplete training.
2.1.c. Experiencing changes in physical capacities.
2.2.External characteristics.
2.2.a. Existence of unfavorable economic conditions.
2.2.b. Existence of unfavorable institutional conditions.
2.2.c. Experiencing undesirable changes in one's family situation.

Problem categories 3.0 and 4.0 each can be further subdivided at least into one additional set of categories, as the taxonomy in Table 1 shows, and possibly even beyond.

Although this taxonomy does not have the detailed etiological and treatment focus that medical taxonomies such as the DSM-III have, it is based on a thorough analysis of career development through the various life stages. It is based on assumptions and observations concerning the theoretically relevant and empirically documented sequences of events that are associated with vocational adequacy. Certainly, many of the problems described in the 1.0 category, decision making, have been studied extensively and have been validated by research in career indecision with the use of instruments like the Career Decision Scale (Osipow et al., 1976) and Holland et al.'s (1980) My Vocational Identity Scale.

Unfortunately, little instrumentation is available to use this taxonomy to assess progress through various vocational developmental stages. So far, only one instrument exists for the establishment stage and none beyond that. Crites (1979) developed the Career Adjustment and Development Inventory, which measures vocational maturity and development in the early to late 30s. The instrument is based on development in the establishment stage. It follows on earlier work of Crites (1978) represented by the Career Maturity Inventory. Crites (1979) assumed that six establishment substages exist. Ranging from least to most mature, these are organizational adaptability, position performance, work habits and attitudes, co-worker relationships, advancement, and career choice and planning. There are 15 items in each scale by which to measure these events. In some of its forms, the instrument also has some more open-ended questions to assess vocational maturity.

Crites proposed that the higher one's score on each scale, the greater maturity the individual has achieved in the establishment task. He also proposed that development occurs in sequence and validated the hypothesis by showing that the mean scores on each scale for a large sample of respondents follow the predicted order: Organizational adaptability is the highest mean, position performance second highest, work habits and attitudes third highest, co-worker relationships fourth, advancement fifth, and career choice and planning sixth and lowest (Crites, 1982).

Thus before a person can develop good co-worker relationships, that person must already have mastered the earlier tasks of organizational adaptability, position performance, and work habits and attitudes. One advantage of this scheme is that it can be used to assess an individual's level of career maturity with respect to the establishment task. For example, if a counselor discovers that an individual who is chronologically and experientially approaching the end of the establishment phase is still dealing with tasks at the organizational adaptability and position performance level, the counselor is thereby guided about interventions and the appropriate criteria to use to evaluate progress in that counseling task.

The potential utility of the Campbell and Cellini taxonomy is enormous. It is the first comprehensive effort to try to understand and differentially diagnose what happens to people in their adult career lives. Conceivably, program developers, career counselors, and others can use the taxonomy both to develop instrumentation to measure career maturity and development (as Crites has done) and to sort out the career problems that people encounter; ultimately, it may be possible to develop systematic interventions designed specifically to deal with problems categorized in the taxonomy.

Given the immense potential of the microprocessor as a means of cognitive intervention, the potential applications of this taxonomy are very impressive. Naturally, much work remains to be done before its potential can bear fruit. Many investigators will need to devote considerable time and thought to developing methods to measure and categorize individuals, to modify the taxonomy as necessary, and to devise the appropriate interventions. That effort is worth making because the taxonomy could provide the basis for a generation of researchers' activities.

Gottfredson's "At-Risk" Concept

A second recent and major development that is useful in understanding the barriers to career development is the application of a concept from the medical literature that has not yet been used extensively in understanding what happens to people in their careers. Gottfredson (in press) has used the concept of being "at risk" to understand the barriers that people from different backgrounds may face in their career development. She has speculated that different groups of people are exposed to varying degrees of risk of career impairment because they possess attributes that can interfere with optimal career development. In her article, Gottfredson discussed several specific groups, including White Anglo-Saxon Protestants, White Ethnics, Blacks, Hispanics, American Indians, Asian Americans, and Jews. She has also identified sex and various handicaps, including visual, auditory, problems with the use of limbs, dyslexia, mental retardation, and mental illness as risk factors.

Among the risk factors that Gottfredson has suggested are three large categories. The first category includes factors that cause a person to be different from the general population. These factors are defined in terms of variables such as intelligence level, poor academic background, poverty, cultural isolation or segregation, functional limitations, and low self-esteem. The second set of factors involves differences within one's own social circle. These include interests typical of the other sex or of a different racial, ethnic, or social class group; social isolation or segregation from one's peers; or differences in intelligence compared to family and peers. The third set of risk factors involves family responsibilities and is subdivided into service as the probable or actual primary caregiver or service as the probable or actual primary economic provider.

According to Gottfredson, it is possible to review the existing literature to determine the degree to which each special group is exposed to events placing them at higher or lower than average risk in terms of career development. Thus, for example, after reviewing the literature, Gottfredson has concluded that White Anglo-Saxon Protestants are probably not at higher than average risk with respect to differences from the general population or differences within their own social circle but that White Anglo-Saxon Protestant men are probably at higher than average risk with respect to service as the primary economic provider and that White Anglo-Saxon Protestant women are at higher than average risk as primary caregivers. This means that because the men are the actual primary economic provider in most cases, they are not as free to seek career opportunities as they might be otherwise. For example, men are not able to give up good jobs to seek self-fulfillment when they must support family members. Similarly, women who provide caregiving are not free to implement careers they might otherwise prefer.

According to Gottfredson, however, White Ethnics may be at higher than average risk with respect to cultural isolation. That is, they probably come from backgrounds that separate them sufficiently from the population at large to create significant barriers to their career development. To continue, Blacks would appear to be at higher than average risk in all of the categories dealing with the differences from the general population except low self-esteem, and Black women in particular are probably at greater risk with respect to caregiving and economic providing than most people, whereas Black men are probably not at higher than average risk on those dimensions.

Gottfredson has analyzed all of the groups noted earlier along these lines. Her analysis is interesting in that it places in a new context the notion of what career development issues various groups may encounter. Certainly, the notion that barriers exist is not new; with respect particularly to women and minority group members, many of these barriers have been previously identified. What is new in the Gottfredson analysis is the notion that some individuals are able to overcome these barriers better than others because of particular personality characteristics. Furthermore, it is useful to know how these barriers interact with other individual characteristics in raising or lowering an individual's exposure to risk—in this case, risk associated with an inability to implement optimal career activities.

The applications of this idea lend themselves not only to research settings in which investigations can be conducted to identify the risk factors associated with membership in particular groups but also to the search for interventions to minimize the risks for members of high-risk groups so that career options can be enhanced. Although one might disagree with Gottfredson's interpretation of the literature, which implies that certain groups may be at more or less risk than other groups, the important contribution of the idea of risk is that it lends itself to a new level of analysis of the problems that various subgroups in our culture may experience with respect to careers.

The Gottfredson at-risk notion and the Campbell and Cellini taxonomy are two significant new ways to construe what happens to people in their careers. Significantly, these two developments cut across theoretical orientations in that they can be applied to individuals from a variety of theoretical reference points.

Identifying Occupational Stress

An example of one of the major occupational problems of adults that has attracted the attention and interest of investigators in recent years is occupational stress and identifying ways to cope with it. A number of models have been proposed to study occupational stress. Some focus on assessing objective events in the work environment; others take a subjective, perceptual approach to understanding work stress (see Lazarus, DeLongis, Folkman, & Gruen, 1985).

My view is that the subjective, perceptual approach is the more useful, because a given objective environmental event may not have the same impact on different people. For example, one worker may find constant deadlines oppressive and stressful, whereas a colleague in the same environment with the same deadlines may thrive on the situation. Thus, Spokane and I (Osipow & Spokane, 1983) have taken the approach that occupational stress is affected by the perceptions individuals have of their work environment and is buffered by individual coping resources. Thus, the degree to which people experience strain or disruption is a function of the occupational stress that they perceive.

Thus, Figure 1, which shows a model of occupational stress and strain, indicates in a schematic fashion the relationship of a variety of events to occupational stress. The key elements are job demands (shown on the left), which may be measured in a variety of ways: (a) by direct observation such as job analysis, (b) by self-reported activities, (c) by self-reported perceptions of work roles, and (d) by ergonomics. These job demands influence and are influenced by family demands; in addition, they are moderated by a variety of personal attributes. In particular, the job demands are ameliorated or exacerbated by the degree to which individuals possess personal, environmental, family, and social resources. These resources serve as buffers (shown by the arrows with dotted lines interposed between job demands and outcomes) that moderate the kinds of outcomes of particular relevance to the understanding of work stress: productivity, satisfaction, and personal well-being, both mental and physical.

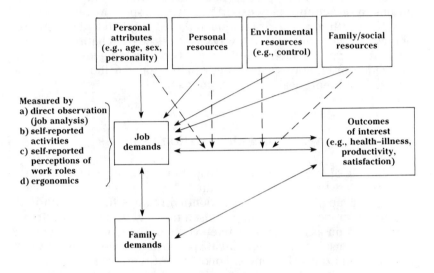

Figure 1. Some factors influencing occupational stress and strain. Hyphenated lines indicate buffering effects.

How People Make Career Choices

Career-development theorists often assume that it is possible to propose a clear understanding of careers and how they develop. Most of the theories, however, are written from an ideal perspective. They describe events as the theorists think they should have been or should be, and sometimes that "should" is misinterpreted to be "what was" or "what is." Further complicating the issue is that theorists also want to predict what will be. Because events—past, present, and future—are so similar to each other, theorists and readers alike fail to differentiate among them appropriately.

Let me try to simplify that idea. Critical examination of many of the career development theories suggests that the theorists truly believe that an orderly approach to career choice is not only possible but actually exists. Ideally, such an orderly process is possible. However, evidence based on years of research by hundreds of investigators convinces me that most individuals do not take a consistently rational, systematic approach to career decision making. Most individuals behave as if each decision is loosely connected to each previous decision, and although they hope that there is some order and plan in their lives, they do not behave as if they believe that is so. The theories describe how it should be done, but not how it is done. Krumboltz (1981) has begun to formulate an approach designed to include the irrational aspects of career decision making.

What advice, then, can be given to aspiring deciders, career counselors, and investigators? What has happened with respect to the assumptions that I reviewed at the beginning of this chapter? Very little in those original assumptions has changed. There is nothing that I said in 1969 about career development that I would not say now. Career development still seems essentially socially bound. Careers are still subject to considerable change over the life span. Career choice and implementation, as well as adjustment, expose individuals to a great many stresses. Abilities still significantly affect how people's careers unfold and their levels of attainment, and the environment appears to provide an important context in which career development takes place.

Subjectively, however, much has changed for the better. What has changed since I wrote my 1969 paper is that researchers can speak to these issues with a considerably higher degree of confidence than previously and can also add a few new ideas that seem to be supported by data.

First, I reiterate the notion of "least resistance" that I proposed some years ago (Osipow, 1969). The least resistance approach holds that given an array of options, people are inclined to pursue those most accessible to them. In the same way that water tends to run downhill, although not always in a straight line, people's careers generally unfold in the most convenient direction. Although there are exceptions, the principle seems to make sense. Although a few individuals work against all odds to achieve unusual and difficult career goals, most people follow the lines open to them by virtue of their unique combination of personality, skills, experience, social background, opportunity, and access.

The analysis in terms of risk factors proposed by Gottfredson is consistent with this view. People are placed at risk as a function of their personal attributes and social class membership. These risk factors make certain options more accessible to them than others. People tend to pursue accessible options rather than remote ones. One of the objectives of career psychologists is to try to help people examine a variety of options and occasionally follow the line of most resistance when a more rigorous course would yield higher benefits. Certainly, there are many routes to the same vocational outcomes. There are multiple career paths people can follow and multiple access routes to the same work settings. At the same time, the same initial occupational commitment can lead to many different outcomes, depending on the choice points encountered along the way and the manner in which the individual chooses to deal with them.

A second idea that can be stated with some assurance is that career decision making is a function of the range of choice in terms particularly of economics, personal resources, and technology. To the degree that any of those three circumstances restrict the number and range of career options people have, there will be less room for decisions by the individual. Those options can shrink to the point where no decisions are possible, as in a *Brave New World* kind of approach where people are bred to assume particular occupational roles; or the options can be so broad and inviting as to create an almost bewildering array of possible decisions. When options are numerous, expectancies regarding satisfaction, implementation of interests, high income, and personal fulfillment are emphasized. When options are few, skills and the implementation of skills are emphasized in career decisions. In times of limited work, people search for ways to use their most highly prized attributes instead of searching for options they themselves will prize. We are at a time in history when options are perceived to be limited (I am not sure if that is a reality), and young deciders are looking more toward emphasizing skills and implementing them in their career decisions than were young people a generation ago, when options appeared to be abundant and people were seeking to implement their interests and find happiness and satisfaction in the intrinsic aspects of their work (Osipow, 1983).

Another principle that seems reasonable is that the amount of *choice activity* varies as a function of the time since the last overt career choice was made. A high school student who is committed to a post-high-school plan will settle down and not appear to be actively pursuing alternatives for a time until that new plan has been started and implemented and begins to decay. Similarly, a person active in the job search market will appear to be inactive for a time, once a job has been found. As the fit of the new job begins to slip, the individual will increase the level of decision activity. With this principle, it is possible to predict cycles of greater and lesser vocational search activity for individuals. One corollary to this, however, is that the amplitude of the activity probably diminishes with age; the amount of activity is likely to be larger at young ages than at older ages (Osipow, 1983).

A reciprocal factor that is involved in the degree of choice activity is *decisional demand,* which seems to be a function of the institution or organization in which the individual is involved, of the individual's age, and of the time since the last decision was made (Osipow, 1983). Thus, certain institutions require many specific decisions frequently, whereas others allow individuals more leisure in reaching closure. Some institutions and organizations require people to commit early;

others permit later decision making and frequent correction of earlier decisions.

Career Counseling

Efforts to understand and predict career behavior are aimed at aiding people to obtain greater satisfaction and effectiveness in career activity. A variety of interventions have been devised to help people choose and implement careers. These interventions are sometimes individual in nature, sometimes programmatic, and sometimes involve assessment and information dispensation. The larger enterprise is called career counseling.

The effectiveness of career counseling, as with psychotherapy, is difficult to document. Several researchers have discussed problems and potential solutions involved in documenting the impact of career counseling efforts. Oliver (1979) indicated that one of the problems is the failure of researchers to specify suitable outcome criteria for career counseling. She suggested some solutions, including the use of multiple criteria; the use of specific as well as global outcome measures; an emphasis on short-term measures; better definitions of the constructs used; the use of instruments with known reliability and validity; an emphasis on nonreactive measures; and better experimental methods, such as the random assignment of subjects to treatments, the use of control groups, and the use of appropriately sized samples.

Fretz (1981) suggested that treatment parameters and client attributes be better described, that treatment costs be reported so that economy of effort can be considered, that two or more treatments be randomly applied to subjects to permit comparison, and that intercorrelations among variables be reported by investigators. Holland, Magoon, and Spokane (1981) identified four common treatment factors used in career interventions. These included occupational information, cognitive rehearsal of vocational aspirations, the acquisition of a cognitive structure for organizing information about the self and occupations, and social support and reinforcement from counselors and others.

Despite its many limitations, career counseling appears to be a potent procedure. Spokane and Oliver (1983) applied meta-analysis to studies published between 1950 and 1980 and involving vocational interventions or using vocational outcome measures. They calculated effect sizes to study the degree to which changes in the desired direction occurred. Their first conclusion was that the average client receiving any type of vocational intervention had an outcome that was better than that of 80 percent of untreated control groups in the 52 studies they analyzed. Second, the outcome status of the average client receiving some kind of group vocational intervention exceeded that of 87 percent of the untreated control subjects. One reason the effect size for group interventions was higher than for individual interventions is that group interventions often employ more extensive treatments, that is, more hours or more sessions.

Their third conclusion was that the outcome status of the average client receiving individual vocational interventions exceeded that of 81 percent of untreated control subjects. Despite the many methodological shortcomings in the career counseling research studied, and with the understanding that published studies tend to be those that have found significant differences, these are still impressive findings, which indicate that career counseling and various vocational interventions have positive effects on clients.

The criteria that are used, however, for defining objectives for career counseling still need sharpening. Career counseling needs to address questions broader than merely identifying career alternatives. Outcomes of a more immediate nature as well as a long-term nature can be addressed. I have listed some of these outcomes (1982), which include improved self-awareness, growth in vocational maturity, the development of a list of practical vocational alternatives, skill development in implementing alternatives, improvement in decision-making skills, improvement in information-seeking skills, and the widening of the individual's career options. Clearly an agenda for research exists for the career psychologist to study ways to improve vocational counseling practice.

Issues for Research

A Master Lecture should outline directions in which a field is headed. There are several issues that should influence the life span practice and research agenda for the near and middle-range future. Issues such as unemployment, underemployment, serial careers, the problems of part-time and temporary workers, disability and compensation, rehabilitation, labor force shifts, and working conditions have rarely been studied from a life span perspective. Other topics have been studied in the life span context and will continue to be important. First, there is the study of career stress and adjustment. I think the focus will be on improved measurement of stress and its outcomes, better interventions to reduce work stress, improved conceptions about work stress in the context of total life stress, and work redesign.

Second, whereas the impact of financial rewards on occupational behaviors has been ignored in the past, there now appears to be increasing interest in studying the effects of money and job security on career choices, adjustment, implemention, stress, and decision making.

Third, sexism and racism continue to be issues of importance. They will be redefined largely in terms of increased attention to assessment issues, questions of equal worth of occupational activities, and discrimination and its effects in the work place (Fitzgerald & Betz, 1983).

A fourth area that has already been studied extensively and that I think will continue to be the focus of considerable attention is mid-career change and multiple careers. This phenomenon will be of increasing interest to researchers and practitioners, because with an increased life span and an inflationary economy, people are working to older ages. In addition, changes in social policy such as in social security will probably cause some people to retire at older ages than they might have otherwise and to continue working after retirement (Olson, 1985). This increase in work life means that many people will be making changes in their career lives over a longer period of time than was the case formerly. Therefore, it will be necessary to know more about the factors that predict career changes in adults and the factors that make career changes easier to accomplish.

A fifth area of investigation that I think will be of increasing importance is the impact of the family context on career decision making and adjustment. It has long been realized that family factors have a significant influence on women's careers. What has not been thought about very much is how these same factors affect men's careers. The concept of being at risk in terms of economic providing suggested by Gottfredson (in press) is one influence of the family context. Another aspect is reflected by the increasing number of studies and books on dual-career families. In *Men in Dual-Career Families* (1985), Gilbert has analyzed the problems that dual-career couples face and the adequacy with which they deal with them. Her study, however, does not reveal an entirely rosy picture.

The last area that appears to be high on the research and practice agenda is leisure and retirement. Again, because of the expanding life span and greater financial resources of many elderly people, preretirement vocational factors that might predict adjustment and satisfaction in retirement are beginning to be examined. Preretirement issues promise to generate a research agenda that will stretch well into the next century. It should be emphasized, however, that retirement programs are not the be-all and end-all. Olson (1981) has noted that although retirement planning programs have seldom been evaluated, they are increasingly being offered by corporations. In addition, however, Olson (1985) found that older adults need career assistance in realms beyond retirement planning. Many older people are actively seeking employment and need help in their search.

Much of this anticipated research agenda is stimulated by the aging population. The baby boom has been a prime factor in determining the research agenda on career development since the 1950s. When the "boomers" were young, education and career entry were studied; as they have aged, a variety of other services have been emphasized. The professional and research agenda will continue to be defined by this population bulge as it goes through the life span.

References

Astin, H. S. (1984). The meaning of work in women's lives: A sociopsy-chological model of career choice and work behavior. *The Counseling Psychologist, 12* (4), 117–126.

Betz, N. E., & Hackett, G. (1981). The relationship of career-related self-efficacy expectations to perceived career options in college women and men. *Journal of Counseling Psychology, 28,* 399–410.

Bijou, S. W. (1976). *Child development: The basic stage of early childhood.* Englewood Cliffs, NJ: Prentice-Hall.

Bordin, E. S., Nachmann, B., & Segal, S. J. (1963). An articulated framework for vocational development. *Journal of Counseling Psychology, 10,* 107–116.

Campbell, R. E., Cellini, J. V., , Shaltry, P. E., Long, A. E., & Pinkos, D. (1979). *A diagnostic taxonomy of adult career problems.* (NIE Project No. G-78-0211). Columbus, OH: National Center for Research in Vocational Education.

Crites, J. O. (1978). Theory and research handbook for the Career Maturity Inventory. Monterey, CA: CTB, McGraw-Hill.

Crites, J. O. (1979). *Career adjustment and development inventory.* College Park, MD: Gumpert.

Crites, J. O. (1982). *Research on the Career Adjustment and Development Inventory.* Paper presented at a colloquium at Ohio State University, Columbus, OH.

Dawis, R., & Lofquist, L. (1984). *A psychological theory of work adjustment.* Minneapolis: University of Minnesota.

Erikson, E. H. (1959). Identity and the life cycle. *Psychological Issues, 1,* 18–64.

Farmer, H. S. (1985). Model of career and achievement motivation for women and men. *Journal of Counseling Psychology, 32,* 363–390.

Fassinger, R. E. (1985). A causal model of college women's career choice. *Journal of Vocational Behavior, 27,* 123–153.

Fitzgerald, L. F. (1980). Nontraditional occupations: Not for women only. *Journal of Counseling Psychology, 27,* 252–259.

Fitzgerald, L. F., & Betz ,N. E. (1983). Issues in the vocational psychology of women. In W. B. Walsh & S. H. Osipow (Eds.), *Handbook of vocational psychology: Vol. 2. Foundations.* Hillsdale, NJ: Erlbaum.

Fitzgerald, L. F., & Cherpas, C. C. (1985). On the reciprocal relationship between gender and occupation: Rethinking the assumptions concerning masculine career development. *Journal of Vocational Behavior, 27,* 109–122.

Fitzgerald, L. F., & Crites, J. O. (1980). Toward a career psychology of women: What do we know? What do we need to know? *Journal of Counseling Psychology, 27,* 44–62.

Fretz, B. (1981). Evaluating the effectiveness of career interventions. *Journal of Counseling Psychology, 28,* 77–90.

Gilbert, L. A. (1985). *Men in dual-career families.* Hillsdale, NJ: Erlbaum.

Gottfredson, L. S. (1981). Circumscription and compromise: A developmental theory of occupational aspirations. *Journal of Counseling Psychology, 28,* 545–579.

Gottfredson, L. S. (1983). Creating and criticizing theory. *Journal of Vocational Behavior, 23,* 203–212.

Gottfredson, L. S. (in press). Special groups and the beneficial use of vocational interest inventories. In W. B. Walsh & S. H. Osipow (Eds.), *Advances in vocational psychology: Vol. 1. Assessment of interests.* Hillsdale, NJ: Erlbaum.

Hackett, G., & Betz, N. E. (1981). A self-efficacy approach to the career development of women. *Journal of Vocational Behavior, 18,* 326–339.

Harren, V. A. (1979). A model of career decision making for college students. *Journal of Vocational Behavior, 14,* 119–133.

Heider, F. (1958). *The psychology of interpersonal relations.* New York: Wiley.

Holland, J. L. (1985). *Making vocational choices* (2nd ed.). Englewood Cliffs, NJ: Prentice-Hall.

Holland, J. L., Daiger, D. C., & Power, P. G. (1980). *Manual for my vocational situation.* Palo Alto, CA: Consulting Psychologists Press.

Holland, J. L., Magoon, T., & Spokane, A. R. (1981). Counseling psychology: Career intervention and related research and theory. *Annual Review of Psychology, 32,* 279–305.

Johnson, R. H. (1978). Individual styles of decision-making: A theoretical model for counseling. *Personnel and Guidance Journal, 30,* 530–536.

Krumboltz, J. D. (1981). Rational career decision making. Colloquium presented at Ohio State University, Columbus, OH.

Lazarus, R. S., DeLongis, A., Folkman, S., & Gruen, R. (1985). Stress and adaptational outcomes: The problem of confounded measures. *American Psychologist, 40,* 770–779.

Lofquist, L. H., & Dawis, R. V. (1969). *Adjustment to work.* Englewood Cliffs, NJ: Prentice-Hall.

Markham, S. (1983). I can be a bum: Knowledge about abilities and life style in behavior. *Journal of Vocational Behavior, 23,* 72–86.

Mitchell, A. M., Krumboltz, J. D., & Jones, G. B. (Eds.) (1979). *Social learning theory of career decision making.* Cranston, RI: Carroll Press.

Oliver, L. W. (1979). Outcome measures in career counseling research. *Journal of Counseling Psychology, 25,* 217–226.

Olson, S. K. (1981). Current status of corporate retirement preparation programs. *Aging and Work, 4,* 175–187.

Olson, S. K. (1985). *In search of innovative life/career planning programs for older adults.* Paper presented at the meeting of the National Council on the Aging, Inc., San Francisco, CA.

Osipow, S. H. (1969). What do we really know about career development? *Proceedings of the National Conference on Guidance Counseling and Placement in Career Development and Education Occupational Decision-Making.* Columbia, MO.

Osipow, S. H. (1982). Research in career counseling: An analysis of issues and problems. *Counseling Psychologist, 10* (4), 27–34.

Osipow, S. H. (1983). *Theories of career development* (3rd ed.). Englewood Cliffs, NJ: Prentice-Hall.

Osipow, S. H., Carney, C. G., Winer, J. L., Yanico, B., & Koschier, M. (1976). *The career decision scale.* Columbus, OH: Marathon Consulting and Press.

Osipow, S. H., Doty, R., & Spokane, A. R. (1985). Occupational stress, strain, and coping across the lifespan. *Journal of Vocational Behavior, 27,* 98–108.

Osipow, S. H., & Spokane, A. R. (1983). *Manual for the occupational environment scales, personal strain questionnaire, and personal resources questionnaire.* Columbus, OH: Marathon Consulting and Press.

Roe, A. (1957). Early determinants of vocational choice. *Journal of Counseling Psychology, 4,* 212–217.

Spokane, A. R. (1985). A review of research on person–environment congruence in Holland's theory of careers. *Journal of Vocational Behavior, 26,* 306–343.

Spokane, A. R., & Oliver, L. W. (1983). In Walsh, W. B., & Osipow, S. H. (Eds.) *Handbook of vocational psychology: Vol. 2. Applications.* Hillsdale, NJ: Erlbaum.

Strong, E. K., Hansen, J. I., & Campbell, D. P. (1985). *Strong vocational interest inventory.* (1985 Revision of the Strong-Campbell Interest Inventory.) Palo Alto, CA: Consulting Psychologists Press.

Super, D. E. (1963). Self-concepts in vocational development. In Super, D. E., Starishevsky, R., Matlin, N., & Jordaan, J. P., *Career development: Self-concept theory* (Research Monograph No. 4). New York: College Entrance Examination Board.

Super, D. E. (1980). A life span, life space approach to career development. *Journal of Vocational Behavior, 16,* 282–298.

Super, D. E., Starishevsky, R., Matlin, N., & Jordaan, J. P. (1963). *Career development: Self-concept theory* (Research Monograph No. 4). New York: CEEB.

Tiedeman, D. V., & O'Hara, R. P. (1963). *Career development and adjustment.* New York: CEEB.

Vondracek, F. W., Lerner, R. M., & Schulenberg, J. E. (1983). The concept of career development in vocational theory and intervention. *Journal of Vocational Behavior, 23,* 179–202.

Vondracek, F. W., Lerner, R. M., Schulenberg, J. E. (in press). *Career development: A life span developmental approach.* Hillsdale, NJ: Erlbaum.

LOIS WLADIS HOFFMAN

WORK, FAMILY, AND THE CHILD

LOIS WLADIS HOFFMAN

Lois Wladis Hoffman obtained her Bachelor's degree from the State University of New York at Buffalo, a Master of Science from Purdue, and a PhD from the University of Michigan in 1958. Her doctoral research was a pioneering investigation of the effects of the employment of mothers on the family. She has maintained an interest in this area over the years and has published two books on the topic, both with Ivan Nye, *The Employed Mother in America* in 1963 and *Working Mothers* in 1974. She has also written several reviews over the years on the effects of maternal employment on the child, lectured on the topic throughout the United States, in Europe and in Asia, and is currently involved in research on the timing of the mother's return to work and mother–infant attachment.

In 1964, she launched the highly regarded series, the *Review of Child Development Research,* Volume 1 coming out in 1964, Volume 2 in 1966. Hoffman was also a pioneer in studying the effects of the father's role on the family and on the child's development. Her first research on this topic was published in 1961. She has subsequently conducted research and written research reviews on the effects of work and parent roles on the family and the child's socialization. Her most recent published work on this topic is a review, "Work, Family and the Socialization of the Child," in Volume 7 of the *Review of Child Development Research.* As part of this same general interest, Hoffman has also studied achievement patterns among women and motivations for parenthood, both with an orientation toward the family structure and the socialization of the child.

Hoffman has been employed at the University of Michigan almost continuously since 1954. Between 1954 and 1960, she was at the Institute for Social Research there, first at the Survey Research Center and later at the Research Center for Group Dynamics. In 1967, she joined the Psychology Department, where she is now Professor of Psychology, in the developmental area. She has received a number of awards and honors, served on the editorial boards of various journals and on government panels, and recently completed a term as President of Division 9 of the APA.

LOIS WLADIS HOFFMAN

WORK, FAMILY, AND THE CHILD

This chapter will deal with the influence of paid work on the family—focusing particularly on the family's child-rearing function. The question that will be addressed is: How does parental employment affect the family in its socialization of the child?

There has been a recent burgeoning of interest in the interface between work and the family, particularly in the impact of the parents' work on their family roles. Increased attention to this topic reflects changes both in the society and in the field of psychology. First, of course, the increased employment of mothers in the United States is one of the most impressive and easily documented of all social changes. Understanding the effects of this on family life and on the child's socialization has become a major concern of the public as well as of the social scientist. Second, there has been an increased interest in the role of fathers. This concern probably reflects the fact that this role, too, may be changing. Although the pace of the change is slower, and the empirical documentation is less clear, it seems that fathers are becoming more involved in child-rearing as a counterpart to the increased involvement of mothers in the labor force. The convergence of roles between the parents—each moving more actively into what was previously the other's sphere—has stimulated interest in what it means for both mothers and fathers to move back and forth between these two major social institutions.

In addition, psychologists seem to have become more involved in studying family dynamics generally. Certainly in clinical psychology, there has been a movement from dealing only with the patient and his or her perceptions to doing therapy with the whole family, considering its ongoing interactions and not only its historical input. And, finally, just as psychology has become more aware that understanding the individual requires analysis of his or her social setting, and particularly the family, so has there also been increasing awareness that to understand the family, one has to understand its position in the larger social setting and its relationship to other social institutions. Perhaps the two major institutions in society are work and the family. Interest in the dynamics between them is a natural outgrowth of this new maturity of social science, as well as a response to the changing roles of men and women.

In this review, only one piece of this will be discussed—the effects of parental employment on the family and the child, though it has been clearly demonstrated that effects occur also in the other direction—the family also affects the job (Crouter, 1984b; Kanter, 1977). Furthermore, the macrotheories proposed by sociologists and economists that deal with this relationship will not be discussed, though the occupational structure of society, the degree of industrialization, and the prevailing economic activities have long been seen by them as the major explanation for the particular prevailing family form and child-rearing patterns (Ogburn & Nimkoff, 1955; Parsons, 1955; Schneider, 1957). Instead, the focus will be on the attempt by psychologists to study the process by which an individual's work affects his or her family relationships.

Most of this research has concentrated on either the mother or the father, not both. Furthermore, the aspect of work considered for each parent has been different: Research on mothers, until recently, looked only at whether a mother was employed; research on fathers either looked at the kind of job held or examined the effects of involuntary unemployment. In fact, however, most of the theories and conceptualizations used in the research on fathers' work can be applied to mothers also, and, with the increased supply of employed mothers for study, several recent investigations have done just that (Crouter, Huston, & Robins, 1983; Miller, Schooler, Kohn, & Miller, 1979; Piotrkowski & Crits-Christoph, 1981; Piotrkowski & Katz, 1982). However, most of the research on mothers has focused on the effects of employment when the worker also has the primary responsibility for child care. Because this pattern still prevails for women but not for men, the bulk of the maternal employment literature is still mother-specific.

For that reason, this presentation will be divided into two parts. In the first part, the discussion will deal with the effects of the parents' work on the family and on the child's socialization more generally. Although most of this research has been conducted with men, the concepts and processes described can apply to both parents. In the second part, specific attention will be given to the effects of the mother's employment.

Part 1: The Concepts and Processes Used in Studying the Effects of Work on the Family and the Child

The Variables Studied

The variables that have been used in studying the effects of work on families and children are listed in Table 1. The first column lists the different ways that work has been conceptualized. The first entry, for example, simply refers to the fact that some researchers have investigated the effects of employment status per se. In the studies of men, the contrast has been between men who are employed and those who have been involuntarily unemployed. Much of this research was carried out during the Depression of the 1930s. During that time there were several classic studies, such as the work of Angell (1936) and Komorovsky (1940), investigating the impact of unemployment on the structure and functioning of the family. These studies documented negative effects in terms of the father's loss of status in the family, the decline of self-esteem, and the family disorganization that resulted from the loss of its traditional pattern of the man as breadwinner outside the home. These researchers also identified variables that enabled some families to maintain their integration in the face of such change. The pre-unemployment state of cohesion in the family was found to be an important supportive force.

A particularly valuable analysis of data originally collected during this era has been carried out by Elder (1974, 1978). Elder used longitudinal data from the Berkeley and Oakland Growth Studies to analyze the impact of the Depression on families and on children's development. The effects on children as observed over the years varied depending on the age of the child at the time of financial loss, the sex of the child, the general economic level of the family as well as the degree of financial loss, and various aspects of the family dynamics. Although Elder's work verified the potential deleterious effects of unemployment, it also revealed possible positive outcomes. For example, the children in the financially affected families who were in early adolescence during the Depression, particularly those who had been middle class before the Depression, showed positive effects from this stress. Compared to youths in the families that were not affected, their subsequent development showed better success educationally, maritally, and in terms of personal satisfaction. The positive effect seemed to be the result of greater responsibility and family cooperation that was imposed upon them as the family coped with the financial loss.

Table 1
Variables Used in Studies of Work, Family, and the Child

Conceptualization of Work	Effects on Family	Child Outcomes
Employed, unemployed, nonemployed	Resources	Social-personal adjustment
Resources provided	Status	Cognitive level
Status of the work	Values and attitudes	Attitudes and values
Behaviors on the job	Division of labor	Coping styles
Values and attitudes engendered	Power relations	Vocational choice
Authority relations	Marital relationship	Preferred marriage patterns
Emotional state engendered	Child-rearing patterns	
a. morale	Parent as model	
b. need satisfaction or arousal	Social activities	
Time and energy involved	Degree of involvement of parent in the family	
Intrinsic stress	Degree of family involvement in the work	
Intrusiveness	Stress	

More recent studies of unemployment have also been conducted. Although most of these have not focused on the family dynamics as intensively as the earlier studies did, they have documented adverse effects on the unemployed worker in ways that clearly have implications for their family dynamics, effects such as depression, hostility, alcoholism, somatic complaints, and loss of self-esteem (Cobb & Kasl, 1977; Kasl & Cobb, 1979; Margolis, 1982; Scholzman & Verba, 1978). Studies have also indicated negative effects on the marriage (Marsden, 1975); less positive attitudes toward children (Sheldon & Fox, 1983); and adverse child outcomes in terms of personal adjustment, coping style, and school performance (Buss & Redburn, 1983;

Morris-Vann, 1982; Werner & Smith, 1982). As in the family studies carried out during the Depression of the 1930s, social support both from within the family and from others served to lessen the impact.

A considerable body of research also reveals an association between paternal job loss and intrafamily violence—wife beating and child abuse (Justice & Duncan, 1977; O'Brien, 1971; Parke & Collmer, 1975; Steinmetz & Straus, 1974). Park and Collmer have noted several mechanisms that may bring about family violence resulting from fathers' unemployment: (a) the greater amount of time the father spends at home, which increases the probability of conflict; (b) a possible increase in the father's discipline role; (c) reaffirmation of the father's power in the face of status loss; and (d) tension from the diminished resources and its accompanying strains.

Whereas studies of unemployment have dealt exclusively with men as workers, studies of nonemployment have dealt exclusively with women. Most of the research on the effects of maternal employment have contrasted simply employment and nonemployment—comparing families where the mother is employed to families where she is not and typically excluding women who are temporarily and involuntarily unemployed. And, as Bronfenbrenner and Crouter (1982) have pointed out in a recent review, it is often assumed that trouble in the family and negative effects on children will result from the father's unemployment but from the mother's employment. Although the assumption about fathers is often supported by the data, sometimes it is not, as the research by Elder shows. The assumption about mothers, however, has rarely been supported by the data as will subsequently be discussed.

The other entries will be explained more briefly in Column 1. "Resources provided" refers to the fact that some researchers have conceptualized work in terms of the money it provides. There are studies that have focused on the role of the worker in the family, which is affected by the fact that the worker is the provider of money, and also studies that have focused on the income that is made available to the family—studies that regard the income level as the dynamic force. An example of the former is the research carried out by sociologists Blood and Wolfe (1960) in the 1950s. Their theory, called a "resource exchange" theory, held that power within the family was determined by the relative resources of its members and that one of the primary resources was money. Thus, employment gave the worker an important resource that increased his or her power in the family. Data were presented to support the hypotheses that the more money the male worker made, the greater was his power in the family and also that a wife's employment increased her power because of the monetary resource it provided. Although the data originally presented supported these hypotheses, they have subsequently been criticized and reanalyzed (Bahr, 1974; Quarm, 1977). The reinterpretation of these results is that monetary resources may increase a parent's power over economic decisions but not power in the family generally. The research that focuses simply on the amount of money that is provided for the family by a parent's employment and analyzes how this income level affects the family functioning and interaction will be discussed again later.

"Status of the work" refers to the idea that different kinds of work have different statuses. The status level of the job, or the social class that is often defined and measured by it, has frequently been the aspect of the work that is studied in relation to family life and child development (Hoffman, 1984b).

"Behaviors on the job" refers to the activities that one engages in while at work, such as the complexity of the work; whether it involves physical drudgery, routine and repetitive operations, or mental effort; whether it involves giving nurturance, teaching, listening to complaints, or selling.

Work is also conceptualized as engendering certain attitudes and values. Through one's work, for example, one often forms attitudes about labor and management and the role of unions. Moreover one's attitudes about various groups can be shaped by work experiences. The experience of working with other races, for example, can affect one's attitudes, the direction being determined by the nature of the work relationships (Miller & Brewer, 1985). In addition, one can gain substantive knowledge through work that changes one's views (Crouter, 1984a).

The next entry in the list is "authority relations." Some workers are told what to do on the job without explanations. Others may be given reasons for their required behavior, or they may be granted autonomy in their work, or they may themselves be in charge. These differences in authority relations are seen as important contributors to styles of interaction in the family.

In many studies work is conceptualized in terms of the emotional state it engenders. Some researchers focus on morale generally— whether work is a source of positive or negative feelings. Others focus more on specific needs that may be aroused at work and then expressed in the family. Still others conceptualize work as meeting or failing to meet certain needs that might otherwise be met in the family.

"Time and energy involved," refers to the amount of time spent on the job and in job-related activities, the scheduling of work time, and the amount of energy that is consumed by work. "Intrinsic stress" refers to the fact that because some jobs are dangerous, insecure, or tension laden, they are in themselves a source of stress to the worker. The job of urban police officer is one often conceptualized in this way (Kroes & Hurrell, 1975; Nordlicht, 1979; Symonds, 1970).

The last item in the column, "intrusiveness," refers to the fact that some jobs intrude into the workers' lives more than others. For example, in a study of coal miners in Australia, Williams (1981) has described the work as intruding on the total structure of the community; as shaping leisure pursuits, friendship patterns, and marital relations; and, by its nature, as drawing men into male cliques and away from their families. Whyte (1956) has described the work of corporate executives as one that shapes the social life of the family and may require a major commitment by the wife to fulfill certain social obligations.

All of the conceptualizations of work listed in the first column have been used in research, some singly, and some in combination. In the second column, the various ways in which the family has been conceptualized are listed, and in the third, the aspects of the child's development that have been considered. For example, a researcher might classify certain jobs in terms of the different behavior patterns required, examine how this affected child-rearing patterns, and then investigate how the affected child-rearing patterns influenced the child's cognitive development. Another researcher might classify work on the basis of the time and energy demanded, see how this affects the degree of the worker's involvement in the family, and examine the impact of this involvement on the child's personal adjustment.

In some cases the variables in the second column are only inferred. In a study of lower-class employed mothers, for example, Piotrkowski and Katz (1982) empirically linked characteristics of the mother's job, namely the opportunity for autonomy and the degree of skill utilized, with certain child behaviors. Higher skill was associated with higher academic performance, whereas higher autonomy was associated with skipping classes. The researchers did not actually obtain measures of the intervening variables, the family patterns that mediated this process, but they inferred that there was a communication in the family that skill was important or that autonomy was to be respected. More often, the variables in the last column are omitted, as, for example, in the studies of unemployment and child abuse, and in several studies that link behaviors on the job or authority relations to child-rearing patterns. The connection between child-rearing patterns and child outcomes that are omitted in these studies may be established by other research in the child development area.

The Processes by Which Work Affects the Family

So far, it is mainly the various ways in which work has been conceptualized in the research that has been described. How work affects the family has been brought in only occasionally to help explicate a particular concept. The question for special consideration now is: What are the processes that link the work variables to the family variables and to the child outcomes? The list that follows includes some of the processes that have been suggested and researched.

1. Work provides material resources that affect the family's economic well-being.

2. Being employed or not employed and the particular occupation confer status that affects the family's status in the community, the worker's status in the family, and the worker's self-concept.

3. Behaviors at work are repeated in the home.

4. Work experiences affect ideas about what qualities are important in adulthood and thus influence child-rearing patterns.

5. Work affects the worker's personality and intellectual functioning and thus influences his or her behavior in the family. The child is affected through parental child-rearing practices and identification with the parent.

6. Authority structures at work are repeated in the family and are reflected in child-rearing patterns.

7. Moods generated at work are carried over to the family.

8. The family may be used as a complementary source of need satisfaction: The worker may seek to satisfy in the family needs unsatisfied or engendered at work.

9. Work takes time, energy, and involvement from the family. In addition to the loss itself, this can lead to stress from overload or guilt.

10. Work can be a source of stress either because of the above processes or because it is intrinsically dangerous or insecure.

Material resources and family well-being. A few of these processes are so obvious that they hardly seem worth noting. For example, work means money, and the fact that a parent is employed, along with the income level of the job, has a direct bearing on the family; it affects the material quality of their lives, their nutrition, the resources available for handling stress, opportunities for education, and economic security. Although this seems self-evident, it is actually an aspect of a parent's employment that is often overlooked, particularly in studies of maternal employment. For example, some of the positive effects of maternal employment, such as the higher cognitive performance scores so often observed among the children of employed mothers in economically disadvantaged populations, may result from the monetary advantage itself. In conditions of poverty, the mother's employment can often make a crucial difference (Cherry & Eaton, 1977; U.S. Department of Labor, 1981).

The monetary aspect of the job may also be part of the explanation for the social class differences in family interaction patterns, child-rearing styles, and child outcomes that have so often been demonstrated in the research (Hoffman, 1984b). The most common operational definition of social class is the father's occupation. In most of these studies, the prestige of the occupation, the nature of the behaviors and authority relations on the job, or the general social milieu that occupational categories imply, is seen as the important aspect of social class. However, the income difference itself sometimes might be the differentiating factor. For example, Kohn (1959a) observed in his early work that in families of blue-collar workers, children were punished for breaking things whether or not the act was intentional, whereas middle-class parents punished their children only for intentional breakage. This observation was tied to an elaborate and important theory of how the authority relations on the job affected child-rearing patterns. However, an alternative hypothesis is that when money is scarce, breakage is more upsetting to parents.

Similarly, many studies over the years have shown that lower-class parents use more power-assertive discipline generally and more physical punishment, give fewer explanations, demand more obedience, and spend less time in child-care activities (Hess & Shipman, 1965; Hill & Stafford, 1978; Hoffman, 1984b). In turn, these patterns have been linked to children's cognitive and moral development. Although there are many explanations for these differences in parenting style, as will be seen later, a contributing factor may simply be the income differences. Lower income means less adequate housing, fewer time-saving facilities, and greater vulnerability to stress. Under such conditions, the more time-consuming and patience-demanding child-rearing techniques used by middle-class parents may also be less available. Thus, the first process listed, that the money provided by work affects the material resources of the family, may not be a fancy theory, but it may be an important one. (For a more extensive discussion of the factors mediating the relation between social class and child-rearing patterns, see Hoffman, 1984b).

Status. In addition to the job being conceptualized in terms of its status, the status conferred by the work has been used to link occupation to the family situation. For example, in studies of the effects of men's unemployment, it is often the loss of status that is important in mediating its impact. The adverse consequences are magnified when unemployment leads to a loss of status in the family or in a father's own eyes. This loss of status may be seen as the link to marital difficulties, child abuse, and alcoholism (Justice & Duncan, 1977; Margolis & Farran, in press; Parke & Collmer, 1975). On the other hand, when the loss of status can be averted, the impact of unemployment is less (Angell, 1936).

Among employed men, the father's particular job may also affect his own sense of status and his status in the family, and this has been found to affect family interaction patterns, sex role concepts, and the son's identification (Mortimer, 1974, 1976; Rosenberg, 1979; Sennet & Cobb, 1972). However, status is not necessarily determined by the absolute level of the father's occupational achievement. The status of the father's job is judged against some reference point—the job of his father or other relatives, the other jobs in the community or in the man's social group, the job he held previously, or the individual's and the family's expectations. A steady job may mean higher status in some families than a $50,000 executive position in others.

Work affects not only the individual's status in the family but also the status and prestige of the family in the community. Many social psychologists and sociologists have argued that the social status of the family is determined largely, if not entirely, by the father's occupation (Hoffman, 1984b). This status has an enormous impact on the response of others to the individual family members. Lynd and Lynd (1937) and Hollingshead (1975) have demonstrated the influence of job-related status on children's peer group and school experiences in two small towns. Even though this effect may be particularly apparent in the smaller communities studied, it is not limited to these sites; it operates in urban areas as well, with significance for the family experience as well as for the child's socialization.

Behaviors at work are repeated in the home. Many empirical studies conceptualize work in terms of the behaviors that are entailed. However, the processes by means of which these behaviors affect family life have been seen in different ways. A number of studies support the hypothesis that a worker tends to act at home the way he or she acts at work—that there is a carryover of style (Gerstl, 1961; Rousseau, 1978; Staines & Pagnucco, 1977; Steinmetz, 1974). In these studies a similarity was found between job activities and activities in the home and in leisure pursuits. In fact, however, it is very difficult to know whether these positive correlations reflect carryover of work patterns or occupational choice. For example, it has been shown that workers who have jobs requiring interpersonal interaction also engage in a high level of interpersonal interaction off the job (Bishop & Ikeda, 1970; Meissner, 1971; Staines & Pagnucco, 1977). Although this has been interpreted as job carryover, it seems just as likely that people who enjoy interpersonal interaction seek jobs where this is possible and spend their off-work hours in the same way. Thus, similarity in behavior in the home and the job may reflect the qualities of the person and not the effect of one setting on the other. The image of the minister who preaches to his family, the salesman who "sells" the behaviors he wants his children to engage in, or the professor who answers his children's questions with a lecture is widely held; but even if the image were unequivocally demonstrated empirically, it would be difficult to show that the behavior in the family was a carryover from work rather than a consistency in personality. To show that the behavior was an effect of the work, it would probably be necessary to conduct either a longitudinal study or one that compared the correlations found for different cohorts on the job to see if the correlations were higher for those who had been on the job longer.

Work affects ideas about desired adult qualities and thus shapes child-rearing patterns. The fourth process listed is one that is assumed in several different theories. It refers to the notion that work affects a person's ideas about what personal qualities are important in life, what traits make for a successful adult adjustment. These ideas influence parents' goals for their children and are reflected in their child-rearing patterns.

The basic assumption involved probably comes originally from anthropology (Barry, Bacon, & Child, 1957). It has been suggested, for example, that in a hunting society, traits that facilitate effective hunting—such as courage, strength, dexterity, and timing—are likely to be encouraged in sons. It is not that parents planfully encourage these traits in order to make their sons good hunters, but rather that in such a society these traits have been associated with the most successful men and have acquired a desirability that seems intrinsic.

This same idea—that occupational roles affect socialization patterns so that children are shaped for similar adult roles—is also invoked in a theory about sex-differentiated child-rearing patterns. Hoffman (1977a) has suggested that sex differences in socialization patterns reflect the traditional expectation that girls will grow up to be mothers and boys will grow up to be breadwinners. Accordingly, girls have been encouraged to develop traits that are consistent with mothering, and their toys and games are miniature versions of the mother role. Boys, by contrast, have been encouraged to develop traits consistent with the occupational roles of society, and their toys and games are miniature versions of occupational roles. With increased employment of women across the life span, however, and with the decrease in family size and in the percentage of the adult years devoted to active mothering, corresponding changes in socialization practices are occurring. As the occupational roles of men and women converge, a corresponding decrease in sex-differentiated child-rearing patterns is predicted.

There are several empirical studies in the work–family area that have implicitly or explicitly assumed this process—that work roles influence the parents' ideas of what qualities are desirable in adults, and their child-rearing patterns reflect these values. However, there are two classic studies in this group, both of which were originally undertaken in the 1950s.

One study was the research of Miller and Swanson (1958). These investigators hypothesized that the child-rearing patterns of parents would reflect values and goals that were consistent with the traits that a man experienced as being valuable in his work. They contrasted two different styles of occupational organization—entrepreneurial and bureaucratic. The entrepreneurial pattern—characterized by smaller business organizations, simple division of labor, and mobility through competition and risk taking—was hypothesized as being consistent with child-rearing patterns that encouraged independent achievement, individual responsibility, and self-control. In contrast, bureaucratic occupational structure—characterized by large organizations, with several levels of authority, greater job security through seniority, and mobility through interpersonal skills and smooth relations within the organization—was hypothesized as being consistent with child-rearing patterns that encouraged accommodation more than self-control, and interpersonal interaction rather than independence. On the whole, the findings supported these hypotheses. When a father was employed in an entrepreneurial setting, the child-rearing patterns in the family were more consistent with the goals of independence, responsibility, and self-control, whereas when the father's occupation was of the bureaucratic type, child-rearing patterns were more permissive and consistent with the goal of developing interpersonal skills, with getting along with others.

This was an important theory. Although the research was less than perfect (the operational definitions of the work settings were too diffuse and included nonwork variables), and subsequent efforts at replication have yielded mixed results (Caudill & Weinstein, 1969; Gold & Slater, 1958), this was one of the first theories that suggested a process to connect the characteristics of a parent's job to child-rearing practices. Furthermore, this theory, like Hoffman's, was tied to the idea of social change. Miller and Swanson (1958) argued that as the American society moved from a predominantly entrepreneurial occupational structure to a predominantly bureaucratic one, the prevailing child-rearing practices would also change in response to the new kinds of personal qualities being demanded for job success.

The other major research, also undertaken originally in the 1950s, was the work of Kohn and his colleagues (Kohn, 1959a, 1959b, 1969; Kohn & Schooler, 1982). Their work has continued up to the present. Their theoretical framework is similar to that of Miller and Swanson in that they assume that through one's job one develops notions of what qualities and values are important for success, and these ideas are embodied in child-rearing patterns. Kohn has concentrated not on the work setting, as Miller and Swanson did, but on the content of the work activities. He has been particularly interested in explicating the observation that there are social class differences in child-rearing styles, and he has sought the explanation in the nature of the work performed by each class. According to Kohn, middle-class or white-collar occupations involve manipulating ideas, symbols, and interpersonal relations and require flexibility, thought, and judgment. Lower-class or blue-collar occupations require manipulating physical objects and are more standardized, less complex, and more supervised. Because of these differences, middle-class fathers would be expected to value self-direction and independence in their children—qualities demanded by their own occupations—whereas lower-class fathers would value obedience and conformity. Kohn's data have supported this prediction, and he has found corresponding differences in reported child-rearing practices: Lower-class parents used more physical punishment and judged their children's misbehavior in terms of the consequences, whereas middle-class parents used more psychological discipline, such as love withdrawal, and judged misbehavior in terms of their children's intent. Kohn and his colleagues also found that when the fathers' jobs involved autonomy and working with people, the parents were more likely to stress achievement, independence, and self-reliance to their children (Pearlin & Kohn, 1966). Kohn's work in this area has continued over a 30-year span and has stimulated investigations by other researchers. In the course of this work, other processes have been suggested for linking work to family patterns and child development. One of these is the fifth process in the list.

Work affects the worker's personality and intellectual functioning and thus influences family behavior, child-rearing, and the child's identification. In some of Kohn's later research, he examined the interplay between work and the adult's personality and intellectual functioning. In a longitudinal design, he tried to disentangle the various relationships between characteristics of the work and personality functioning. This analysis suggested that when work involves substantive complexity, the worker's intellectual flexibility increases over the years. (Kohn & Schooler, 1978). This research differs from Kohn's previously discussed work in that it suggests that the work experience influences not only child-rearing values and practices but also the worker's personality and cognitive functioning (Elder, 1984). The process involved here also differs from the third process listed because it is not simply a repetition of the work behavior in the home but an effect on the worker's personality.

Other research also documents the effects of work on personal functioning. For example, Crouter (1984a) studied workers in a manufacturing plant that involved worker participation in decision making and problem solving, to see how their work experience affected their lives. Among the changes reported were an increase in interpersonal skills, communication skills, and listening ability. In addition, several studies support the hypothesis that paid employment increases a mother's self-confidence (Birnbaum, 1975; Feld, 1963; Feree, 1976).

Neither Kohn, in this later work, nor the other researchers traced the changes in the workers through to their family interactions, but the studies clearly imply such effects. Furthermore, it seems likely that their children's development would be affected, because the changes identified in the workers might be expected to influence both their child-rearing behavior and the model that they present to the child. Nevertheless, the links connecting the effects of work on the parent's personality to family interaction and to the socialization process have not been adequately empirically examined.

Authority structures at work are repeated in the family and reflected in child-rearing patterns. The hypothesis that authority relations on the job are replicated by the worker in the home comes mainly from the literature that focuses on social-class differences in child-rearing patterns. A repeated finding over the years is that lower-class parents rely on ascribed power to influence their children more than do middle- or upper-class parents. Thus, they are more likely to say "Do it," "Because I say so," or "That's the rule." They are more likely to use what M. L. Hoffman (1960) has called "power assertive techniques." They are less likely, on the other hand, to give reasons for the requirement, try to induce the child to become intrinsically motivated to comply, or attend to extenuating circumstances that the child might bring out, all of which are more characteristic of middle- and upper-class parents (Bernstein, 1961, 1964; Bronfenbrenner, 1958; Cohen & Hodges, 1963; Hess and Shipman, 1965, 1967; M.L. Hoffman, 1960; Kohn, 1959a, 1959b, 1980; Waters & Crandall, 1964).

This style of parent–child interaction has been seen as reflecting the parent's own experience in society generally, and particularly his or her experiences on the job (Hess, 1970; Hoffman, 1984b). The lower-class parent's supervisor on the job is not likely to explain the basis for rules and requirements, and, since the lower-class person is not likely to participate in the setting up of rules or to be involved in the overall operation, it is quite likely that he or she is not familiar with the substantive rationale of the workplace and its functioning. Its rules may thus often seem arbitrary and absolute. Because a lower-class adult is more likely to have authoritarian, rule-governed experiences, his or her views of the social order are affected, and so are his or her asymetric power interactions in the family. In short, the hypothesis is that the lower-class worker expresses in the family the same authority relations he or she experiences on the job, but this time he or she is the authority. This process is not suggesting a frustration–aggression model but rather a cognitive model: That is the way authority is expressed.

The effects of such discipline techniques on the children have been well researched. Discipline based on the assertion of power and rules rather than on explanation, reasoning, and induction have been empirically linked to lower performance on cognitive tasks, reading readiness, and verbal development (Bernstein, 1964; Hess, Shipman, Brophy, & Baer, 1968), and to aggressiveness, externalized rather than internalized morality, and to a less flexible, humanistic moral orientation (M.L. Hoffman, 1960; M.L. Hoffman & Saltzstein, 1967). Among the processes seen as connecting the lower-class style of discipline to these outcomes are that (a) they engender in the child a sense of inefficacy, (b) they fail to communicate rationality in life, and (c) they do not provide verbal enrichment (Hoffman, 1984b).

Although the link between social class and discipline styles has been established empirically, and the link between discipline styles and the child's cognitive and moral development has also, the hypothesis that it is the authority experiences on the job that are important has not. There are many other aspects of lower-class life, including similar authority relations in the society generally, that might also be involved. Kohn (1959a, 1959b, 1963) has tried to show that the power position on the job is the crucial variable, but it is very difficult to disentangle the other interrelated variables such as education, money, and other aspects of lower-class life. It seems likely, however, from this work, that the authority experiences on the job are a contributing factor.

The study by Crouter (1984a), already mentioned, adds further confirmation to the idea that the authority relations on the job affect authority relations in the family. When she asked the workers in a plant that actively engaged workers in management decision making what some of the effects of this experience were, they actually described how their own experiences in democratic decision making had led them to begin using similar procedures with their children. Here are some of the responses:

> I have a 16-year-old son and I use some of the things we do at work with him instead of yelling. We listen better here, we let people tell their side.

> I say things to my [8-year-old] daughter that I know are a result of the way we do things at work. I ask her, "What do you think about that?" or "How would you handle this problem?"

> In terms of dealing with my family, I'm more willing to get their opinions. We hold "team meetings" at home to make decisions. (pp. 81–82)

Moods at work are carried over to the family. If any link between work and the family seems to have been documented, it is the idea that moods generated at work are carried over to the family. So many studies have shown a positive correlation between a worker's mood at work and his or her mood at home that several researchers have concluded that this is the major process by which a parent's work experience affects family functioning (Piotrkowski, 1979; Staines, 1980). The problem with this research, however, is that one cannot infer from the data that the mood engendered at work affects the mood at home. In most cases, the research uses self-report measures. It is quite possible that people who report positive mood states in one setting also report positive states in another. Nor does the problem lie simply in the use of self-report measures. Even if the mood states were tapped more objectively in the two settings, a positive correlation could simply indicate consistency in individuals. It may be that more studies report evidence for mood carryover from work to the home than report the alternative hypothesis—that workers seek compensatory gratification in the two settings—because many of the positive correlations found in these studies are spurious relationships. Because individuals tend to be consistent both in reporting moods and in experiencing them, it is easier to find positive correlations but more difficult to interpret what they mean.

An interesting approach to testing the hypothesis of mood carryover is suggested by the research of Repetti (1985). Although this study had a different focus, the measures employed, and the findings, suggest an alternative way of studying mood carryover. Repetti was interested in seeing how social relations at work affected the worker's psychological well-being. To measure how satisfying the work situation was, she did not simply rely on the subject's report. Instead, she selected workers in comparable jobs but different work settings and had co-workers rate the quality of the social relations. Thus she had two measures of social relations at work: (a) an average of the co-workers' ratings of the social environment and (b) the individual's own rating of the social environment. Both related positively to the individual's self-reported psychological well-being (levels of depression, anxiety, and self-esteem). The fact that the group perception also related to the individual's psychological well-being gives considerable strength to the idea that there was a mood-generating aspect to the employment situation and not just a consistency within the individuals studied. Causality can be more confidently inferred from this design. Adding some measure of the mood-generating potential of the work situation would improve the design of the mood-carryover studies.

The family may be used as a complementary source of need satisfaction. One mechanism postulated as linking the father's occupation with his family role is the frustration–aggression model: The job creates frustrations that the father takes out in the family. A man may be on the bottom of the power hierarchy at work, but he is on the top at home; aggression engendered on the job that cannot be expressed there for fear of negative sanctions is displaced to the safer target, the family. The idea of parental authority over children as a compensation for power frustration at work has come up in the work of Blau and Duncan (1967) and of Hoffman and Manis (1979), and some empirical support has come from research by McKinley (1964). Particularly at the higher socioeconomic levels, McKinley found that fathers low in autonomy in their work were more likely to be hostile and severe with their sons. In a study of lower-income families, Rainwater (1965) has presented data suggesting that an occupationally frustrated father may take out his frustrations on his wife, whereas Hoffman's data (M.L. Hoffman, 1960) suggest that power assertiveness by the father over the wife leads to assertiveness by the mother over the child in what appears to be a pecking order.

The idea of the family as fulfilling complementary needs, needs unsatisfied or aroused at work, does not necessarily imply a negative effect on the family, as in the frustration–aggression hypothesis. In Hoffman's work on the value of children to parents (Hoffman & Hoffman, 1973; Hoffman & Manis, 1979; Hoffman, Thornton, & Manis, 1978), children are seen as satisfying psychological needs that are not met by other aspects of life. Although these may be needs for power, they may also be needs for morality, for self-esteem, for a sense of accomplishment, for affiliative satisfaction, or for fun and stimulation. This research suggests that to the extent that these needs are not satisfied on the job, the parent may seek to satisfy them in the family. Energy, effort, warm interaction, high performance standards, enthusiasm, and joy may thus go into parenting because the job is not an alternative source of gratification.

The idea that the family may serve as a compensation for work experiences implies that the parent's behavior and moods will be different at work and in the family. This is a very different prediction than would be made from the ideas of mood carryover or behavior carryover. It is not useful, however, to think of the compensation hypothesis as competing with the carryover hypotheses. Both patterns have been shown to occur. A more useful direction for research would be to investigate when one process is likely to operate and when the other.

Work steals time, energy, and involvement. Of the various processes that have been seen as linking work to the family, probably the one most commonly invoked is the idea that the time, energy, and involvement that a parent spends on work is not available to the family. Long hours and overinvolvement in work are seen as diminishing the quality of family life, as impairing the marital relationship, and as disturbing parent–child relationships—both because of the non-availability of the worker to the family and because of the stress for the worker. A substantial body of research bears on this hypothesis, particularly with respect to mothers but also with respect to fathers. Summarizing these data, however, is complicated because the relationships are not linear, they differ for various subgroups (education making a particular difference), and the effects depend on what aspect of the husband–wife or parent–child interaction is being considered. Furthermore, the patterns for mothers may be different from those for fathers.

In general, the findings seem to indicate that this process does operate, but it is not a linear relationship. When work is excessively time consuming and involving, family involvement may be diminished, but there is no simple correlation between the number of hours worked and the degree of participation in family activities and interpersonal relationships for either parent (Clark & Gecas, 1977; Clark, Nye, & Gecas, 1978; Crouter & Huston, 1985; Robinson, 1977). For fathers, detrimental effects have been shown to occur for professionals and executives who are overinvolved in their work (Heath, 1977; Mortimer, 1980); for those whose work requires that they spend long periods—weeks and months—away from the family (Cotterell, 1985; Lynn & Sawrey, 1959; Tiller, 1958); and for night-shift workers whose working hours prevent them from being home when their school-aged children are present (Landy, Rosenberg, & Sutton-Smith, 1969; Mott et al., 1965).

For mothers, the variations in the amount of time spent in paid employment are much greater than for men, but there are no studies focusing on women who are overinvolved in work. Studies indicate that not only is there not a linear relationship between the number of hours spent at work and involvement in family activities and child care (Crouter & Huston, 1985) but also that part-time work seems to be associated with more positive marital relationships, attitudes toward children, and child outcomes than either nonemployment or full-time employment (Bronfenbrenner & Crouter, 1982; Hoffman, 1984a; Hoffman & Nye, 1974). Furthermore, although it is true that employed mothers spend less time in housework, child care and leisure time with their husbands than do nonemployed mothers (Hill & Stafford, 1978; Pleck & Rustad, 1980; Robinson, 1980), the data indicate that they compensate, in part, for the employment time by setting aside special periods for their children, cutting down on sleep and personal leisure, and using more time-saving housework procedures and outside help. The effort at compensation is particularly marked for college-educated mothers (Goldberg, 1977; Hill & Stafford, 1978; Hoffman, 1958, 1984a; Pederson, Cain, Zaslow, & Anderson, 1982).

Nevertheless, although there is no evidence for the mother's work time and involvements as mediating a general negative effect, this may be a process that links maternal employment to some of the child outcomes. For example, it has often been observed that the daughters of employed mothers are more independent, and it is possible that the mothers' time at work contributes to this pattern (Hoffman, 1984a, 1984b; Piotrkowski & Repetti, 1984). For both mothers and fathers, time and involvement in work may be curvilinear in their effects. A certain amount may enhance family relationships, but too much may be detrimental.

Stress. There can be little doubt that one of the processes by which work experiences can affect the family is through the stress that is sometimes engendered. In fact, every one of the concepts listed in the first column of Table 1 can produce stress in the worker: unemployment, too little money, low status, unpleasant tasks on the job, values engendered on the job that are incongruent with the work experience itself or other aspects of one's life, a lack of control and autonomy at work, frustration or low morale, excessive time and energy demands, the intrinsic stress of the job and physical danger, and intrusiveness (Cobb & Kasl, 1977; House, 1981; Kasl, 1974; Mortimer & Sorensen, 1984; Quinn & Staines, 1979; Wells, 1982). In addition, work can also lead to stress through its interaction with the family situation. For example, in the case of maternal employment, stress is likely to occur when the family situation is particularly demanding, as when there are five or more children in the family, a handicapped child, or inadequate substitute child care (Hoffman, 1984a).

Furthermore, there is also abundant evidence that the worker's stress can have adverse consequences for the marital relationship, parent–child interactions, and child outcomes (Burke & Weir, 1981; Buss & Redburn, 1983; Elder, 1984; Parke & Collmer, 1975; Steinmetz & Straus, 1974; Werner & Smith, 1982).

It is interesting to note in considering stress as an intervening process that several studies have indicated that boys are more vulnerable than girls to parental and family stress (Block & Block, in press; Elder, 1984; Hetherington, 1979; Hinde, 1985; Hoffman, 1984a; Werner & Smith, 1982). Studies of family stress that is not work related (Block & Block, in press; Hetherington, 1979) as well as studies of fathers' unemployment and of mothers' employment have shown more adverse consequences for sons than for daughters (Bronfenbrenner & Crouter, 1982; Elder, 1984; Hoffman, 1980, 1984a; Ray & McLoyd, in press; Werner & Smith, 1982). There are also some preliminary findings that suggest that when parents are under stress, their interactions with sons are more likely to be adversely affected than are their interactions with daughters (Elder, 1984; Hetherington, 1979; Hinde, 1985). Furthermore, studies of maternal employment in families with preschool children indicate that employed mothers have more positive and more active interactions with their daughters than do nonemployed mothers but less positive and less active interactions with their sons (Bronfenbrenner, Alvarez, & Henderson, 1982; Stuckey, McGhee, & Bell, 1982; Zaslow, Pederson, Suwalsky, & Rabinovich, 1983). One of the possible explanations for this pattern is that boys are more active and noncompliant than girls, and this may be particularly difficult for parents when they are under stress (Hoffman, 1984a). It is also possible that because boys are seen as sturdier and less vulnerable than girls (Hoffman, 1972), they are more likely to be the targets of the parents' frustration.

Future directions. In describing the various processes that seem to provide an explanation for how the parent's work affects the family and the child, it has been possible to cite some research that illustrates each. These are not competing hypotheses in the sense that if one is true, the other is not. They are all true to some extent. What it has not been possible to cite is research that tries to see *when* one process is more likely to operate than another. In fact, in only a few cases has the process actually been made explicit in the research and incorporated into a guiding theory. Too little attention has been given to *how* the work experiences affect the family and when one pattern rather than another is likely to prevail. As interest in the connection between work and the family grows, more attention should be directed to these issues.

Part 2: The Effects of Maternal Employment

The research described in Part 1 has been primarily research on the effects of fathers' work. However, in describing the concepts that have been used and the processes by which the father's work has been seen to affect the family, some of the maternal employment research has also been cited and most of the theories and conceptualizations could be applied to studies of mothers' work. In fact, however, the great bulk of the research on maternal employment has dealt only with one conceptualization of work—Is she employed or nonemployed?—and only about half of the processes have actually been involved in the maternal employment studies, almost none that deal with the actual work experience or the particular job.

The research on the mother's work is different from that on fathers, of course, largely because it is the mother who has had the primary responsibility for homemaking and child care, and she still does. Furthermore, it is only recently that large numbers of mothers have been in the labor force, and even now, almost 40 percent of the mothers with children under 18 still are not. It is, therefore, only natural that interest focuses on the employment–nonemployment difference itself, and that the process most often implied in this research is the one listed ninth earlier in the chapter: Work takes time from the family. What are the effects of this?

So, in Part 2, the effects of maternal employment on the family will be examined as a separate issue. Before reviewing this research, however, some preliminary comments are needed.

Methodological Problems

A great deal of research on the effects of maternal employment has been done over the years. It varies widely in quality. Too often reviewers summarize these results as though all studies were equal, but in fact, some research has glaring inadequacies. Once it has been presented uncritically in a review, it becomes part of the body of accepted knowledge and is referred to in subsequent publications and in innumerable doctoral dissertations. Some of the most common methodological problems in this work will be pointed out here in the hope that it will be useful in doing research on this topic and in interpreting published reports.

Controls. The most common methodological error is failure to control on extraneous variables. Employed mothers are different from nonemployed mothers in other ways besides the sheer fact of employment status. They are more likely to be from lower income groups, but within their social class they are better educated. They are more likely to be divorced; if currently married, they are more likely to have been previously divorced. They have fewer children and older children. They are more likely to be Black. Studies must control on these variables lest the results reflect not differences in employment but differences in one or more of these other factors. The research literature is full of reported effects of maternal employment that close examination of the data reveals are related not to employment at all, but rather to single-parent or lower-class status (e.g., Ginsberg, Milne, Myers & Rosenthal, 1984; Hansson, O'Connor, Jones, & Blocker, 1981).

The problem of inadequate controls can also be quite subtle. For example, there are studies in which the sample consists of adolescent children all of whom have currently intact two-parent families. The analysis, however, is interested in preschool employment and correlates the mother's employment status during the child's preschool years with the child's current cognitive or emotional level. On the surface, the design seems appropriate. In fact, however, it is likely that many of the mothers who were employed during the child's preschool years were divorced at that time, even though they have subsequently remarried. This is particularly likely in a retrospective study, because, until recently, it was unusual for a mother to be employed during a child's preschool years, and a very disproportionate percentage of these employed mothers were divorced. Thus, it is difficult to know whether the correlates of employment during preschool years in this design reflect the mothers' employment or the absence of fathers. (Heyns & Catsambis, 1985).

Subgroup analysis. Controlling on interfering variables, however, is not enough. Often it is necessary to use them as the basis for separate subgroup analysis. Maternal employment does affect family life and child development, but it operates in complex ways. The effects vary depending on social class, race, sex of child, age of child, the attitudes of both parents, whether it is a one-parent or a two-parent family, the nature of the employment, and a host of other variables. To reveal these patterns, the analysis has to consider the various groups separately (Hoffman, 1963a, 1974).

Changing times. Another problem concerns the fact that maternal employment patterns have changed markedly over the years. The results of any empirical study are valid only for the situation that prevailed at the time the data were collected. One has to be very cautious, then, in generalizing the findings of research from the 1950s and 1960s to the present. For example, whereas employed mothers of the past responded with guilt and overmothering, as one study in the 1950s showed (Hoffman, 1961a), guilt is less likely to be the response now that maternal employment is so prevalent. In fact, more recent data suggest that nonemployed mothers may be on the defensive today, and to justify their nonemployment, they may be overmothering (Hoffman, 1980). This problem applies not only to studies published 20 years ago but also to present analyses of longitudinal data that were collected 20 years ago. They may be revealing effects of maternal employment that no longer prevail.

The point that maternal employment patterns and the social setting generally have changed over the years is important not only for methodological reasons but substantively as well. To understand the effects of maternal employment today, it is necessary to consider the social context. Final preliminary comments pertain to this issue.

Table 2
Labor Force Participation Rates of Mothers
With Children Under 18, 1940–1984

Year	% of Mothers
1984	60.5
1982	58.5
1980	56.6
1978	53.0
1976	48.8
1974	45.7
1972	42.9
1970	42.0
1968	39.4
1966	35.8
1964	34.5
1962	32.9
1960	30.4
1958	29.5
1956	27.5
1954	25.6
1952	23.8
1950	21.6
1948	20.2
1946	18.2
1940	8.6

Source: U.S. Department of Labor, 1977; U.S. Department of Commerce, 1979; U.S. Department of Labor, 1981; U.S. Department of Labor, 1985 (data supplied by E. Waldman, Senior Economist).

Social Change

The steady rise in maternal employment rates over the years is clearly illustrated in Table 2. The pattern, rare in 1940, had become modal by 1978 and has been found to be more prevalent at each new reading. There are, of course, differences in employment rates for mothers of different-aged children, and Table 3 shows what the current rates are. Rates are higher when there are no preschool children and when there is no husband in the family. And yet, for the past 15 years, more than half of the mothers of school-aged children, in families where the husband is present, have been employed. Even this rate climbs every year; in 1984 it was over 65 percent. It was over 76 percent when no husband was present and there were only school-aged children in the family. The most rapid recent gains in employment rates have been, however, among the mothers of preschoolers. In 1984, the employment rate for women who lived with their husbands and had preschool children was almost 52 percent, a rate nearly triple the 1960 rate of 19 percent. Even among mothers of preschoolers under three who are living with their husbands, 45 percent were employed.

Table 3
Percentage of Mothers in the Labor Force
by Marital Status and Age of Child 1984

Marital Status of Mother and Age of Child	Percentage Employed
Mothers with children 6–17 only	
Married, husband present	65.4[a]
Widowed, divorced, separated	76.5[b]
Mothers with children under 6	
Married, husband present	51.8[c]
Widowed, divorced, separated	53.2
Mothers with children under 3	
Married, husband present	48.3[d]
Widowed, divorced, separated	45.0

[a] Of these, 65.8% were full time, 29.2% were part time, and 5.0% were "unemployed but looking."

[b] Of these, 73.4% were full time, 14.7% were part time, and 11.9% were "unemployed but looking."

[c] Of these, 58.9% were full time, 32.2% were part time, and 8.9% were "unemployed but looking."

[d] Of these, 57.8% were full time, 32.8% were part time, and 9.4% were "unemployed but looking."

Source: U.S. Department of Labor, Bureau of Labor Statistics. Data supplied by E. Waldman, Senior Economist.

A change as impressive as this increase in the employment of mothers occurs not in isolation but as part of a complex pattern. The increased employment rates are a response to some new events, accompanied by other responses to these events, and the cause of still other changes. It is the nature of social systems that change in one part involves a change in other parts. One must therefore consider the total pattern to see how maternal employment fits into the picture.

American family life has undergone so many transformations in recent years that the context within which maternal employment is now occurring is different from in the past. Technological developments—including clothes dryers, no-iron fabrics, disposable diapers, home freezers, and processed foods of good quality—have drastically diminished the amount of work necessary for operating a household; family size is smaller; marital instability has increased the necessity for women to establish occupational competence; economic pressures in general have increased; women's educational levels have risen; the adult roles for which children are being socialized are different; the prevailing social values have changed (Hoffman, 1984b). Today full-time mothers as well as employed mothers may feel a need to justify their role, and the role of full-time mother is a less satisfying one according to a number of recent studies (Birnbaum, 1975; Feree, 1976; Gold & Andres, 1978a, 1978b; Kessler & McRae, 1982; Veroff, Douvan, & Kulka, 1981). The role of the present-day nonemployed mothers may be as new as the role of the majority of present-day mothers, who are employed. It is even difficult to know which represents more of a continuity with the nonemployed mother of the past. It is possible that the individual child in today's employed-mother household receives as much attention as the individual child in yesterday's nonemployed-mother household—work filling in the time previously spent on the extra household responsibilities and the additional children, whereas today's nonemployed mother represents the really new pattern. There are data from the national time-use studies that suggest that the full-time homemaker has more free time than in previous years (Pleck & Rustad, 1980; Robinson, 1977, 1980). We do not know if she also has more child-interaction time than has ever been common previously, but it is possible. It is important to keep in mind when employed-mother families are compared to nonemployed-mother families that neither represents the traditional pattern.

The discussion of the effects of maternal employment on the family and the child is organized under three general headings: (a) the husband–wife relationship, which includes the marital relationship, the relative power of the husband and wife, and the division of labor; (b) the mother's morale, which includes general levels of satisfaction or happiness and the degree of stress; and (c) the parent–child interaction patterns. For each of these, the studies of how they are affected by maternal employment and what the significance of these effects are for the child are reviewed.

Husband–Wife Relationship

Three aspects of the husband–wife relationship have been examined to see how they relate to the mother's employment: the marital relationship, power relations, and the division of labor. Most of the studies of the marital and power relationship were conducted during the 1950s and 1960s. The one clear conclusion that emerged from these studies was that it is very complicated. Measuring either marital satisfaction or power is difficult, and each dimension consists of many components that do not necessarily covary. Furthermore, the relation between each of these and maternal employment requires consideration of other mediating conditions.

The marital relationship. The studies that have examined the relation between the mother's employment status and some measure of marital happiness, satisfaction, or adjustment have generally found that a negative relation is more likely to prevail if the sample is lower class, if the father is the reporter, if the study was conducted earlier (in the 1950s or early 1960s), if the mother indicates that she prefers not to work, and if the father opposes her employment. Positive effects on the marriage are more often indicated if the sample is middle class, if the sample is educated, if the mother is the reporter, if the study was conducted recently, if the mother wants to work, and if the work is part time (Axelson, 1970; Burke & Weir, 1976; Feld, 1963; Nye, 1963, 1974; Orden & Bradburn, 1969). In studies that have measured specific aspects of the relationship rather than marital satisfaction generally, both the husband and wife have reported better communication and agreement about behavior and values in the employed-mother families (Aldous, 1969; Burke & Weir, 1976).

Some studies have explored the possibility that when the mother's occupational status is superior to her husband's, there is a stress on the marriage. Although it depends on the attitudes of the couple, this pattern has been noted to result in no stress, in no stress as long as the husband's salary is higher, in divorce, in withdrawal of the woman from the labor force, and in pregnancy as a reaffirmation of femininity and marital solidarity and as an excuse for the woman to withdraw partially from employment (Hoffman, 1977b; Philliber & Hiller, 1983; Piotrkowski & Repetti, 1984; Safilios-Rothschild, 1976).

Finally, data indicate a higher divorce rate for families with employed wives (Sawhill, Peabody, Jones, & Caldwell, 1975). At least part of the explanation for this relation, however, seems to be that the monetary resource and the woman's wage-earning ability enable the divorce to take place. In some cases, in fact, the employment was undertaken to make a divorce possible.

The quality of the parents' marriage does affect the child's development, but since there is no clear effect of maternal employment on the marital relationship, this does not seem to be an important link between employment and child outcomes. Furthermore, although divorce has been shown to have deleterious consequences for children, these consequences are not more serious than growing up in a conflict-laden home (Hetherington & Camara, 1984). Thus, to the extent that maternal employment merely facilitates a wanted divorce, its effects are at least not negative.

There are, however, some data to indicate the role of a mother's employment in the divorce situation. In a study of the impact of divorce on preschool children, Hetherington (1979), found that when a mother had been employed since well before the divorce, her employment helped her to cope more effectively both psychologically and economically. Her interaction with her child was therefore less distressed, and adverse consequences for the child were diminished. On the other hand, it was particularly difficult for a child when the mother started work at the time of the divorce. Whereas the new job helped the mother in some way, such as providing self-esteem and new social contacts, her employment was difficult for the child because it increased the disruption in routines caused by the divorce and thereby added to the child's losses.

Husband–wife power. Studies of the husband–wife power relationship were popular in the 1950s and 1960s, but marital power was difficult to conceptualize, let alone measure (Bahr, 1974; Hoffman & Lippitt, 1960; Safilios-Rothschild, 1970). It was most often defined in terms of who made various decisions, or who made the decision when there were conflicting views, or who decided about the other's behavior. In the more sophisticated studies, a distinction was made between control over major family decisions and control over household activities and child care (Bahr, 1974; Hoffman, 1963b). In general, these studies indicated that maternal employment did increase the wife's power over major decisions, particularly economic decisions, and decreased her power over routine household decisions and child care. The former was more marked in lower-class families; the latter was more likely to occur when the husband increased his activity in these areas (Bahr, 1974; Hoffman, 1963b, 1983; Quarm, 1977). All of this was complicated, however, by the interaction of other variables. For example, Hoffman (1963b) found that an employed wife's endorsing a male-dominance ideology could have a counteractive influence; that is, some employed women assumed a lower power profile lest their employment disturb the marital relationship.

Very little research of this sort has been conducted in recent years, however, following perhaps several critical reviews which pointed up the complexities of this issue (Bahr, 1974; Safilios-Rothschild, 1970). A few more recent studies have looked at maternal employment and the negotiation process between the husband and wife (Chafetz, 1980; Scanzoni, 1978). Chafetz has suggested that maternal employment increases both egalitarianism and conflict between the spouses.

Although no one has studied it to any extent, it seems likely that employment increases a wife's power particularly when she would otherwise be at the very low end of the power distribution. The ability to earn wages can increase her self-esteem and enable her to feel less totally dependent on her husband. Thus, she is able to assert herself more. Both the divorce literature and the fact that increased power from employment is more common in the lower-class groups are consistent with this hypothesis.

The possibility that maternal employment may move the couple toward a more egalitarian relationship may have significance for the child's development. Studies indicate that children of employed mothers are less likely to see women as incompetent than are children of full-time homemakers (Baruch, 1972a; Vogel, Broverman, Broverman, Clarkson, & Rosenkratz, 1970). Furthermore, daughters of employed women are more likely to name their mother as the person they most admire or would like to be like when grown (Baruch, 1972b; Douvan, 1963). It is possible that both of these patterns are related to the mother's higher status in the family and more active role in family decisions. Although there are no data that show a direct relationship between maternal employment and the daughter's self-esteem, there are data that show that the daughters of employed mothers are more likely to have higher occupational goals and to attain more professional success. This may also be mediated in part by having a mother who seems more effective and influential in the family.

Some studies have found, however, but only in the lower or blue-collar class, that sons of employed mothers, in comparison with sons of nonemployed mothers, are less likely to name their fathers as the person they most admire. It is possible that this reflects a lower status of fathers in this group. In the blue-collar class, there may still be a perception that the mother's employment implies a failure on the part of the father. In fact, the mothers in this group do originally enter the labor force at a time when the father's income is seen as inadequate. As attitudes toward maternal employment change in accordance with its actual prevalence, this pattern may disappear. Studies do not indicate, incidentally, any adverse consequences on cognitive or socioemotional indices for sons of employed mothers in this socioeconomic group.

The division of labor. Probably the most clearly demonstrated effect of maternal employment is a modest increase in the participation of fathers in household tasks and child care. Every study for the past

30 years that has exercised adequate controls has found that when the mother is employed, the father helps more with household tasks and child care. This effect has been found in studies from the 1950s (Bahr, 1974; Blood & Hamblin, 1958; Hoffman, 1963b; Nolan, 1963; Powell, 1963) through the present (Baruch & Barnett, 1981; Gold & Andres, 1978b; Pleck & Rustad, 1980; Robinson, 1978; Crouter & Huston, 1985; Crouter, Huston, & Robins, 1983), and it has been found with every kind of measure. The effect is not great; mothers still maintain the li-oness' share, but it is statistically significant. This effect is more pronounced when the mother is employed full time, when there is more than one child, and when there are no older children in the household, particularly no older daughters (Hoffman, 1963b; Powell, 1963; Walker & Woods, 1976). Furthermore, some studies indicate the effect is more pronounced when the wife's income approaches the husband's (Model, 1981; Scanzoni, 1978). The fact that husbands of employed mothers are more active in household tasks and child care also appears to be a causal relationship, and not merely a selective factor, because the relationship holds even when sex role ideology is controlled (Hoffman, 1963b; Crouter & Huston, 1983), and it is frequently reported by parents as an effect of employment, (Gottfried, Gottfried, & Bathurst, 1985; Hoffman, 1958, 1983).

The only research in which this effect has not been apparent are some of the earlier national time-use studies, studies in which respondents keep records of how they spend their time. These studies often did not control on whether there were children, the number of children, or their ages. Because employed mothers had fewer and older children, families spent fewer hours on household tasks and child care. Thus, the fact was obscured that more hours were spent by fathers in employed-mother families than in *comparable* families with nonemployed mothers. More recent time-use studies, however, have exercised better empirical controls, and the pattern has emerged in this work (Crouter & Huston, 1985; Crouter, Huston, & Robins, 1983; Hoffman, 1983; Pleck & Rustad, 1980). Lamb (1981) has suggested that there may also be an increase in the father's responsiveness in this area.

One interesting exception to this general pattern has come out of the research on infancy (Pederson, Cain, Zaslow, & Anderson, 1982). In a study of parent–infant interaction, home observations were carried out during the late afternoon, just after dual-career couples returned from work. The data indicated that during this time, employed mothers, compared to full-time homemakers, had high levels of parent–infant interaction, whereas their husbands were low in comparison to the husbands of full-time homemakers. In the full-time homemakers' families, this time was the special period for the father to play with the baby, whereas in the employed-mother families this was a time when the mothers made up for their absence at work while their husbands helped by handling other household demands. Because of the priority assigned to the working mother's relationship to the infant, fathers were squeezed out of the time when fathers traditionally attend to the baby while the mother turns to other activities. Except for this interesting finding, however, fathers of infants and very young children, like fathers of older children, are more active generally in child care when mothers are employed (Hoffman, 1984a).

The effects of maternal employment on the traditional division of labor in the family is important in several respects. In particular, it is likely that this is one of the routes by which maternal employment operates to diminish sex role traditionalism. The employment of a mother calls for some accommodation by the father. Although the response has been modest, there has been some, and this, in turn, diminishes the traditionalistic ideology in families and in society generally. The repeated finding that the children of employed mothers hold less stereotyped attitudes about sex roles than do the children of nonemployed mothers (Douvan, 1963; Gold & Andres, 1978c; Hartley, 1960; Miller, 1975; Vogel et al., 1970) may be at least partly explained by the intermediating effect on the parental division of labor.

The greater participation of the father in child care may itself be an important factor in a child's development, but the nature of the effect is very difficult to extrapolate from the existing data on fathers (Lamb, 1979). For example, the absence of the father seems to affect cognitive development adversely (Radin, 1976), but that does not necessarily mean that a modest increase in the father's role would have a positive effect. The high involvement of fathers in child care has been found to be associated with an increase in social competence (Biller, 1976; Hoffman, 1961b), particularly in boys. And, indeed, many studies do find the children of working mothers higher in social competence (Hoffman, 1979), but it may not be sound to apply this research on fathers to the maternal employment situation. The problem in generalizing any of the existing data on the father's effect is that these studies are generally dealing with an increment or decrement in total parent involvement. In the employed mother situation, it is a switch from the traditional pattern, but not necessarily a total gain in parent attention. Gold and Andres (1978b, 1978c; Gold, Andres, & Glorieux, 1979) have suggested that the major effect of the father's participation in child care in the dual-wage family is to offset any possible adverse effects from the mother's time at work. In particular, they suggested that the occasionally observed pattern of lower academic performance by sons of employed mothers in the middle class is counteracted when there is an increase in the father's role. Further research is needed, however, to understand what the effects are of having the child-rearing role shared rather than mother dominated.

The Mother's Morale

An aspect of family life that is often seen as linking the mother's employment status to the effects on the child is the mother's emotional state, or "morale." There are two seemingly conflicting views. One is that employment can enhance a woman's life, providing stimulation, self-esteem, adult contacts, and escape from the repetitive routines of housework and child care, and by this route she can be a better mother to her child. The other is that the dual roles of worker and mother are stressful, and, as a result, the quality of mothering is diminished. In fact, of course, both patterns operate—sometimes in the same mother.

A morale boost. As indicated earlier, the role of the full-time mother in America has changed. The decrease in required homemaking time and in the number of children in the family have made this pattern seem to many women an insufficient contribution to the family and an inadequate use of their abilities. This feeling is heightened by the woman's awareness that she could use her time to earn money for the family—money that the family often needs to maintain an acceptable standard of living. Rising educational levels for women have increased both the ability and the motivation to obtain employment, and the current instability of marriage has made many women feel a need to establish occupational competence. In addition, present living arrangements have increased the full-time homemaker's isolation from other adults. Finally, there have been changes in America about what an individual should expect from life. In this context, it is not surprising that most studies comparing the personal life satisfactions of employed and nonemployed mothers find a higher level of satisfaction among the employed. This has been found for professional women (Birnbaum, 1975) and for blue-collar workers (Feree, 1976), in national samples (Veroff, Douvan, & Kulka, 1981) and in more homogeneous ones (Feldman & Feldman, 1973; Gold & Andres, 1978a, 1978b; Kessler & McRae, 1982).

Because studies indicate that the mother's mood does affect her children, even infants (Yarrow, 1979), it is reasonable to conclude that maternal employment may often have a positive effect on the child because it improves the mother's own sense of well-being. One approach to this issue has been the idea of role congruence. Several studies have investigated the hypothesis that when there is congruence between the mother's actual employment status and her desired employment status, that is, when there is satisfaction with her role whether it is as employed mother or as full-time homemaker, higher quality mother–child interaction results, with positive effects on the children. The data are consistent with this hypothesis, but it is not an easy one to prove empirically. Studies with infants, as well as with older children, have consistently demonstrated that a mother's satisfaction with her employment status relates positively to the quality of mother–child interaction and also to various indices of the child's adjustment and abilities (Farel, 1980; Hock, 1980; Schubert, Bradley-Johnson, & Nuttal, 1980; Stuckey et al., 1982; Yarrow, Scott, DeLeeuw, & Heinig, 1962). The difficulty lies in demonstrating the direction of causality. Although maternal satisfaction may be the reason for the positive mother–child interaction, it may also reflect the relationship with the child and the mother's awareness that the child is doing well. Difficulties with the child, on the other hand, could cause the mother's discontent. Attempts to prove this hypothesis over the years have shown improvements in design and measures, but none has succeeded in demonstrating the direction of causality.

Stress. In the research on fathers, stress is most often seen as being engendered by the job situation itself; in the research on mothers, stress is seen to be engendered by the combination of work and family roles. Because the employed mother still has the major responsibility for housework and child care, she is frequently seen as being under stress from work overload.

It is not necessarily true, however, that employed mothers are under more stress than are nonemployed mothers. Although they put in considerably more work hours than the full-time homemaker (Pleck & Rustad, 1980) and typically complain that there is "not enough time in the day" (Birnbaum, 1975), in studies that compare stress indicators, psychosomatic symptoms, and depression, the employed mothers tend to score lower (Burke & Weir, 1976; Kessler & MacRae, 1982).

Nevertheless, it is true that the dual role involves considerable strain. The possibility that maternal employment can become stressful and have adverse consequences for the child increases when there are several preschool children, a handicapped child, inadequate substitute child care, an absence of adult support, or the chronic illness of either parent. Unfortunately, however, these same conditions can increase the economic and psychological need for the mother's employment. Part-time employment can be an appropriate compromise when the family situation involves stress for either full-time employment or full-time mothering. As has already been noted, several studies have found that part-time employment is associated with more positive outcomes for family life and child development than either full-time pattern (Hoffman, 1984a, 1984b).

Mother–Child Interaction

The final aspect of family life to be discussed is the mother–child interaction. As already indicated, employed mothers do spend less time in child care, as one would assume, but the differences are less pronounced if only direct contact is considered. For example, in one study of preschool children, there was no difference in the amount of direct interaction time, but there was a difference in indirect contact—when the mother and child were within voice range but not involved in one-to-one interaction (Goldberg, 1977). College-educated employed mothers, in particular, try to compensate for their employment by setting aside special time for the children and by cutting down on sleep and personal leisure (Baruch & Barnett, 1981; Hill & Stafford, 1978).

Infants. Much of the most recent work on maternal employment has been concerned with the very young child, and the studies of mother–child interaction have concentrated particularly on the infant. Several studies have used behavioral observations to measure the quality of the mother–infant interaction. The results of these studies are not entirely consistent. The samples were not random, and the patterns found seem to vary with the nature of the sample. Most of the differences that have been found, however, seem to suggest that the employed mother is more attentive, particularly verbally. (See Hoffman, 1984a).

Two of these studies, carried out by independent researchers, showed the sex differences already described: In employed-mother families, parents were more interactive with girls, whereas in nonemployed-mother families, parents were more interactive with boys (Stuckey et al., 1982; Zaslow et al., 1983). Support for this pattern also comes from a study of three-year-olds that involved interviews with mothers. Mothers who were employed full time described their daughters but not their sons in the most positive terms. The opposite pattern was found for the nonemployed mothers (Bronfenbrenner, Alvarez, & Henderson, 1984).

Several studies of maternal employment effects on infants have examined the attachment relationship between the mother and child. The security of the attachment relationship is an important concept in developmental psychology and has been shown to relate to the child's social competence at later ages (Sroufe, 1983). It is measured by a standard laboratory procedure developed by Mary Ainsworth (Ainsworth, Blehar, Waters, & Wall, 1978). In none of the studies that has compared employed and nonemployed mothers on the security of the mother–infant attachment has a difference been found (Chase-Lansdale, 1981; Hock, 1980; Hoffman, 1984a; Schwartz, 1983; Vaughn, Gove, & Egeland, 1980). There are two studies that tried to see if a change in the mother's employment status resulted in a change in the attachment relationship. In one study it was found that when the mother entered the labor force, there was a change in the security of attachment, but the change was as likely to go in one direction as the other—toward security or toward insecurity (Thompson, Lamb, &

Estes, 1982); in the other study no change was found (Owen, Easterbrooks, Chase-Lansdale, & Goldberg, 1984). Thus, judging from the studies of attachment so far, maternal employment does not seem to be a powerful variable. In current investigation, however, researchers are looking at the timing of the mother's return to work to see if a return during the period of attachment formation, in the second half of the first year or early in the second, is more disturbing to the relationship than a return either earlier or later (Weinraub & Hoffman, personal communication).

School-aged children and independence training. The data on school-aged children seem to indicate that employed mothers are more likely to encourage independence in their children than are nonemployed mothers (Hoffman, 1974). This pattern may be, in part, an adaptation to the working-mother role: An independent child can cope more adequately in the mother's absence. It also, however, may reflect a difference in the psychological state of employed and nonemployed mothers. Some studies suggest that the nonemployed mother, because of the social changes already described, may overinvest in the mother role since it is the only one from which she derives a sense of self-worth. She needs to feel needed. In Birnbaum's (1975) study of educated women, the full-time homemakers indicated anxiety as their children moved toward independence, because they felt it signaled the end of their major role.

For daughters, the greater encouragement of independence by employed mothers seems to be a clear advantage. Several studies have indicated that in the traditional family, dependency is encouraged in girls. This pattern has been seen as a source of excessive affiliative concerns, an interference with the development of independent coping skills, and a barrier to top performance (Hoffman, 1972, 1977a). The daughters of employed mothers, by contrast, have been found to be high achievers, as already noted, and several studies have found that they also had higher scores than daughters of nonemployed mothers on various measures of socioemotional adjustment (Almquist & Angrist, 1971; Ginzberg, 1971; Gold & Andres, 1978a; Tangri, 1972). One of the explanations for the generally positive impact of maternal employment on daughters is the greater independence training they receive.

It is not clear, however, whether the greater encouragement of independence offered by employed mothers is an advantage or a disadvantage for boys. Boys traditionally are encouraged to be independent (Hoffman, 1979) and so any additional push in this direction might be more than is appropriate for their developmental level. To the extent, then, that employed mothers are giving *boys* more independence than has been traditionally given, this may be too much. There are some data, however, that suggest that at least part of the difference between the employed mothers and the nonemployed is because the nonemployed do not encourage independence in their sons as has been the case traditionally. This is consistent with the idea that the full-time homemaker today feels a need to justify her choice. She may be inadvertently encouraging dependency in her children—sons as well as daughters.

Consistent with this second interpretation, Moore (1975) found that sons of full-time homemakers, at early adolescence, were more inhibited and conforming, but also performed better in school. The pattern suggests that they may have been "over-socialized," in the way girls have previously been described (Hoffman, 1972). On the other hand, the lower school performance of boys with employed mothers in the Moore study could be seen as resulting from too much independence. Bronfenbrenner and Crouter (1982) have suggested that the sons of working mothers may, perhaps because of their independence, become particularly involved in peer groups whose influence may undermine adult socialization.

These different hypotheses have been proposed to explain an interesting pattern in the employed-mother studies. A considerable amount of research has examined differences between the children of employed and nonemployed mothers on various indices of cognitive performance. The results vary according to social class. Among lower-class, economically pressed families, differences fairly consistently favor the employed mother's children (Cherry and Eaton, 1977). Among blue-collar families, there are either no differences or differences that also favor the employed mothers' children. In the middle class, however, for boys only, several studies have found that maternal employment is associated with lower IQ scores or lower school performance (Gold & Andres, 1978b, 1978c; Hoffman, 1980). It is not clear from the data whether the better performance of the middle-class boys in the nonworking-mother families reflects differences in ability that have long-term significance or whether it reflects a greater conformity to adult authority that would influence elementary school performance but would have a different impact at higher academic levels (Gold, 1978a; Hoffman, 1972). Further information about the nature of these differences is needed before it can be decided whether the middle-class homemakers' sons are being oversocialized—that is, whether they are being given too little encouragement toward independence training or whether the employed mothers' sons are being given too much.

For both the high achievement pattern of working mothers' daughters and the lower elementary-school performance of the middle-class working mothers' sons, other explanations have also been proposed, but the difference in independence training that tends to accompany the mother's employment status seems to be one of the important links to these child outcomes.

Household responsibilities. Children of employed mothers are more likely to have regular household responsibilities than are children of nonemployed mothers. This is particularly true for older elementary-school children and high-school students, girls, and first-born children (Douvan, 1963; Propper, 1972; Trimberger & Maclean, 1982; Walker, 1970). In one study of elementary-school children that was conducted in the 1950s (Hoffman, 1963a), employed mothers who enjoyed their work showed a pattern that indicated they were going out of their way to see that their employment did not inconvenience their children; and in these families, the children actually helped less in the house than did a matched sample of children from families with nonemployed mothers. But, in general, except when guilt intervenes, working mothers' children have more household responsibilities. This pattern is clearly adaptive for families of employed mothers. Some studies have indicated that the children may complain about these tasks (Trimberger & MacLean, 1982), and it can obviously be overdone, but there is considerable evidence that having household responsibilities enhances ego development and self-esteem in children (Clausen, 1966; Elder, 1978; Johnson, 1969; Medrich, 1981; Smokler, 1975; Woods, 1972).

Rule-governed households. This is also some evidence, but it is scanty, that in lower-class families, mothers employed full time are more likely to have rule-governed households, a pattern that also seems adaptive in that it would enable the family to function better in the mother's absence. In a study of lower-class Black families, Woods (1972) found that the mothers who were employed full time were more likely to show consistency between principles and practice in their discipline, and Yarrow and her colleagues (Yarrow et al., 1962) found a similar pattern among lower-class White families. It has already been noted that several studies of low-income populations have shown advantages, particularly cognitive advantages, for the children of employed mothers. One previous suggestion was that the money itself that has been added by maternal employment may be part of the explanation, but it is possible that the firmer, more rule-governed pattern also mediates this outcome.

It must be pointed out, however, that although the data show a correlation, they do not necessarily indicate that the positive outcomes noted in the children are a result of the mother's employment. In this situation, where the mother's employment seems so necessary, it may be that a selective factor is operating: The mothers who are better copers, more organized, or under less stress may be the ones most likely to seek employment, and their children may fare better for these reasons. Similarly, it is possible that their structured discipline is simply part of this same pattern—another manifestation of their coping ability rather than a causal link.

Summary and Conclusions

In the second part of this review the research dealing with the effects of the mother's employment on the family and the child has been examined with particular attention to the husband–wife relationship, the mother's morale, and the mother–child interaction. With respect to the husband–wife relationship, the data do not indicate any clear association between employment status and the affective bond, but there is some empirical support for an increase in egalitarianism, rather than husband dominance, in the families with employed mothers and clear support for a modest increase in the father's participation in household tasks and child care. It was suggested that the greater role of employed mothers in family decisions may be part of the explanation for the finding that the daughters of employed women are more likely to see women as competent and effective and to name their mothers as their adult models, whereas the less traditional division of labor in the family may be a link to the less stereotyped sex role attitudes of working mothers' children.

Research on the effects of employment on morale indicates that employment can provide either a psychological boost or a stress. Most studies do indicate a higher level of satisfaction among employed mothers, but stress can result when the demands of the dual role are excessive. Several researchers have tried to show that when there is congruence between the actual role and the woman's desired role, there are positive effects on the child, but the direction of causality is ambiguous in this research.

In considering mother–child interaction, it was noted that although employed mothers have less time with their children, the quality is not diminished and may be enhanced. Preliminary data suggest that employed mothers may have more positive interactions with infant daughters, whereas nonemployed have more positive interactions with infant sons. Data suggest that the employed mothers are more likely to encourage independence in their children, a pattern seen to give clear advantages for daughters but possibly disadvantages for sons. Two other differences were noted: Employed mothers' children are more likely to have household responsibilities, and this has been found to relate to self-esteem and ego development in children; and in the lower class, there is some limited evidence that the full-time employed mothers have more rule-governed households, which could be a link to the higher cognitive performance of children from low-income families.

One observation that can be made from these findings is that several family patterns that are associated with maternal employment seem to be beneficial for daughters: the more egalitarian power between parents, which may lead daughters to hold the female status in higher esteem, the less traditional division of labor, which may lead daughters to hold a less restricted view of their own role; the fact that mothers provide models more consistent with the roles the daughters themselves are likely to occupy; the greater encouragement of independence; and the possibility that daughters receive more parental attention even as infants. The picture for sons, however, is less clear. Bem (1975) has suggested that diminished sex role stereotypes may benefit both boys and girls; but data suggest that in the blue-collar class, the mother's employment may diminish the father's status in his sons' eyes. The greater independence training may not be an advantage for boys, and some studies suggest that it is in the nonworking-mother family that young sons receive more attention. It is possible that the greater involvement of fathers in child care is an advantage for boys and that the household responsibilities and rule-governed households would benefit both sexes, but the situation for sons is more mixed than for daughters. The outcome data on children are consistent with this: In the studies that have found a difference between employed and nonemployed mothers' children, the employed mothers' daughters seem to fare better, but the sons have shown a more complicated picture, with differences occurring in either direction.

Because the emphasis here has been on differences found, there has not been a discussion of the differences not found. In fact, however, most studies comparing the children of employed and nonemployed mothers do not find significant differences. These include studies of the developmental level of infants (Hoffman, 1984a) and many of the studies of cognitive and emotional development in older children (Gottfried, Gottfried, & Bathurst, 1985; Heyns, 1982; Heyns & Catsambis, 1985). Studies have been undertaken comparing television-viewing patterns of the children, but no meaningful differences have been revealed (Messaris & Hornik, 1983). And, although there is a great deal of interest in this question in the mass media, there are no good data on differences in the amount of unsupervised time or how this time is spent (Hoffman, 1980, 1984b).

The mother's employment in itself does not seem to be a robust variable. In any study of the effects of work on the family and the child, however, it is necessary to consider the many other aspects of the situation that are involved. Failure to find an effect does not mean there is not one. It may simply mean that the various conditions that can alter the outcome have not been specified. It is clear that both men's work and women's work affect their family life and their children's development, but tracing this influence through, both theoretically and empirically, requires considering the various steps in the causal connection and the conditions that intervene. There is a great deal of research yet to be done.

References

Ainsworth, M., Blehar, M., Waters, E., & Wall, S. (1978). *Patterns of attachment.* Hillsdale, NJ: Erlbaum.

Aldous, J. (1969). Occupational characteristics and male's role performance in the family. *Journal of Marriage and the Family, 31,* 707–712.

Almquist, E. M., & Angrist, S. S. (1971). Role model influences on college women's career aspirations. *Merrill-Palmer Quarterly, 71,* 263–279.

Angell, R. E. (1936). *The family encounters the Depression.* New York: Scribner.

Axelson, L. (1970). The working wife: Differences in perception among Negro and white males. *Journal of Marriage and the Family, 32,* 457–464.

Bahr, S. J. (1974). Effects on power and division of labor in the family. In L. W. Hoffman & F. I. Nye (Eds.), *Working mothers* (pp. 167–185). San Francisco: Jossey-Bass.

Barry, H. A., Bacon, M. K., & Child, I. L. (1957). A cross-cultural survey of some sex differences in socialization. *Journal of Abnormal and Social Psychology, 55,* 8.

Baruch, G. K. (1972a). Maternal influences upon college women's attitudes toward women and work. *Developmental Psychology, 6,* 32–37.

Baruch, G. K. (1972b, April). *Maternal role pattern as related to self-esteem and parental identification in college women.* Paper presented at the meeting of the Eastern Psychological Association, Boston, MA.

Baruch, G. K., & Barnett, R. C. (1981). Fathers' participation in the care of their preschool children. *Sex Roles, 7,* 1043–1055.

Bem, S. I. (1975). Sex-role adaptability: One consequence of psychological androgyny. *Journal of Personality and Social Psychology, 31,* 534–643.

Bernstein, B. (1961). Social class and linguistic development: A theory of social learning. In A. H. Halsey, J. Floud, & C. A. Anderson (Eds.), *Economy, education and society* (pp. 78–96). New York: Free Press.

Bernstein, B. (1964). Elaborated and restricted codes: Their social origins and some consequences. In J. Gumperz & D. Hymes (Eds.), The ethnography of communication. *American Anthropologist Special Publication, 66,* 55–69.

Biller, H. B. (1976). The father and personality development: Paternal deprivation and sex-role development. In M. E. Lamb (Ed.), *The role of the father in child development* (pp. 89–156). New York: Wiley.

Birnbaum, J. A. (1975). Life patterns and self-esteem in gifted family-oriented and career-committed women. In M. S. Mednick, S. S. Tangri, & L. W. Hoffman (Eds.), *Women and achievement* (pp. 396–419). Washington, DC: Hemisphere.

Bishop, D. W., & Ikeda, M. (1970). Status and role factors in the leisure behavior of different occupations. *Sociology and Social Research, 54,* 190–208.

Blau, P. M., & Duncan, O. D. (1967). Men's work and men's families. In *The American occupational structure.* New York: Wiley.

Block, J., & Block, J. H. (in press). A longitudinal study of personality and cognitive development. In S. Mednick & M. Harway (Eds.), *Longitudinal research in the United States.* New York: Plenum Press.

Blood, R. O., & Hamblin, R. L. (1958). The effect of the wife's employment on the family power structure. *Social Forces, 36,* 347–352.

Blood, R. O., Jr., & Wolfe, D. M. (1960). *Husbands and wives.* Glencoe, IL: Free Press.

Bronfenbrenner, U. (1958). Socialization and social class through time and space. In E. Maccoby, T. Newcomb, & R. Hartley (Eds.), *Readings in social psychology* (pp. 400–425). New York: Holt.

Bronfenbrenner, U., Alvarez, W. F., & Henderson, C. R., Jr. (1984). Working and watching: Maternal employment status and parents' perceptions of their three-year-old children. *Child Development, 55,* 1362–1378.

Bronfenbrenner, U., & Crouter, A. (1982). Work and family through time and space. In S. B. Kamerman & C. D. Hayes (Eds.), *Families that work: Children in a changing world* (pp. 39–83). Washington, DC: National Academy Press.

Burke, R. J., & Weir, T. (1976). Relationship of wives' employment status to husband, wife, and pair satisfaction and performance. *Journal of Marriage and the Family, 38,* 279–287.

Burke, R. J., & Weir, T. (1981). Impact of occupational demands on nonwork experiences. *Group and Organizational Studies, 6,* 472–485.

Buss, T., & Redburn, F. S. (1983). *Mass unemployment: Plant closings and community mental health.* Beverly Hills, CA: Sage.

Caudill, W., & Weinstein, H. (1969). Maternal care and infant behavior in Japan and America. *Psychiatry, 32,* 12–43.

Chafetz, J. S. (1980). Conflict resolution in marriage: Toward a theory of spousal strategy and marital dissolution notes. *Journal of Family Issues, 1,* 397–441.

Chase-Lansdale, P. L. (1981). Effects of maternal employment on mother–infant and father–infant attachment *Dissertation Abstracts International, 42,* 2562, (University Microfilms No. DEN81-25083).

Cherry, R. R., & Eaton, E. L. (1977). Physical and cognitive development in children of low-income mothers working in the child's early years. *Child Development, 48,* 158–166.

Clark, R. A., & Gecas, V. (1977, April). *The employed father in America: A role competition analysis.* Paper presented at the annual meeting of the Pacific Sociological Association, San Francisco, CA.

Clark, R. A., Nye, F. I., & Gecas, V. (1978). Work involvement and marital role performance. *Journal of Marriage and the Family, 40,* 9–22.

Clausen, J. A. (1966). Family structure, socialization and personality. In L. W. Hoffman & M. L. Hoffman (Eds.), *Review of child development research* (Vol. 2, pp. 1–54). New York: Russell Sage Foundation.

Cobb, S., & Kasl, S. (1977). *Termination: The consequences of job loss* (Publication No. 77-224). Washington, DC: U.S. Department of Health, Education and Welfare.

Cohen, A., & Hodges, H. (1963). Characteristics of the low blue-collar class. *Social Problems, 10,* 4.

Cotterell, J. L. (1985, April). *Work and community influences on the quality of childrearing.* Paper presented at the biennial meeting of the Society for Research in Child Development, Toronto, Ontario.

Crouter, A. C. (1984a). Participative work as an influence of human development. *Journal of Applied Developmental Psychology, 5,* 71–90.

Crouter, A. C. (1984b). Spillover from family to work: The neglected side of the work–family interface. *Human Relations, 37,* 425–441.

Crouter, A. C., & Huston, T. (1985, April). *Social psychological and contextual antecedents of fathering in dual-earner families.* Paper presented at the biennial meeting of the Society for Research in Child Development, Toronto, Ontario.

Crouter, A. C., Huston, T., & Robins, E. (1983, October). *Bringing work home: Psychological spillover from work to the family.* Paper presented at the meeting of the National Council on Family Relations, St. Paul, MN.

Douvan, E. (1963). Employment and the adolescent. In F. I. Nye & L. W. Hoffman (Eds.), *The employed mother in America* (pp. 142–164). Chicago: Rand McNally.

Elder, G. H., Jr. (1974). *Children of the Great Depression. Social change in life experience.* Chicago: University of Chicago Press.

Elder, G. H., Jr. (1978). Approaches to social change and the family. *American Journal of Sociology, 84.* 1–38.

Elder, G. H. (1984). Families, kin, and the life course: A sociological perspective. In R. D. Parke (Ed.), *The family: Review of child development research* (Vol. 7, pp. 80–136). Chicago: University of Chicago Press.

Farel, A. N. (1980). Effects of preferred maternal roles, maternal employment, and sociographic status on school adjustment and competence. *Child Development, 50,* 1179–1186.

Feld, A. (1963). Feelings of adjustment. In F. I. Nye & L. W. Hoffman (Eds.), *The employed mother in America* (pp. 331–352). Chicago: Rand McNally.

Feldman, H., & Feldman, M. (1973). *The relationship between the family and occupational functioning in a sample of rural women.* Ithaca, NY: Cornell University Press.

Feree, M. (1976). Working-class jobs: Housework and paid work as sources of satisfaction. *Social Problems, 23,* 431–441.

Gerstl, J. E. (1961). Leisure, taste, and occupational milieu. *Social Problems, 9,* 56–68.

Ginsberg, A., Milne, A. M., Myers, D. E., & Rosenthal, A. S. (1984). *Single parents, working mothers and the educational achievement of school children* (Contracts No. 300-80-0778 and No. 300-83-0211). Washington, DC: U.S. Department of Education.

Ginzberg, E. (1971). *Educated American women: Life styles and self-portraits.* New York: Columbia University Press.

Gold, D., & Andres, D. (1978a). Developmental comparisons between adolescent children with employed and nonemployed mothers. *Merrill-Palmer Quarterly, 24,* 243–254.

Gold, D., & Andres, D. (1978b). Developmental comparisons between 10-year-old children with employed and nonemployed mothers. *Child Development, 49,* 75–84.

Gold, D., & Andres, D. (1978c). Relations between maternal employment and development of nursery school children. *Canadian Journal of Behavioral Science, 10,* 116–129.

Gold, D., Andres, D., & Glorieux, J. (1979). The development of Francophone nursery school children with employed and nonemployed mothers. *Canadian Journal of Behavioral Science, 11,* 169–173.

Gold, M., & Slater, C. (1958). Office, factory, store, and family: A study of integration setting. *American Sociological Review, 23,* 64–74.

Goldberg, R. J. (1977, March). *Maternal time use and preschool performance.* Paper presented at the meeting of the Society for Research in Child Development, New Orleans.

Gottfried, A. E., Gottfried, A. W., & Bathurst, K. (1985, August). *Maternal employment and young children's development: A longitudinal investigation.* Paper presented at the meeting of The American Psychological Association, Los Angeles, CA.

Hansson, R. O., O'Connor, M. E., Jones, W. H., & Blocker, T. J. (1981). Maternal employment and adolescent sexual behavior. *Journal of Youth and Adolescence, 10,* 55–60.

Hartley, R. E. (1960). Children's concepts of male and female roles. *Merrill-Palmer Quarterly, 6,* 83–91.

Heath, D. B. (1977). Some possible effects of occupation on the maturing of professional men. *Journal of Vocational Behavior, 11,* 263–281.

Hess, R. D. (1970). Social class and ethnic influences on socialization. In P. Mussen (Ed.), *Carmichael's manual of child psychology* (Vol. 2, pp. 457–558). New York: Wiley.

Hess, R. D., & Shipman, V. C. (1965). Early experience and the socialization of cognitive modes in children. *Child Development, 34,* 869–886.

Hess, R. D., & Shipman, V. C. (1967). Cognitive elements in maternal behavior. In J. P. Hill (Ed.), *Minnesota symposia on child psychology* (Vol. 1, 57–81). Minneapolis: University of Minnesota Press.

Hess, R. D., Shipman, V. C., Brophy, J., & Baer, D. (1968). *The cognitive environment of urban preschool children.* Chicago: Graduate School of Education, University of Chicago.

Hetherington, E. M. (1979). A child's perspective. *American Psychologist, 34,* 851–858.

Hetherington, E. M., & Camara, K. A. (1984). Families in transition: The processes of dissolution and reconstitution. In R. D. Parke (Ed.), *The family: Review of child development research* (Vol. 7, pp. 398–439). Chicago: University of Chicago Press.

Heyns, B. (1982). The influence of parents' work on children's school achievement. In S. B. Kamerman & C. D. Hayes (Eds.), *Families that work: Children in a changing world* (pp. 229–267). Washington, DC: National Academy Press.

Heyns, B., & Catsambis, S. (1985). Working mothers and the achievement of children: A critique. *Sociology of Education, 18,* 308–321.

Hill, C. R., & Stafford, F. P. (1978). *Parental care of children: Time diary estimates of quantity, predictability, and variety* (Working paper series). Ann Arbor: University of Michigan, Institute for Social Research.

Hinde, R. A. (1985, April). *Categorizing individuals: A method linking clinical and developmental psychology.* Paper presented at the biennial meeting of the Society for Research in Child Development, Toronto, Ontario.

Hock, E. (1980). Working and nonworking mothers and their infants: A comparative study of maternal care-giving characteristics and infant social behavior. *Merrill-Palmer Quarterly, 26,* 79–101.

Hoffman, L. W. (1958). *The effects of maternal employment on the division of labor and power structure of the family.* Unpublished doctoral dissertation, University of Michigan, Ann Arbor.

Hoffman, L. W. (1961a). Effects of maternal employment on the child. *Child Development, 32,* 187–197.

Hoffman, L. W. (1961b). The father's role in the family and the child's peer group adjustment. *Merrill-Palmer Quarterly, 7,* 97–105.

Hoffman, L. W. (1963a). Effects on children: Summary and discussion. In F. I. Nye & L. W. Hoffman, (Eds.), *The employed mother in America* (pp. 190–214). Chicago: Rand McNally.

Hoffman, L. W. (1963b). Parental power relations and the division of household tasks. In F. I. Nye & L. W. Hoffman (Eds.), *The employed mother in America* (pp. 215–230). Chicago: Rand McNally.

Hoffman, L. W. (1972). Early childhood experiences and women's achievement motives. *Journal of Social Issues, 28,* 129–156.

Hoffman, L. W. (1974). Effects of maternal employment on the child: A review of the research. *Developmental Psychology, 10,* 204–228.

Hoffman, L. W. (1977a). Changes in family roles, socialization, and sex differences. *American Psychologist, 32,* 644–657.

Hoffman, L. W. (1977b). Fear of success in 1965 and 1974: A reinterview study. *Journal of Consulting and Clinical Psychology, 45,* 310–321.

Hoffman, L. W. (1979). Maternal employment: 1979. *American Psychologist, 34,* 859–865.

Hoffman, L. W. (1980). The effects of maternal employment on the academic attitudes and performance of school-age children. *School Psychology Review, 9,* 319–336.

Hoffman, L. W. (1983). Increased fathering: Effects on the mother. In M. Lamb & A. Sagi (Eds.), *Social policies and legal issues pertaining to fatherhood* (pp. 167–190). Hillsdale, NJ: Erlbaum.

Hoffman, L. W. (1984a). Maternal employment and the young child. In M. Perlmutter (Ed.), *Parent–child interaction and parent–child relations in child development. The Minnesota Symposia on Child Psychology* (Vol. 17, pp. 101–128). Hillsdale, NJ: Erlbaum.

Hoffman, L. W. (1984b). Work, family, and the socialization of the child. In R. D. Parke (Ed.), *The family: Review of child development research* (Vol. 7, pp. 223–282). Chicago: University of Chicago Press.

Hoffman, L. W., & Hoffman, M. L. (1973). The value of children to parents. In J. T. Fawcett (Ed.), *Psychological perspectives on fertility* (pp. 19–76). New York: Basic Books.

Hoffman, L. W., & Lippitt, R. O. (1960). The measurement of family life variables. In D. Goslin (Ed.), *Handbook of research methods in child development* (pp. 945–1013). New York: Wiley.

Hoffman, L. W., & Manis, J. D. (1979). The value of children in the United States: A new approach to the study of fertility. *Marriage and the Family, 42,* 583–596.

Hoffman, L. W., & Nye, F. I. (1974). *Working mothers.* San Francisco: Jossey-Bass.

Hoffman, L. W., Thornton, A., & Manis, J. D. (1978). The value of children to parents in the United States. *Population Behavioral, Social, and Environmental Issues, 1,* 91–131.

Hoffman, M. L. (1960). Power assertion by the parent and its impact on the child. *Child Development, 31,* 129–143.

Hoffman, M. L., & Saltzstein, H. D. (1967). Parent discipline and the child's moral development. *Journal of Personality and Social Psychology, 5,* 45–57.

Hollingshead, A. B. (1975). *Elmtown's youth and Elmtown revisited.* New York: Wiley.

House, J. (1981). *Work stress and social support.* Reading, MA: Addison-Wesley.

Johnson, C. L. (1969). *Leadership patterns in working and non-working-mother middle-class families.* Unpublished doctoral dissertation, University of Kansas. (University Microfilms No. 96–11)

Justice, B., & Duncan, D. F. (1977). Child abuse as a work-related problem. *Journal of Behavior Technology, Methods and Therapy, 23,* 53–55.

Kanter, R. M. (1977). *Work and family in the United States: A critical review of research and policy.* New York: Russell Sage Foundation.

Kasl, S. V. (1974). Work and mental health. In J. O'Toole (Ed.), *Work and the quality of life: Resource papers for work in America.* Cambridge, MA: MIT Press.

Kasl, S. V., & Cobb, S. (1979). Some mental health consequences of plant closing and job loss. In L. A. Ferman & J. P. Gordus (Eds.), *Mental health and the economy* (pp. 99–122). Kalamazoo, MI: W. E. Upjohn Institute for Employment Research.

Kessler, R. C., & McRae, J. A., Jr. (1982). The effects of wives' employment on the mental health of married men and women. *American Psychological Review, 47,* 216–227.

Kohn, M. L. (1959a). Social class and the exercise of parental authority. *American Sociological Review, 24,* 352–366.

Kohn, M. L. (1959b). Social class and parental values. *American Journal of Sociology, 64,* 337–351.

Kohn, M. L. (1963). Social class and parent–child relationships: An interpretation. *American Journal of Sociology, 68,* 471–480.

Kohn, M. L. (1969). *Class and conformity: A study in values.* Homewood, IL: Dorsey Press.

Kohn, M. L. (1980). *Persönlichkeit, beruf und soziale schichtung: Ein Bezugsrahmen* [Personality, occupation, and social situation: A frame of reference]. Heidelberg: Klett-Cotta.

Kohn, M. L., & Schooler, C. (1978). The reciprocal effects of the substantive complexity of work and intellectual flexibility: A longitudinal assessment. *American Journal of Sociology, 84,* 24–52.

Kohn, M. L., & Schooler, C. (1982). Job conditions and personality: A longitudinal assessment of their reciprocal effects. *American Journal of Sociology, 87,* 1257–1286.

Komorovsky, M. (1940). *The unemployed man and his family.* New York: Dryden Press.

Kroes, W. H., & Hurrell, J. J. (1975). *Job stress and the police officer: Identifying stress reduction techniques.* Washington, DC: Public Health Service, Department of Health, Education and Welfare.

Lamb, M. E. (1979). Paternal influences and the father's role: A personal perspective. *American Psychologist, 34,* 938–943.

Lamb, M. E. (1981). Fathers and child development: An integrative overview.

In M. E. Lamb (Ed.), *The father's role in child development* (rev. ed., pp. 1-90). New York: Wiley.

Landy, F., Rosenberg, B. G., & Sutton-Smith, B. (1969). The effects of limited father absence on cognitive development. *Child Development, 40,* 941–944.

Lynd, R. S., & Lynd, H. M. (1937). *Middletown in transition: A study in cultural conflicts.* New York: Harcourt, Brace.

Lynn, D., & Sawrey, W. L. (1959). The effects of father-absence on Norwegian boys and girls. *Journal of Abnormal and Social Psychology, 59,* 258–262.

Margolis, L. (1982). *Helping the families of unemployed workers.* Chapel Hill: University of North Carolina, Bush Institute for Child and Family Policy.

Margolis, L., & Farran, D. (in press). Unemployment: The health consequences for children. *North Carolina Medical Journal.*

Marsden, D. (1975). *Workless: Some unemployed men and their families.* Baltimore, MD: Penguin.

McKinley, D. G. (1964). *Social class and family life.* New York: Free Press.

Medrich, E. (1981). *The serious business of growing up: A study of children's lives outside of school.* Berkeley: University of California Press.

Meissner, M. (1971). The long arm of the job: A study of work and leisure. *Industrial Relations, 10,* 239–260.

Miller, D. R., & Swanson, G. E. (1958). *The changing American parent.* New York: Wiley.

Miller, J., Schooler, C., Kohn, M. L., & Miller, K. A. (1979). Women and work: The psychological effects of occupational conditions. *American Journal of Sociology, 85,* 66–94.

Miller, N., & Brewer, M. B. (Eds.). (1985). *Groups in contact: The psychology of desegregation.* New York: Holt, Rinehart & Winston.

Miller, S. M. (1975). Effects of maternal employment on sex-role perception, interests, and self-esteem in kindergarten girls. *Developmental Psychology, 11,* 405–406.

Model, S. (1981). Housework by husbands. *Journal of Family Issues, 2,* 225–237.

Moore, T. W. (1975). Exclusive early mothering and its alternatives. *Scandinavian Journal of Psychology, 16,* 256–272.

Morris-Vann, A. (1982, September). Hard times for kids of the unemployed. *ASCA Counselor,* 3-4.

Mortimer, J. T. (1974). Patterns of intergenerational occupational movements: A smallest-space analysis. *American Journal of Sociology, 79,* 1278–1299.

Mortimer, J. T. (1976). Social class, work, and the family: Some implications of the father's occupation for familial relationships and sons' career decisions. *Journal of Marriage and the Family, 38,* 241–256.

Mortimer, J. T. (1980). Occupation–family linkages as perceived by men in the early stages of professional and managerial careers. In H. Z. Lopata (Ed.), *Research in the interweave of social holes: Women and men* (Vol. 1, pp. 99–117). Greenwich, CT: JAI Press.

Mortimer, J. T., & Sorensen, G. (1984). Men, women, work, and family. In K. M. Borman, D. Quarm, & S. Gideonse (Eds.), *Women in the workplace: Effects on families* (pp. 139–167). Norwood, NJ: Ablex.

Mott, P. E., et al. (1965). *Shift work: The social, psychological, and physical consequences.* Ann Arbor: University of Michigan Press.

Nolan, F. L. (1963). Rural employment and husbands and wives. In F. I. Nye & L. W. Hoffman (Eds.), *The employed mother in America* (pp. 122–124). Chicago: Rand McNally.

Nordlicht, S. (1979). Effects of stress on the police officer and family. *New York State Journal of Medicine, 79,* 400–401.

Nye, F. I. (1963). Adjustment of the mother: Summary and a frame of reference. In F. I. Nye & L. W. Hoffman (Eds.), *The employed mother in America* (pp. 384–400). Chicago: Rand McNally.

Nye, F. I. (1974). Husband–wife relationship. In L. W. Hoffman & F. I. Nye (Eds.), *Working mothers* (pp. 186–206). San Francisco: Jossey-Bass.

O'Brien, T. E. (1971). Violence in divorce-prone families. *Journal of Marriage and the Family, 33,* 292–298.

Ogburn, W. F., & Nimkoff, M. F. (1955). *Technology and the changing family.* New York: Houghton Mifflin.

Orden, S. R., & Bradburn, N. M. (1969). Working wives and marital happiness. *American Journal of Sociology, 74,* 391–407.

Owen, M. T., Easterbrooks, M. A., Chase-Lansdale, L., & Goldberg, W. A. (1984). The relation between maternal employment status and the stability of attachments to mother and to father. *Child Development, 55,* 1894–1901.

Parke, R. D., & Collmer, C. W. (1975). Child abuse: An interdisciplinary analysis. In E. M. Hetherington (Ed.), *Review of child development research* (Vol. 5, pp. 509–590). Chicago: University of Chicago Press.

Parsons, T. (1955). The American family: Its relation to personality and the social structure. In T. Parsons & R. F. Bales (Eds.), *Family, socialization and interaction process* (pp. 84–107). Glencoe, IL: Free Press.

Pearlin, L. I., & Kohn, M. L. (1966). Social class, occupation, and parental values: A cross-national study. *American Sociological Review, 31,* 466–479.

Pederson, F. A., Cain, R., Zaslow, M., & Anderson, B. (1982). Variation in infant experience associated with alternative family role organization. In L. Laosa & I. Sigel (Eds.), *Families as learning environments for children.* New York: Plenum Press.

Philliber, W. W., & Hiller, D. V. (1983). Relative occupational attainments of spouses and later changes in marriage and wife's work experience. *Journal of Marriage and the Family, 45,* 161–170.

Piotrkowski, C. S. (1979). *Work and the family system: A naturalistic study of working-class and lower-middle-class families.* New York: Free Press.

Piotrkowski, C. S., & Crits-Christoph, P. (1981). Occupational life and women's family adjustment. *Journal of Family Issues, 2,* 126–147.

Piotrkowski, C. S., & Katz, M. H. (1982). Indirect socialization of children: The effects of mothers' jobs on academic behaviors. *Child Development, 53,* 1520–1529.

Piotrkowski, C. S., & Repetti, R. L. (1984). Dual-earner families. *Marriage and Family Review, 7,* 99–124.

Pleck, J., & Rustad, M. (1980). *Husbands' and wives' time in family work and paid work in the 1975–1976 study of time use.* Unpublished manuscript, Wellesley College Center for Research on Women.

Powell, K. S. (1963). Family variables. In F. I. Nye & L. W. Hoffman (Eds.), *The employed mother in America.* Chicago: Rand McNally.

Propper, A. M. (1972). The relationship of maternal employment to adolescent roles, activities, and parental relationships. *Journal of Marriage and the Family, 34,* 417–421.

Quarm, D. E. A. (1977). *The measurement of marital powers.* Unpublished doctoral dissertation, University of Michigan, Ann Arbor.

Quinn, R. P., & Staines, G. L. (1979). *The 1977 quality of employment survey.* Ann Arbor: University of Michigan, Institute for Social Research, Survey Research Center.

Radin, N. (1976). The role of the father in cognitive/academic and intellectual development. In M. E. Lamb (Ed.), *The role of the father in child development* (pp. 237–276). New York: Wiley.

Rainwater, L. (1965). *Family design: Marital sexuality, family size, and contraception.* Chicago: Aldine.

Ray, S. A., & McLoyd, V. C. (in press). Fathers in hard times: The impact of unemployment and poverty on paternal and marital relations. In M. Lamb (Ed.), *The father's role: Applied perspectives.* New York: Wiley.

Repetti, R. L. (1985). *The social environment at work and psychological well-being.* Unpublished doctoral dissertation, Yale University, New Haven, CT.

Robinson, J. P. (1977). *Change in Americans' use of time: 1965–1975.* Cleveland, OH: Cleveland State University, Cleveland Communications Research Center.

Robinson, J. P. (1978). *How Americans use time: A sociological perspective.* New York: Praeger.

Robinson, J. P. (1980). Housework technology and household work. In S. F. Bern (Ed.), *Women and household labor* (pp. 92–124). Beverly Hills, CA: Sage.

Rosenberg, Morris. (1979). *Conceiving the self.* New York: Basic Books.

Rousseau, D. M. (1978). The relationship of work to nonwork. *Journal of Applied Psychology, 63,* 513–517.

Safilios-Rothschild, C. (1970). The study of family power structure: A review 1960–1969. *Journal of Marriage and the Family, 32,* 539–552.

Safilios-Rothschild, C. (1976). Dual linkages between the occupational and family systems: A macro-sociological analysis. *Signs, 1,* 51–60.

Sawhill, I. V., Peabody, G. E., Jones, C. A., & Caldwell, S. B. (1975). *Income transfers and family structure* (Urban Institute Working Paper No. 979–03). Washington, DC: Urban Institute.

Scanzoni, J. H. (1978). *Sex roles, women's work, and marital conflict.* Lexington, MA: Heath.

Schlozman, K. L., & Verba, S. (1978). The new unemployment: Does it hurt? *Public Policy, 16,* 333–358.

Schneider, E. V. (1957). *Industrial society.* New York: McGraw-Hill.

Schubert, J. B., Bradley-Johnson, S., & Nuttal, J. (1980). Mother–infant communication and maternal employment. *Child Development, 51,* 246–249.

Schwartz, P. (1983). Length of day care attendance and attachment behavior in 18-month-old infants. *Child Development, 54,* 1073–1078.

Sennett, R., & Cobb, J. (1972). *The hidden injuries of class.* New York: Knopf.

Sheldon, A., & Fox, G. L. (1983, April). *The impact of economic uncertainty on children's roles within the family.* Paper presented at the meeting of the Society for the Study of Social Problems, Detroit, MI.

Smokler, C. S. (1975). Self-esteem in pre-adolescent and adolescent females (Doctoral dissertation, University of Michigan, 1975). *Dissertation Abstracts International, 35,* 3599B. (University Microfilms No. TS2 75-00-813).

Sroufe, L. (1983). Infant–caregiver attachment and patterns of adaptation in preschool: The roots of maladaption and competence. In M. Perlmutter (Ed.), *Minnesota Symposium on Child Psychology* (Vol. 16, pp. 33–59). Hillsdale, NJ: Erlbaum.

Staines, G. L. (1980). Spillover versus compensation: A review of the literature on the relationship between work and nonwork. *Human Relations, 33,* 111–129.

Staines, G. L., & Pagnucco, D. (1977). Work and non-work: Part II: An empirical study. In Survey Research Center, *Effectiveness in work roles: Employee responses to work environments* (Vol. 1). Ann Arbor, MI: Institute for Social Research.

Steinmetz, S. K. (1974). Occupational environment in relation to physical punishment and dogmatism. In S. Steinmetz & M. Strauss (Eds.), *Violence in the family.* New York: Dodd Mead.

Steinmetz, S. K., & Straus, M. A. (Eds.). (1974). *Violence in the family.* New York: Dodd Mead.

Stuckey, M. R., McGhee, P. E., & Bell, N. J. (1982). Parent–child interaction: The influence of maternal employment. *Developmental Psychology, 18,* 635–644.

Symonds, M. (1970). Emotional hazards of police work. *American Journal of Psychoanalysis, 2,* 155–160.

Tangri, S. S. (1972). Determinants of occupational role innovation among college women. *Journal of Social Issues, 28,* 277–299.

Thompson, R. A., Lamb, M. E., & Estes, D. (1982). Stability of infant–mother attachment and its relationship to changing life circumstances in an unselected middle-class sample. *Child Development, 53,* 144–148.

Tiller, P. O. (1958). *Father absence and personality development in children of sailor families* (Nordisk Psykologi's Monographs, Series No. 9). Oslo: Bokhjrnet.

Trimberger, R., & MacLean, M. J. (1982). Maternal employment: The child's perspective. *Journal of Marriage and the Family, 44,* 469–474.

U.S. Department of Commerce, Bureau of the Census. (1979, April). *Population profile of the United States, 1978, population characteristics* (Current Population Reports, Series P-20, No. 336). Washington, DC: U.S. Government Printing Office.

U.S. Department of Labor, Bureau of Labor Statistics. (1981). *Marital and family characteristics of workers: March 1980* (ASI 6748-58, news release on microfiche). Washington, DC: U.S. Department of Labor.

U.S. Department of Labor, Women's Bureau. (1977). *Working mothers and their children.* Washington, DC: U.S. Government Printing Office.

Vaughn, B. E., Gove, F. I., & Egeland, B. (1980). The relationship between out-of-home care and the quality of infant–mother attachment in an economically disadvantaged population. *Child Development, 51,* 1203–1214.

Veroff, J., Douvan, E., & Kulka, R. (1981) *The inner American: A self-portrait from 1957 to 1976.* New York: Basic Books.

Vogel, S. R., Broverman, I. K., Broverman, D. M., Clarkson, F., & Rosenkrantz, P. (1970). Maternal employment and perception of sex roles among college students. *Developmental Psychology, 3,* 384–391.

Walker, K. E., & Woods, M. (1976). *Time use: A measure of household production of family goods and services.* Washington, DC: American Home Economics Association.

Walker, K. E. (1970). How much help for working mothers? The children's role. *Human Ecology Forum, 1,* 13–15.

Waters, E., & Crandall, V. J. (1964). Social class and observed maternal behavior from 1940–1960. *Child Development, 35,* 1021–1032.

Wells, J. A. (1982). Objective job conditions, social support and perceived stress among blue-collar workers. *Journal of Occupational Behavior, 3,* 79–94.

Werner, E., & Smith, R. (1982). *Vulnerable but invincible.* New York: McGraw-Hill.

Whyte, W., Jr. (1956). *The organization man.* New York: Doubleday.

Williams, C. (1981). *Open cut.* Sydney: Allen and Unwin.

Woods, M. B. (1972). The unsupervised child of the working mother. *Developmental Psychology, 6,* 14–25.

Yarrow, L. (1979). Emotional development. *American Psychologist, 34,* 951–957.

Yarrow, M. R., Scott, P., DeLeeuw, L., & Heinig, C. (1962). Childrearing in families of working and non-working mothers. *Sociometry, 25,* 122–140.

Zaslow, M., Pederson, F. A., Suwalsky, J., & Rabinovich, B. (1983, April). *Maternal employment and parent–infant interaction.* Paper presented at the meeting of the Society for Research in Child Development, Detroit, MI.